I0823122

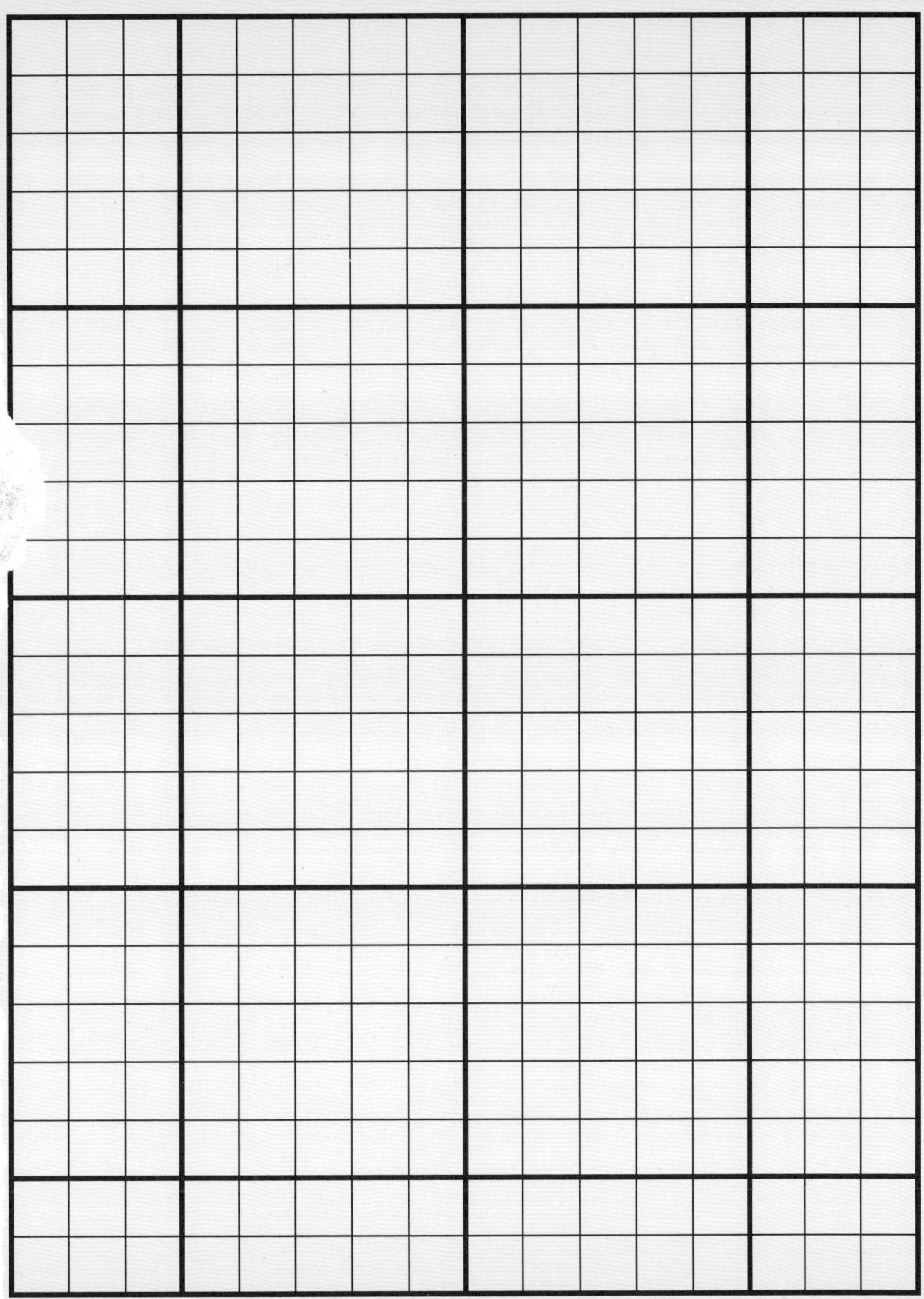

A BOOK ON ZINES

NEW AESTHETICS IN ZINE DESIGN

First published and distributed by
viction workshop ltd.

viction:ary™

viction workshop ltd.
Unit C, 7/F, Seabright Plaza,
9–23 Shell Street,
North Point, Hong Kong SAR
Url: www.victionary.com
Email: we@victionary.com

@victionworkshop
@victionworkshop
Bē @victionary
@victionary
小红书 @Victionary Books

Edited and produced by viction workshop ltd.
Creative Direction: Victor Cheung
Design: Scarlet Ng
Editorial: Ynes Filleul, YL Lim
Coordination: Kristine Ng, Katherine Wong
Production: Bryan Leung
Typeface: Stefan Simple by Dinamo

ISBN 978-988-70660-5-7
Printed and bound in China

A BOOK ON ZINES

NEW AESTHETICS
IN ZINE DESIGN

INDEX

006–008

009–240

072,136,184

241–299

300–303

PREFACE

Zines have always lived slightly to the side of things. They exist in the margins, on folding tables at book fairs, in backpacks and coat pockets, passed hand to hand rather than pushed through formal channels. They are modest in scale but expansive in spirit — a space where ideas can be tested, obsessions indulged, and voices heard without permission or polish. In an age defined by speed, optimisation, and endless digital output, the zine remains insistently human: slow enough to feel, small enough to care about, and tactile enough to remember.

A Book on Zines is born from that impulse. It gathers together a wide range of independent publications from around the world, each shaped by its maker's curiosity, constraints and convictions. Some are rough and immediate, others meticulously crafted; some are playful, others deeply personal. What unites them is not a single aesthetic or ideology, but a shared belief in publishing as an act of agency — the idea that making and distributing a zine can still be a meaningful, no matter how small the print run.

Historically, zines have thrived wherever there is a need to speak outside dominant systems. From punk and protest movements to personal diaries and visual experiments, they have long offered a platform for stories that do not fit neatly into mainstream publishing. That intimate, self-reflective lineage continues in Núria Balinha's Consider This My New Year's Message (pp. 064-065), an eight-page zine exploring the fantasy of personal change and the reluctance to commit to the work it demands. Inspirational texts are layered over photographs saturated in vibrant colour, capturing the tension between motivation, intention and inaction. In a different register, Jonathan Mak's 247 Drawings From Home (pp. 058-061) compiles handwritten notes left by his parents over the years — recurring heart drawings photographed, categorised and edited into a tender study of familial love, memory and everyday affection. Here, the zine becomes both archive and offering.

The projects featured in this book also demonstrate how format can fundamentally shape reading. Mew Imashuku's Kumonodaira Plateau (pp. 158-163), created during a stay deep in the Japanese Northern Alps, takes the form of an accordion book in which poetry and photography occupy opposing sides and cannot be viewed simultaneously. The reader must choose a perspective, moving between contrasting experiences, while a specially designed cover accommodates the fully extended photographic form. Structure becomes narrative.

Material experimentation appears throughout. Maruto Ardi's SMARTPHONE (pp. 024-025), published by Extensive Publishing, treats the book as a constructed object. Using playing cards as pages and a no-glue binding system, the project embraces minimal printing and everyday materials. Phone photographs of ordinary objects are slotted into place, encouraging readers to engage with the book as both artwork and tactile encounter. In Holycrap's An Emojious Odyssey of the Gluttonous Omnivores (pp. 200-205), the zine is housed within a cardboard box replicating a traditional Singaporean takeaway container. The entire package is placed inside a specially printed 'Rubbish' plastic bag and accompanied by disposable chopsticks and a mock receipt, blurring the boundary between publication, ephemera and performative object.

Zines also operate as tools of documentation and preservation. SomethingMoon Design's Searching for Design Files: City, Theatre (pp. 164-165) examines the hidden role of archives within graphic design. Drawing from theatre-based urban projects, it brings drafts, images and documents into public view, reframing design files as active agents of meaning and positioning documentation itself as artistic practice. Similarly, Grafis Nusantara Vol.1: Koleksi

Label dan Stiker (pp. 192-195) gathers Indonesian vintage labels and stickers from the 1970s to 1990s—cigarette, batik and tea labels alongside religious and cartoon stickers—highlighting the visual richness of everyday graphics across the archipelago. The publication functions simultaneously as cultural record and design reference.

Many of the contributors included here speak of zines as spaces of freedom; places to think aloud, to test ideas without commercial pressure, or to document what might otherwise be overlooked. Because zines are often self-published and produced in small editions, the process remains visible. Imperfections are not edited out but embraced; misalignment, variation and manual labour become part of the reading experience. The result is a form of publishing that feels intimate and direct, carrying the presence of its maker in every decision.

At the same time, A Book on Zines does not romanticise the format as purely nostalgic or anti-digital. Many of the practices featured move fluidly between analogue and digital tools, treating software and print as collaborators rather than opposites. What distinguishes the zine is not the rejection of technology, but the refusal of scale, speed and permanence as default values. A zine marks a moment of thought in time. Once made, it does not need to be updated, optimised or endlessly reproduced to justify its existence or prove its worth.

This book is intended as both a document and an invitation. For those already immersed in zine culture, it offers a snapshot of contemporary independent publishing across geographies, disciplines and sensibilities. In bringing these works together, A Book on Zines celebrates the quiet resilience of a medium that continues to adapt without losing its core values. These pages hold experiments, fragments and finished thoughts alike. They are evidence that, even now, the simplest printed object can still carry weight — not because it is perfect or permanent, but because it was made with intention.

ADD TO CART
ALFIE WHEATLEY
BIANCA FORISCHI
BROOS STOFFELS
CAN CAN PRESS
CAN YANG
CHEN LUO
CHENGJIE LI (NLIEECHI)
DTAN STUDIO
ÉLISE RIGOLLET OFFICES
EMPIRE BOOKS
EXTENSIVE PUBLISHING—COPYRIGHT/RESERVED
FOR&ST
GRAFIS NUSANTARA
HOLYCRAP
HOUTH
HOWFUL
HSIAN-JUNG CHEN
JONATHAN MAK
KOSEKO DESIGN & PRESS
LONELY KIDNEY
LUANA LLOYD
MEANTIME
MEW IMASHUKU
NOPATTERN STUDIO
NÚRIA BALINHA
PAY2PLAY
PETR PERSIK
RACHEL SENDER
RIVERSBED
SITING YAO
SOCIOTYPE
SOMETHINGMOON DESIGN
STUDIO DE RONNERS
STUDIO ELANA SCHLENKER
TESS SMITH-ROBERTS
TYPE01
TYRONE WILLIAMS
VICTORIA ROSSELLI
WAN CHAOFAN
WUTHIPOL UJATHAMMARAT

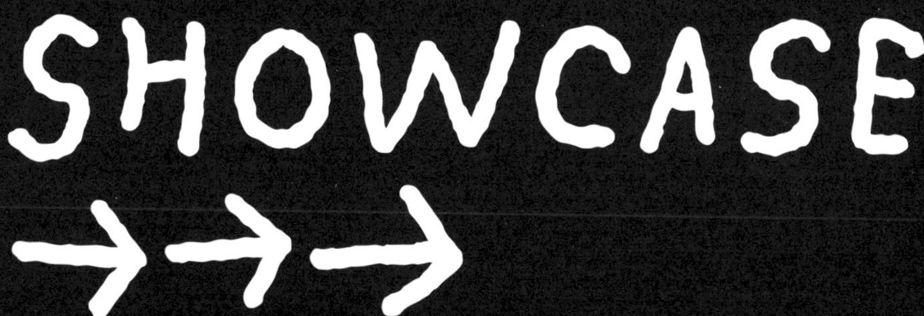

COVER UP

Cover Up is a handcrafted photographic pamphlet that examines exterior tilework through sequencing and material focus. The design highlights repetition, surface texture, and architectural rhythm, balancing visual charm with unease. Through careful image curation and the zine format itself, it frames tile mosaics as both decorative pattern and latent structural risk.

DESIGN	SIZE	PUBLISHER	FEATURES
Wuthipol Ujathammarat	100mm x 100mm	Wuthipol Ujathammarat	Multi-folded, white card stock printing

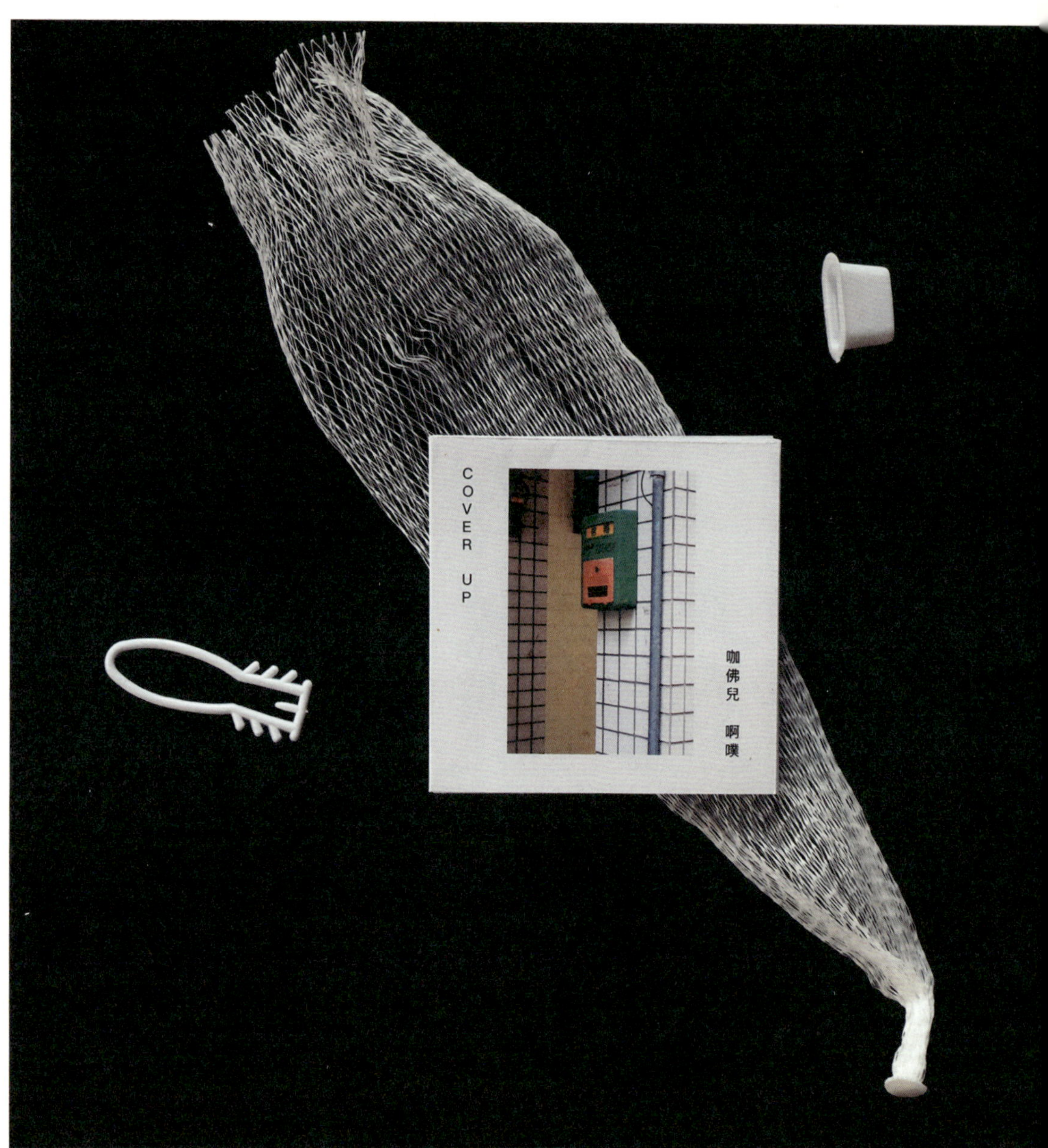
COVER UP
咖佛兒 啊噗

KYOTO SANPO NICHIJO

Kyoto Sanpo Nichijo by Nlieechi is a palm-sized accordion-fold zine compiling scenes observed during his fifth year of living in Kyoto. Organised according to compositional orientation and the passage of time, the work is divided into two volumes — upper and lower — capturing the quiet rhythm of everyday walks.

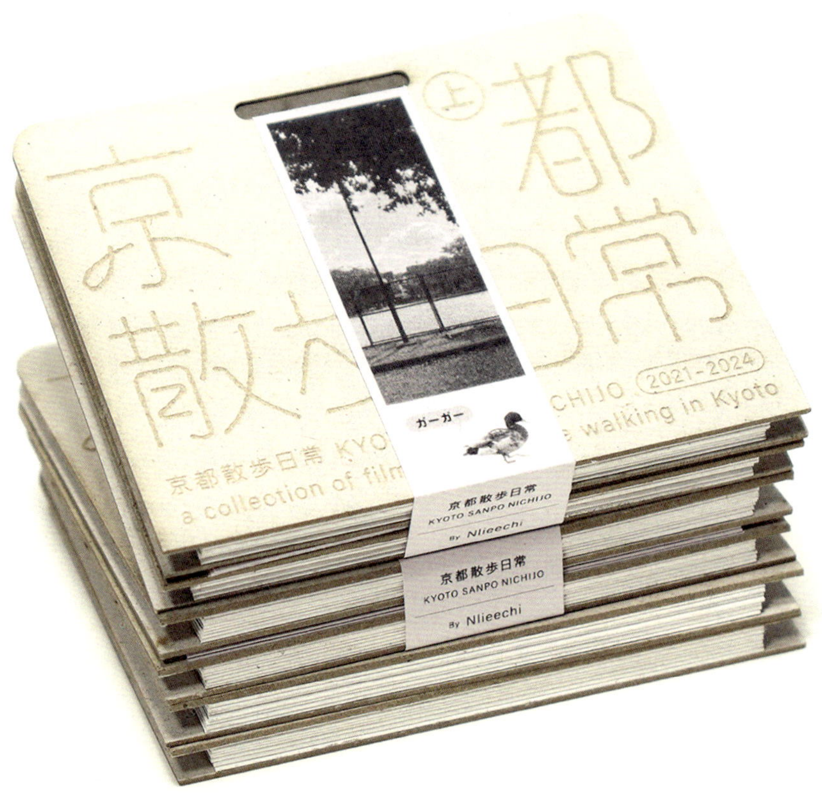

DESIGN	SIZE	PUBLISHER	FEATURES
Chengjie Li (Nlieechi)	68mm x 385mm	Chengjie Li (Nlieechi)	Accordion binding, laser-cut cover, Risograph printing

京 都
散歩日常

京都散步日常 KYOTO SANPO NICHIJO (2021-2024)
a collection of film photos while walking in Kyoto

京都散步日常 KYOTO SANPO NICHIJO (2021-2024)

今年是我在京都生活的第四年。京都是一个适合散步的城市，我总会带着相机，沿着鸭川，漫无目的地游走在这座城市里。对着同一条河流或是远方的同一座山，我也许拍下了许多张相同的照片，但面对着这悠闲宁静的光景，每次收获的感动却是不同的。这本 zine 便是对我在京都的日常散步时光的小小总结。

This is my fourth year living in Kyoto, a city perfect for wandering. I always take my camera along as I stroll along the Kamo River, aimlessly roaming through this city. Perhaps I have taken countless photos of the same river or the same mountain in the distance, but each time, I am moved in a different way by the tranquil beauty around me. This zine is a small collection, a reflection of these daily walks and the quiet moments they bring.

By Nlieechi 2024.10

9 出町柳 | Demachiyanagi
2023.8
11 西陣 | Nishijin
2024.6
12 五条 | Gojo
2023.7
13 鴨川 | Kamogawa
2023.10

UMI

UMI is the first zine created after Nlieechi began a new chapter of life in Japan. Visits to the seaside became a quiet ritual, with train journeys leading to solitary walks and photographs along the shore. The publication is divided into three sections based on coastal landmarks, echoed by three blue threads sewn onto the cover, representing each documented coastline.

DESIGN	SIZE	PUBLISHER	FEATURES
Chengjie Li (Nlieechi)	350mm x 150mm	Chengjie Li (Nlieechi)	Thread sewn-glued binding, screen-printed cover

TOO BIG A BEAN FOR TOO SMALL A PIE

Too Big a Bean for Too Small a Pie is a series of 200 miniature ceramic fèves by Hsian Jung Chen, packaged in a paper box with a Galette des Rois recipe. Hand-sculpted and uniquely glazed, each piece is sold blind through a bookstore vending machine. Inspired by the Galette des Rois tradition, one buyer also receives a cake baked by the artist.

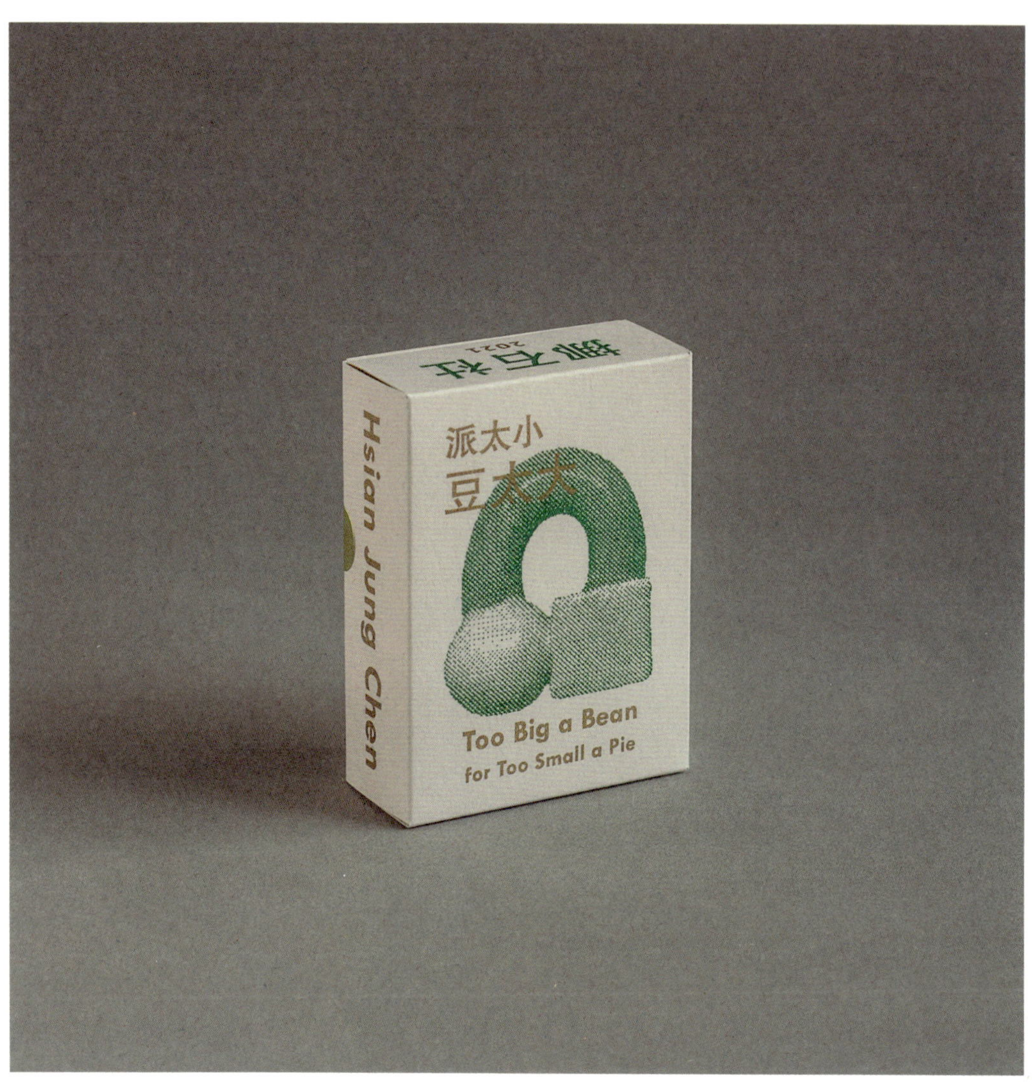

DESIGN	SIZE	PUBLISHER	FEATURES
Hsian-Jung Chen & Son Ni	70mm x 95mm x 30mm	nos:books	Art box packaging, limited-edition ceramic multiples, Risograph printing

Receipe
for
Galette des Rois

派太小

Too Big a Bean

豆太大

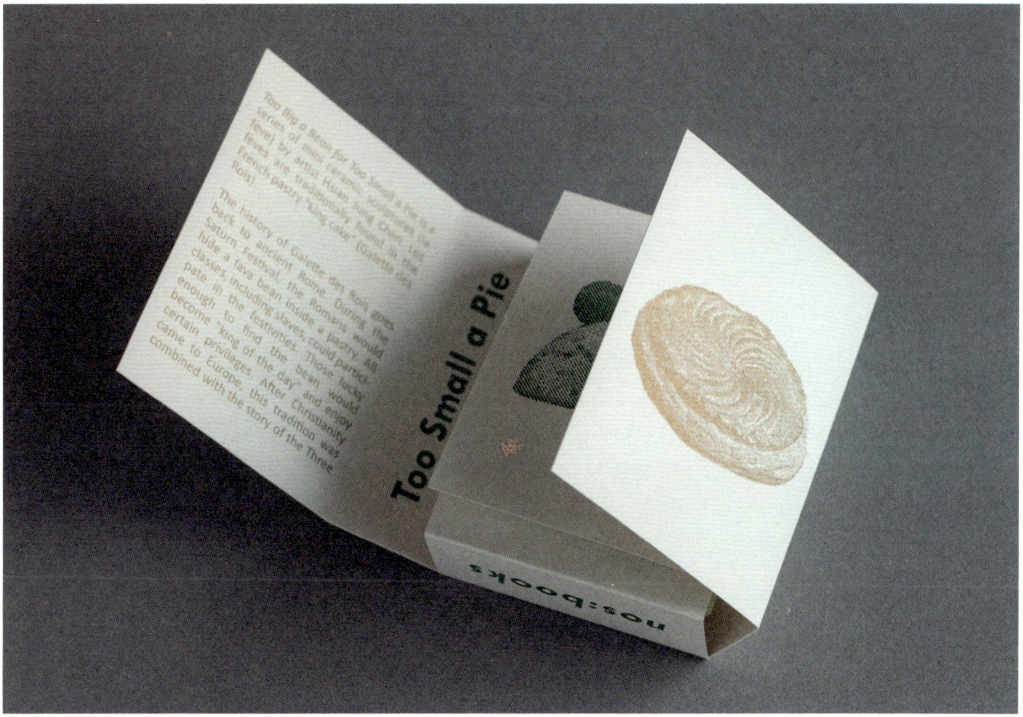
Too Small a Pie
nos:books

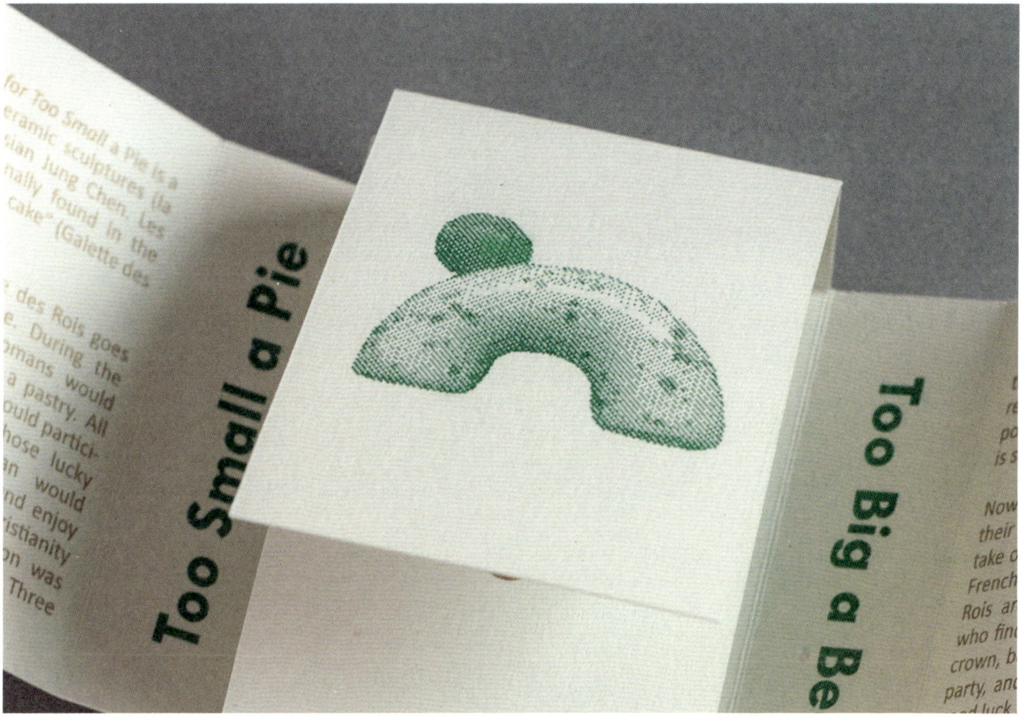
Too Small a Pie
Too Big a Be

SMARTPHONE

SMARTPHONE by Maruto Ardi treats the book as a constructed object. Using playing cards as pages and a no-glue binding system, the project embraces minimal printing and everyday materials. Phone photographs of ordinary objects invite readers to engage with the book as both artwork and tactile experience.

DESIGN

Maruto Ardi

SIZE

176mm x 250mm x 20mm

PUBLISHER

Extensive Publishing—
COPYRIGHT/RESERVED

FEATURES

Manual binding on playcards

GOLDEN STORY

Golden Story by Nlieechi is a handmade zine shaped like a cigarette packet, produced using silkscreen and Risograph printing. Playing on the reflective ritual of lighting a cigarette, it presents images as fragments of memory, inviting readers to unfold each page and project their own recollections into the work.

DESIGN
Chengjie Li (Nlieechi)

SIZE
40mm x 90mm

PUBLISHER
Chengjie Li (Nlieechi)

FEATURES
Loose sheets, tobacco packaging, Risograph printing

HANG

Hang documents the Thai practice of improvised laundry-drying as an urban design language. Through photography and sequencing, everyday clothes racks become ad hoc installations shaped by spatial constraints, sunlight, and DIY logic. The project reframes vernacular problem-solving as visual composition — where colour, placement, and structure transform necessity into an unintentional yet vivid form of urban design.

HANG

DESIGN	SIZE	PUBLISHER	FEATURES
Wuthipol Ujathammarat	150mm x 100mm	Wuthipol Ujathammarat	Saddle-stitched binding, digital film transfer printing on canvas fabric

peculiarly become an artistic norm. A public display of 'hanging laundry' is a common urban vernacular that cannot go unnoticed on an unclouded day. It decorates our city streets with evocative palettes in the midst of obscurely inventive clothes racks, often assembled with everyday objects or hung on an unexpected placement.
This peculiar behaviour of 'hanging laundry' in a public space is notably influenced by a confined architectural space; particularly the modern day flats without a balcony, and outdated homes that are cramped up in little treets. Consequently, the homeowners are motivated to improvise the hanging of laundry by adapting an outside space where there would be a fleeting moment of direct sunshine.
Through a DIY spirit with an endless possibility, these homeowners continue to reveal new approaches to 'hanging laundry' in the most inventive and ridiculous way possible. The craft is effortless, with merely an assembly of household objects to form a clothes rack. Yet the placement often requires a level of

HAPPYLAND

Happyland is a popsicle-shaped zine documenting Bangkok's former amusement park district through saturated Risograph printing. Using vivid colour and geometric compositions, it reframes retro-futurist urban fragments into a playful, dystopian visual narrative. The design amplifies architecture through abstraction, turning neighbourhood remnants into a metaphorical, hyper-coloured urban landscape.

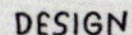

DESIGN	SIZE	PUBLISHER	FEATURES
Wuthipol Ujathammarat	90mm x 50mm	Wuthipol Ujathammarat	Hand-folded binding, Risograph printing

SUNSET SAMPLES

Sunset Samples by Elana Schlenker is an ongoing studio project investigating colour, pattern and production processes. Drawing on photographed sunsets, each image is separated into three halftone colour channels, with patterns manipulated layer by layer. The compositions become increasingly abstract as the halftone scale expands throughout the publication.

DESIGN	SIZE	PUBLISHER	FEATURES
Elana Schlenker	108mm x 279mm	Elana Schlenker	Saddle-stitched binding, Risograph printing

BEST FRIENDS

Best Friends is a self-initiated zine by American photographer Mark Leibowitz, with publication design and logotype by Élise Rigollet, who is a designer and art director based in Paris and Lisbon. The zine explores friendship through its many forms and emotional layers, presenting an intimate and nuanced portrait of personal relationships.

DESIGN	SIZE	PUBLISHER	FEATURES
Élise Rigollet Offices	14mm x 22.8mm x 0.8mm	Mark Leibowitz	Stapled binding

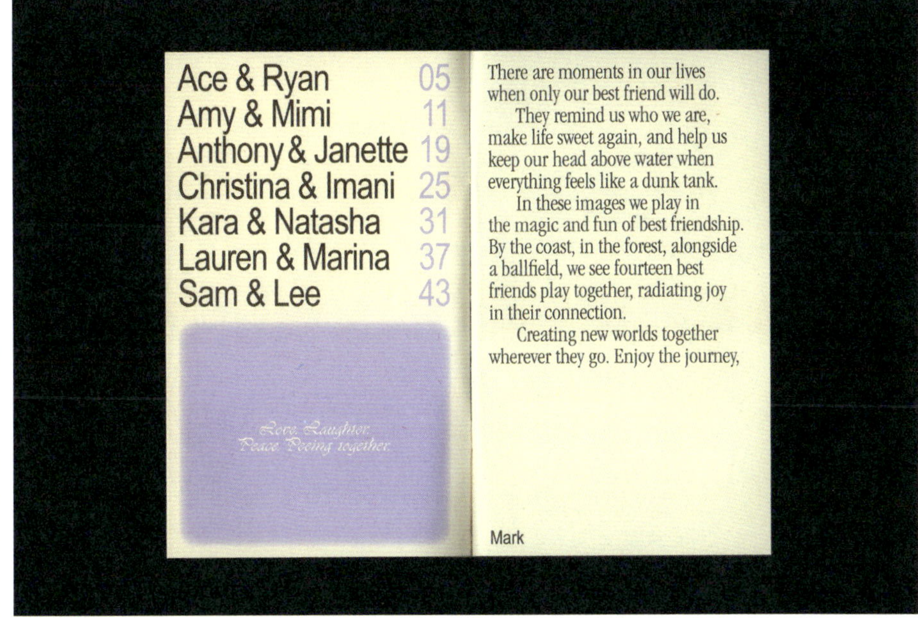

Amy & Mimi

You're beautiful.

Unstoppable. True.
Always bigger.
Always better.
Let's light a cigarette
and really talk.

ch.06
Lauren Marina
p.40

PLAY SERIES 2 『GO OUTSIDE』

GO OUTSIDE translates backpacking essentials into silkscreen-printed imagery. Made from Tyvek, the book integrates a mat into a single piece and includes recipe and image cards, highlighting material experimentation and portability.

DESIGN
the object

SIZE
740mm x 900mm (Unfolded)
120mm x 170mm (Folded)

PUBLISHER
ADD TO CART

FEATURES
Singer-sewn binding, silkscreen-printed Tyvek, integrated book-and-mat structure

PLAY SERIES 2
GO OUTSIDE

OBSERVING OBJECTS

Observing Objects is a photography project that treats mobile image-making as a constraint. Using the smartphone's immediacy and intimacy, it focuses on small subjects through close framing and casual composition, embracing informality and limitation while positioning accessibility and observation as structural elements.

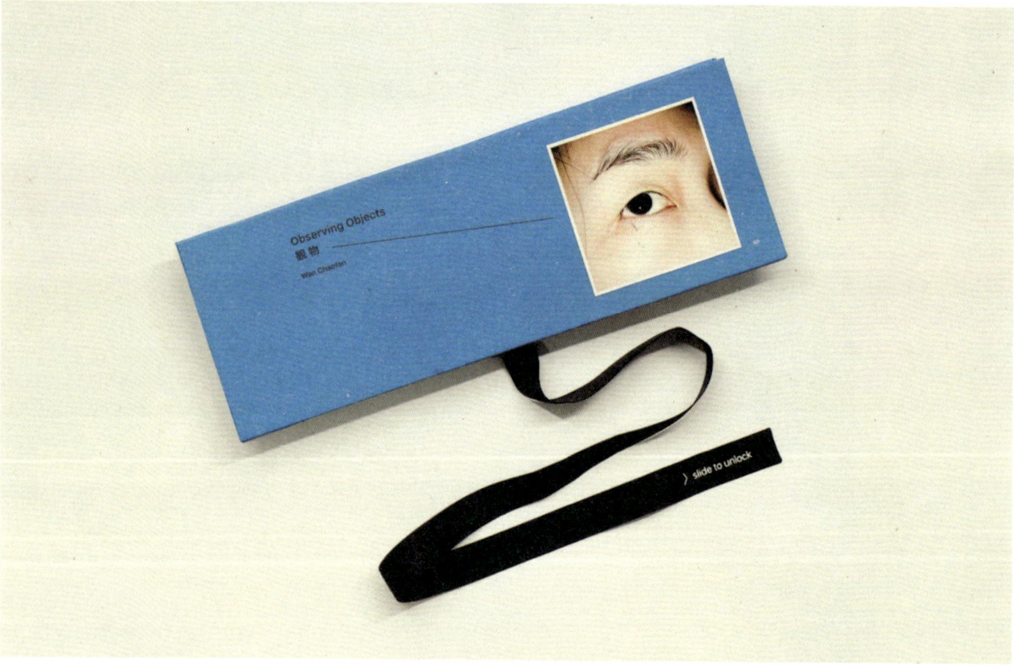

CONCEPT & PHOTOGRAPHY
Wan Chaofan

SIZE
253mm x 89mm x 18mm

PUBLISHER
Wan Publishing

FEATURES
Accordion binding, hard cover, Acrylic slipcase

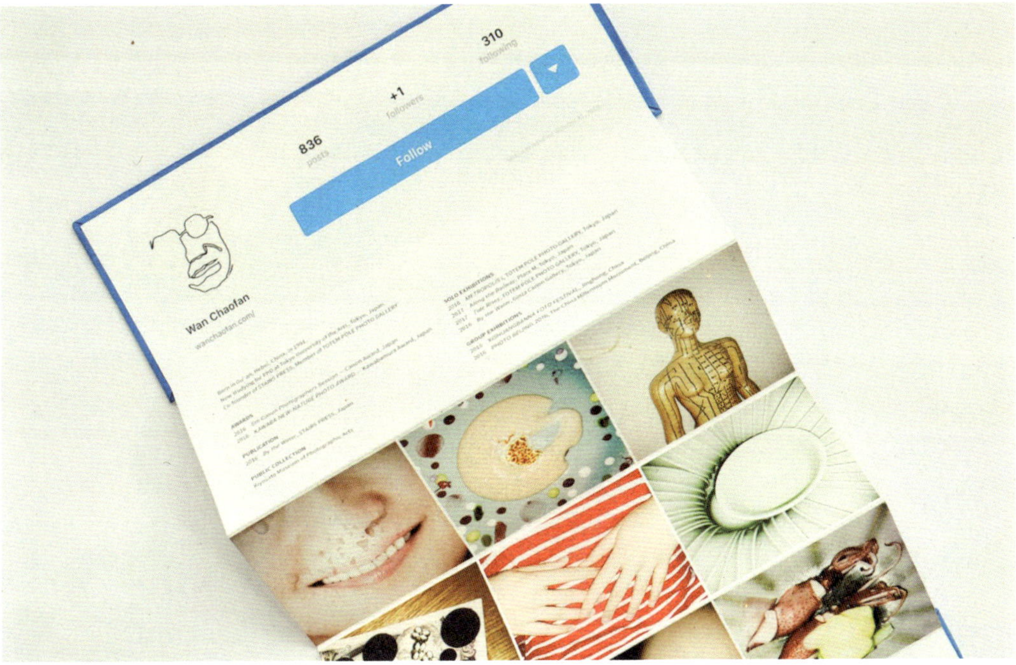

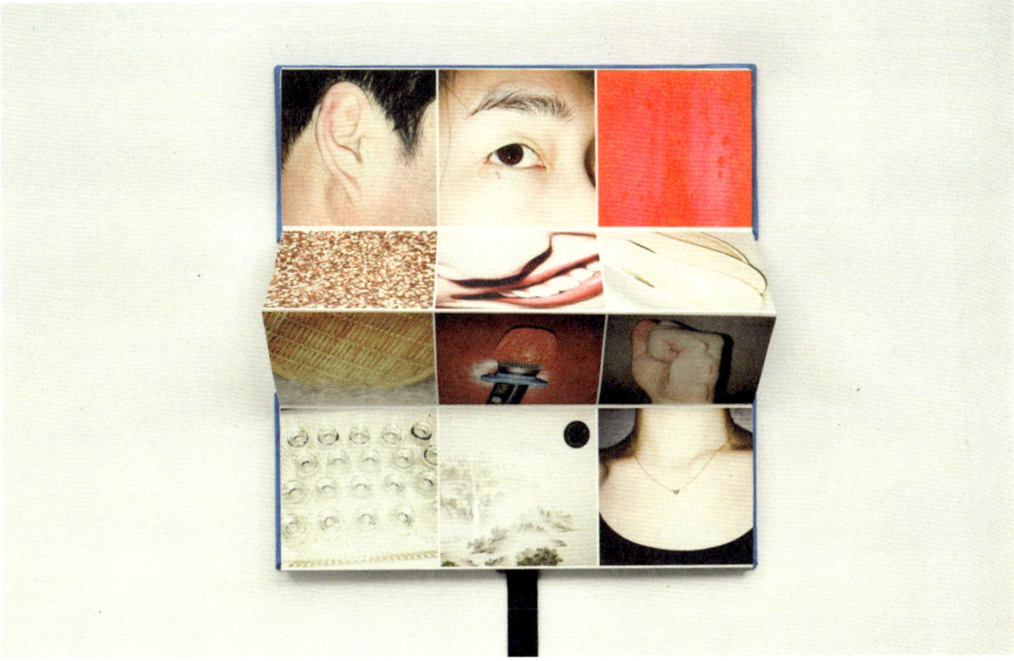

BLURRED ECHOES

Blurred Echoes brings together photographs recovered by Nlieechi after years of being lost. The publication gathers fragments of everyday life, rendered as fading memories through hazy imagery and the soft obscurity of ink. Printed in four-colour Risograph, the work reflects on loss, recovery and the fragile persistence of memory.

DESIGN
Chengjie Li (Nlieechi)

SIZE
120mm x 190mm x 13mm

PUBLISHER
Chengjie Li (Nlieechi)

FEATURES
Hot melt binding, hot-stamped cover, Risograph printing

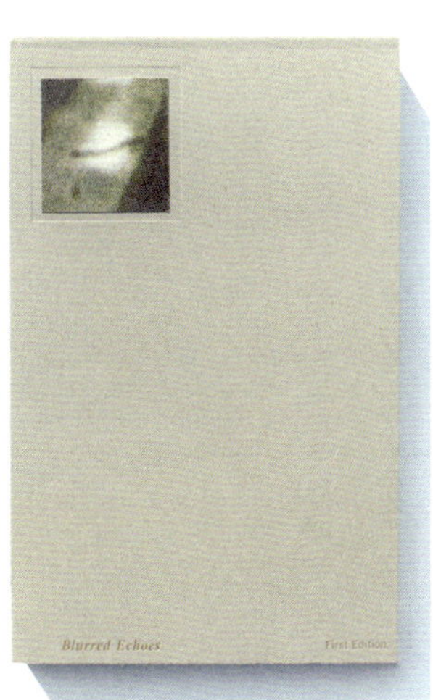

GIKO NOTE

GIKO Note by HOWFUL is a collaboration with Getty Images Korea that approaches photography as a sensorial experience rather than mere information. Through colour, visual rhythm and atmosphere, it translates the time and mood of images onto paper. More than a writing tool, it offers a space to pause, observe and let personal reflections unfold within its margins.

DESIGN
Boda Keem, Inhye Park

SIZE
102mm x 175mm

PUBLISHER
HOWFUL

FEATURES
Saddle-stitched binding, offset printing

LESBIAN SLANG IN CHINESE

Lesbian Slang in Chinese is a queer feminist publication comprising an A6 folded zine and a dictionary-style book, printed in orange and green Risograph inks on Crushcorn paper. Presenting six and forty terms respectively, the bilingual project translates and contextualises Chinese lesbian slang, bridging linguistic and cultural gaps for both Chinese and English-speaking audiences.

DESIGN	SIZE	PUBLISHER	FEATURES
Siting Yao	105mm x 148mm	Siting Yao	Folded binding, two-colour Risograph printing

“铁T救火”

The term "铁T救火"(Dykes Save The Day) originates from a story shared by a guest on the entertainment show "康熙来了" (Kangxi Lai Le). In the story, when a gay bar caught fire, the "铁T" (strong and powerful dykes) from the lesbian bar across the street took the initiative to extinguish the fire, showcasing a spirit of mutual assistance within the LGBTQ+ community.

“铁T救火”源于一则小故事，该故事曾在娱乐节目《康熙来了》中被嘉宾讲述。故事情节中，当同性恋酒吧着火时，街对面的女同性恋酒吧中的“铁T”挺身而出，主动承担了救火任务，展现了性少数群体之间互相帮助的精神。

kes Save The Day

Pillow Princess

The Chinese term "枕头公主" (pillow princess) comes from English. A pillow princess is a slang phrase that describes someone, mostly an LGBTQ woman, who prefers to receive sexual stimulation more than they do to give it.

“枕头公主”来源于英语 Pillow Princess，是一个俚语短语，通常用来描述某人，主要指的是 LGBTQ 女性，她们更喜欢接受性刺激而不是主动提供。

lei si

“蕾丝边”

The edge of lace

LESBIAN
SAVE THE DAY

la la
"拉拉" La La

The term "拉拉 (pronounced as la la)" in Chinese context serves as a colloquial and affectionate nickname specifically referring to lesbians. It's a unique linguistic creation stemming from the phonetic approximation of the English word "lesbian" into Chinese. This term carries a sense of intimacy and camaraderie within the LGBTQ+ community in China.

"拉拉（la la）"在中文语境中作为一种昵称，特指女同性恋者。这个术语源自将英文单词"lesbian"的开头部分音译为中文。它在中国 LGBTQ+ 社群中常被用来自称或称呼别人。

The term "蕾 丝 边 (lěi sī biān)" in Chinese context is a nickname used to refer to lesbians. This term originated from the Chinese phonetic approximation of the English word "lesbian," with "蕾 丝 边" sounding similar to "lesbian" when pronounced in Mandarin Chinese. "= 蕾 丝" means "lace" and "边" means "edge," so together they translate to "the edge of lace."

"蕾丝边"(lěisī biān)是一种用于装饰的边缘，通常用于女性服装。有趣的是，这个词的发音与英文单词"lesbian"（女同性恋）相近，在中文语境中常被用来指代女同性恋。

lei si bian
"蕾丝边"
The edge of lace

ti
"替"
T

The term "替 /T" typically refers to the "top" in a lesbian relationship, representing the partner who takes on a more dominant or active role, akin to the traditional male role. The term is derived from the English word "tomboy."

"替 /T" 通常指的是女同性恋的 "top"，即在刻板印象的同性关系中扮演传统主动角色的一方。这个词源于英文单词 "tombooy"，表示在性关系中扮演主动或更支配的角色。

po
"婆"
P

On the other hand, "婆 /P" refers to the "bottom" in a lesbian relationship, representing the partner who takes on a more submissive or passive role, akin to the traditional female role. The term is derived from the English word "Prettygirl."

"婆 /P" 则是指女同性恋的 "bottom" 一方，即在刻板印象同性关系中扮演被动角色的一方。这个词源于英文单词 "prettygirl"。

247 DRAWINGS FROM HOME

247 Drawings From Home is a self-initiated zine by Jonathan Mak, compiled from handwritten notes left by his parents over the years. Featuring recurring heart drawings, the notes were photographed, categorised by theme and style, and edited into an exploration of familial love, memory and everyday affection.

DESIGN	SIZE	PUBLISHER	FEATURES
Jonathan Mak	115mm x 225mm x 4mm	Jonathan Mak	Saddle-stitched binding, Risograph printing

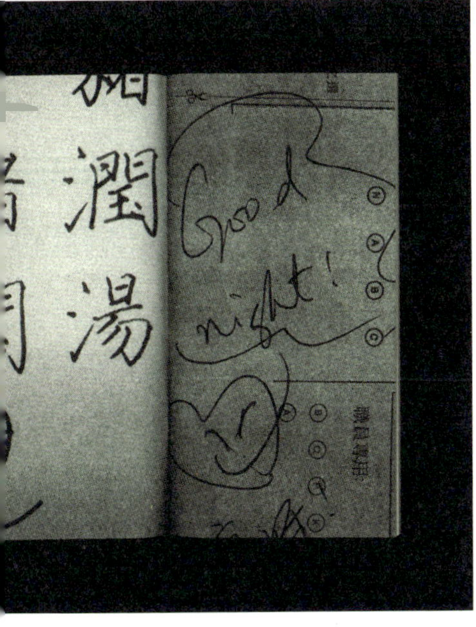

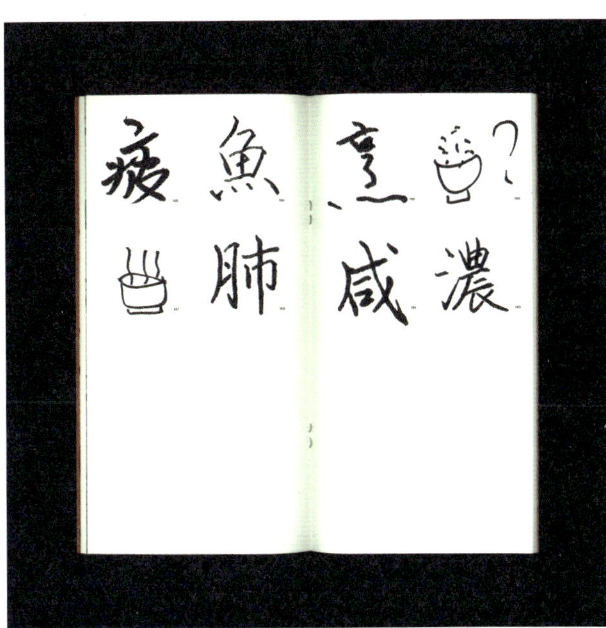

247 drawings
from home

KITSCH examines new aesthetics in contemporary Chinese society through photography, drawing and observational graphesis. Investigating kitsch in urban life and consumer culture, it layers images and critical texts to explore tensions between mass imagery and personal perception as an artefact and aesthetic object.

DESIGN
Can Yang

SIZE
148mm x 210mm

PUBLISHER
Can Yang

FEATURES
Saddle-stitched binding

CONSIDER THIS MY NEW YEAR'S MESSAGE

Consider This My New Year's Message is an eight-page zine by Núria Balinha exploring the fantasy of personal change and the reluctance to commit to the work it demands. Inspirational texts are overlaid on photographs saturated with vibrant colour, reflecting the tension between motivation, intention and inaction.

closed mouths don't get fed.

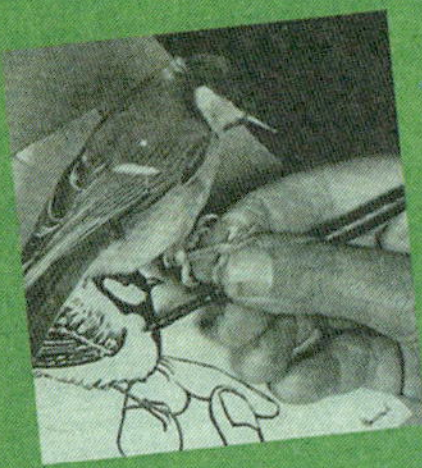

I just hear a lot of people complaining about their lives without even trying to change anything.

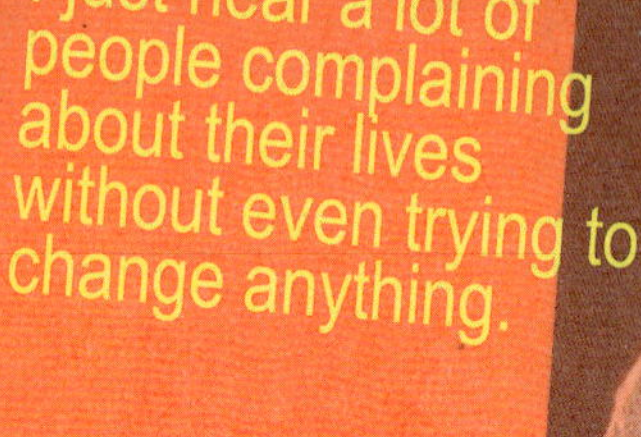

without trying to c

anything.

DESIGN
Núria Balinha

SIZE
74mm x 210mm x 3mm

PUBLISHER
Núria Balinha

FEATURES
Saddle-stitched binding, soft cover

If you are not gonna change the way you live, the way you things, the way you feel react, how do you expect to change?

do your best. You have the possibility to.

consider this a New Year's message!

Park Slope Food Coop
782 Union Street, Brooklyn, NY 11215
Good Food at Low Prices for
Working Members through Cooperation
Since 1973
PARK SLOPE FOOD COOP
4.76 F
5.37 F
5.64 F
1.94 F
EARTH BALANCE BUTTERY SPREAD - SOY FREE
4.62 F
1.62 F

STOP

Park Slope Food Co-Op Members at Odds Over Plastic Bag 'Phaseout'
Can the Park Slope Food Coop Survive?
The Grocery Store Where Produce Meets Politics
Park Slope Food Coop Members Arrested After Allegedly Stealing $18,000 Worth Of Groceries
HEADLINES OVER

GOOD FOOD
AT LOW PRICES.

WELCOME TO THE PARK SLOPE FOOD COOP

FOR WORKING MEMBERS
THROUGH COOPERATION.

DEAR FRIEND, For 51 years, the Park Slope Food Co-op has been making fresh, wholesome food available to all through sweat-equity. More than 10 years before Gwenyth Paltrow goopified kale, we (well, not me) were already selling ten cases of 24 bunches or more per week. Some ~~customers~~ members call the co-op their home, others call it the worst shopping experience inthe tri-state area.

This zine is an invitation to share the Park Slope Co-op experience with you, member or non-member. Because we never would otherwise, unless you work a shift ever six weeks.

Please also note this has no affiliation with The Linewaiters' Gazette.

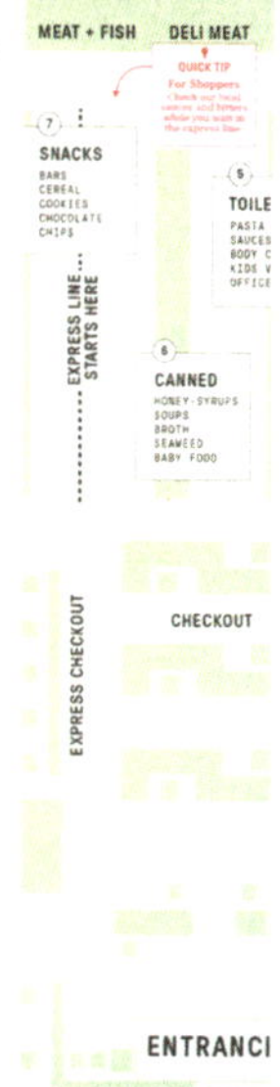

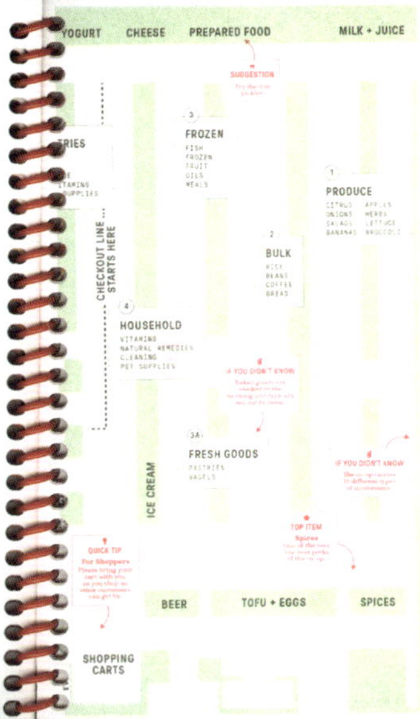

It's Sunday, March 2nd at the Co-op. It's a high of 72 degrees, the warmest day of the season. A foray into summer. Some people cleary did not check the weather.

WHAT'S IN SEASON?

Just a few of spring's harvested crops available now at the co-op.

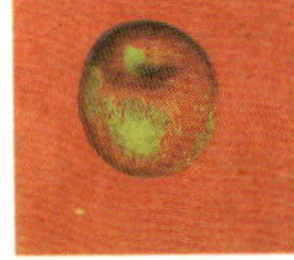

① **WATERMELON RADISH**
Can be enjoyed raw, pickled, or sliced over a salad.

② **ARTICHOKE**
Rich in fiber and antioxidants! Just don't eat the skin, please.

③ **MORELS**
A very earthy and nutty mushroom. They are quite pricey due to their very short growth period.

④ **ENVY APPLE**
Not only are they primarily sweet, but balanced with a slight tanginess and floral nuances.

PERK OF THE LIFTING SHIFT

I NEVER HAVE TO DEAL WITH CUSTOMERS.

OFFICE SHIFT DUTIES

FREELANCE

BEWARE OF THE ENTRANCE DESK SHIFT

FREELANCE

I WAS WORKING AT THE ENTRANCE ...

STOCKING THE BAKED GOODS: YOU'VE BEEN WARNED.

RECURRING

SPECIAL DUTIES ON THE WALKING SHIFT

FREELANCE

THE FRENCH SHIFT

RECURRING

PEOPLE. THEY'RE VERY EXCLUSIVE ABOUT WHO GETS TO WORK THAT SHIFT. I'M LEARNING FRENCH NOW.

NEW MEMBER TIP

FREELANCE

SIGN UP FOR A STOCKING SHIFT TO GET ACQUAINTED WITH ALL OF THE CO-OP'S UNIQUE ITEMS!

GOOD PEOPLE HANDLE GOOD BEER

FREELANCE

"WEARING A RED AND BLACK FLANNEL"THE BEST SHIFT I'VE EVER WORKED. AND I'VE WORKED THEM ALL. THE PEOPLE ARE KIND THAT'S

LET'S TALK SHIFT

MEMBERS GIVE REAL-LIFE ADVICE ON SHIFTS THEY'VE WORKED, COMMON WATCH-OUTS TO LOOK OUT FOR, AND NOT SO COMMON TASKS.

ALL I CAN ASK FOR IN A SHIFT.

THE ONCE MOST IMPORTANT SHIFT

NO LONGER AVAIL

BACK WHEN THE CO-OP WAS CASH ONLY, THE CASH NEEDED TO BE WALKED AND DEPOSITED A FEW BLOCKS DOWN AT 10 PM. NOW THAT I THINK ABOUT IT, THAT WAS A PRETY SCARY RESPONSIBILITY.

HOW TO SECURE A RECURRING CHECKOUT SHIFT

RECURRING

SIGN UP FOR EVERY POSSIBLE WAIT LIST. PRAY.

I'm a man...
where's the
man vitamins?
*passive
aggressive
request about
nutritional
yeast*
OVERHEARD ON THE INTERCOM
Do we have penis gummies?
BANANZA
COSTA RI

ROQUEFORT
Marrekesh
Garlic
Stuffed
HABANERO

PEELED
PHYSALIS
125g
STORAGE AT 0° TO 4° C

VALUES
TO $5.98
OUR PRICE
$4.07
PRODUCT Gooseberries
ORIGIN Colombia
SEASON Summer
PARK SLOPE
FOOD CO-OP
VALUES
TO $5.98
OUR PRICE
$4.07

IRRELEVANT LIFE PHOTOS — A ZINE ABOUT OBSERVING

Irrelevant life photos is a multidisciplinary zine exploring passive observation through photography and print. Focusing on overlooked details such as shadows, discarded objects and quiet spaces, it elevates everyday moments into a minimalist, meditative narrative, revealing subtle beauty within the ordinary.

one month of irrelevant photos for others, but not to [me] that found some meaning & beauty on these so perhaps - who knows - it will have some meaning & beauty for you too

DESIGN	SIZE	PUBLISHER	FEATURES
Luana Lloyd	60mm x 160mm x 10mm	Luana Lloyd	Saddle-stitched binding

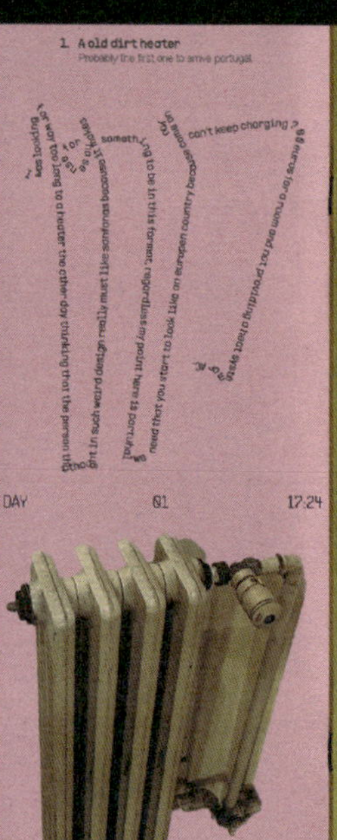

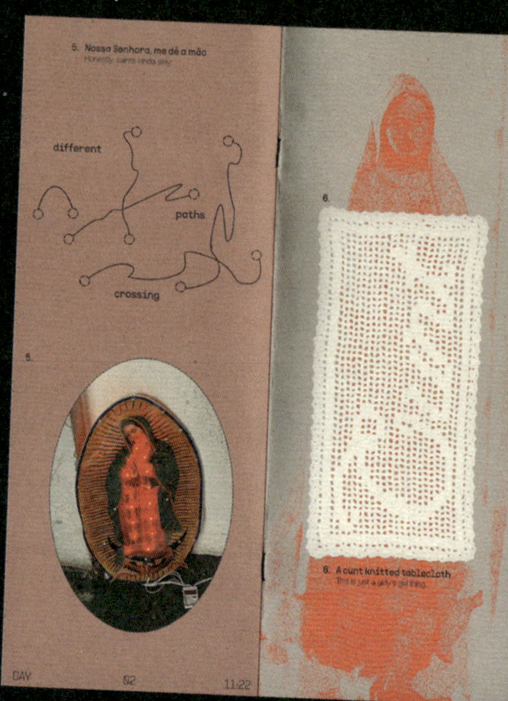

Q&A ①

WHAT DO YOU THINK ZINES CAN DO THAT BOOKS, MAGAZINES, OR DIGITAL MEDIA CAN'T?

"Zines offer an approachable, low-barrier way to share and spread ideas. I love the immediacy of having something physical you can hand to someone or slip into a pocket. Zines can carry knowledge, political views, or creativity and art. They live on shelves and walls, get tucked into drawers and boxes, and reappear years later to be rediscovered. Digital media, ironically, lasts forever on servers and hard drives, but it's much harder to bump into a forgotten PDF than a zine you stumble upon while cleaning a drawer. And unlike anything digital, zines don't require technology to be read. When the servers crash, the zines will still be here."

— RACHEL SENDER

"For us, the printed medium will never die because we believe there is so much more depth to a story when you can touch, feel, flip through, and perhaps even smell actual paper. Having something tangible that you can read and reread at any point adds to the dynamism. With zines, stories and experiences are told in a manner very different from conventional books. You can add a myriad of materials and even objects within the zine, allowing the reader to physically engage with the work and, at times, interact with the story, becoming more emotionally attached to what they are reading."

— HOLYCRAP

"What I love about zines is that they can be about absolutely anything: a short-lived idea you want to explore, a topic you've been meaning to dig into, something funny, or simply something visually pleasing. For me, a zine has no rules — it can be whatever you want it to be. They're low-cost, quick to produce, and immediate. They create space for experimentation, where the process can remain visible and imperfections become part of the story."

— DTAN STUDIO

"Zines are defined by their immediacy and freedom. Unbound by market demands, institutions, or fixed formats, they can respond quickly to emotions, ideas, and social conditions. Compared with books and magazines, they feel more intimate and experimental; compared with digital media, they offer tactility and chance. Rather than pursuing perfection, zines preserve roughness and uncertainty, capturing an authenticity rarely found in other media."

— HOUTH

"Zines offer greater freedom in production as they can be made in small batches by hand, and be tailored to different circumstances."

— WAN CHAOFAN

"ZINES ALLOW US TO CREATE WITHOUT OVER-THINKING. THEY LET US MOVE QUICKLY FROM IDEA TO FINISHED OBJECT, ENJOYING THE PROCESS RATHER THAN GETTING CAUGHT UP IN EXPECTA-TIONS OR PRESSURE."

— ADD TO CART

"A ZINE MARKS A SPECIFIC MOMENT IN TIME. ONCE PUBLISHED, IT NEEDS NO UPDATES, TECHNOLOGY, OR MAINTENANCE TO EXIST."

— STUDIO ELANA SCHLENKER

"Zines offer a freedom that books, magazines, and digital formats rarely allow. Traditional publishing often comes with high costs, large print runs, and distribution challenges, which can be restrictive for independent artists. With zines, those barriers fall away. Small print runs allow experimentation with materials, formats, and printing methods, turning the medium into a playground for testing ideas. Easy, flexible distribution—often hand to hand—supports raw, honest voices, making independence in form and storytelling the true power of zines."

— EXTENSIVE PUBLISHING — COPYRIGHT/RESERVED

"For me, the strength of zines lies in their accessibility and their potential for self-publishing. A zine is one of the most democratic forms of publication. Anyone can make one, and anyone can share their voice without needing permission from institutions, budgets, or algorithms. That openness creates a unique space for experimentation, niche ideas, and communities that might otherwise be overlooked."

— SITING YAO

"There's less pressure when it comes to zines — whether that's coming up with a concept or design, I believe anyone can make a zine! The rules that come with designing a book or a magazine get thrown out the window a bit."

— VICTORIA ROSSELLI

"Zines can do things that books, magazines, or digital media just can't. They're fast, personal, and don't need anyone's permission. You can make a zine today about whatever you're feeling or seeing, and share it tomorrow. That immediacy creates a raw honesty you rarely get in bigger publications. They also travel hand-to-hand — picked up in small shops, traded at events, passed between friends. That physical connection builds community in a very real way. Most importantly, zines give space to voices and stories that usually get overlooked. For us at Grafis Nusantara, that means preserving small pieces of Indonesian culture and everyday graphics that might disappear. Zines make those 'small' stories visible and meaningful."

— GRAFIS NUSANTARA

"Zines are easy to make, and anyone can use them to share ideas. I don't think the tool itself matters that much — a zine is simply the quickest way to capture what you're thinking in the moment and share it straight away. Once it's printed on paper, people can physically feel the words and images. That tactile quality is something books, magazines and phones just can't replicate."

— SOMETHINGMOON DESIGN

"I think zines are a special way of holding more experimental bodies of work, that perhaps books and magazines don't do. The beauty with zines is that they often don't have to hold a narrative and can be totally visual-driven. I often think of a zine as a blank canvas, to do anything or create anything you want, without financial pressure of committing to a larger publication. Every zine I have often come across always has a more experimental nature to them than other mediums."

— ALFIE WHEATLEY

"Zines are a fast, affordable way to publish work and challenge the rules of what a publication can be. Being your own client, publisher, and sometimes printer gives full control over every aspect of the process."

— BROOS STOFFELS

"I BELIEVE ZINES ARE THE FASTEST AND MOST HONEST CHANNEL TO THE HUMAN EXPERIENCE. THEY DON'T NEED TO BE SERIOUS; THEY JUST NEED TO BE FELT IN THE MOMENT. THAT KIND OF UNPREDICTABILITY IS ONLY ATTAINABLE THERE."

— NÚRIA BALINHA

"ZINES MAY BE INHERENTLY THROWAWAY, BUT THE WORLD IS UNDENIABLY RICHER FOR THEM. THEIR EPHEMERALITY AND UNDERGROUND NATURE MAKE THEM PRECIOUS ARTEFACTS LONG AFTER THE MOMENT HAS PASSED. ESPECIALLY WITHIN POLITICALLY CHARGED ARTISTIC MOVEMENTS — SUCH AS PUNK ZINES LIKE 'J.D.S' OR 'BIKINI KILL' — THEY CAN BECOME RARE PRIMARY DOCUMENTS OF MOMENTS OF CHANGE."

— SOCIOTYPE

"Zines are a great way to express any artistic idea with complete freedom and at low cost. There are no rules about what you can include or how to structure them. They offer a way to explore both small and big ideas in a physical format, without taking things too seriously."

— TYRONE WILLIAMS

"A zine occupies the space between a book and an Instagram account, neither as permanent as the former nor as ephemeral as the latter. It has its own kind of 'weight' as a medium. Social media content has been turned into books, and certain books might work better as zines, or vice versa. Ideas can take different forms as long as we play to the strengths of each format, and there's an intimacy to zines that's hard to beat."

— JONATHAN MAK

"To me, zines are a highly personal form of expression. They allow for experimental ideas and unfinished states, and I believe they preserve the creator's sincerity. A zine can exist for only a small audience; it can even be printed as a single copy, created solely for oneself."

— RIVERSBED

"Zine-making allows spontaneity and fluidity, often supported by short print runs that encourage flexibility in materials and binding. This creates a tactile, personal quality unique to zines."

— ÉLISE RIGOLLET OFFICES

"In today's publishing landscape, the boundaries between media are increasingly blurred. However, the true distinction of the zine lies in its nature of provocation and questioning. Zines serve as a powerful personal statement medium — they are fundamentally driven by an urgent idea or message that often bypasses the need for mainstream approval, allowing for highly experimental concepts and formats that are challenging or impossible to execute in mass-produced publications. In short, zines are where the most subversive, unfiltered, and formally audacious ideas find their voice."

— FOR&ST

"I think what zines can do—what books, magazines, or digital media often can't—is allow creators to design the most suitable form for a work precisely because zines are not premised on mass production. When making books or magazines, the need to print and distribute a certain number of copies inevitably places practical constraints on format and production. Digital media, too, is strongly shaped by the screen as a framework, which can limit decisions around tactility and material presence. By contrast, because zines can exist in small editions, they make it possible to think freely from the outset about what form best serves the work itself — without having to begin from the assumptions of large-scale production or distribution. In my own project *Kumonodaira*, for example, I printed text right up to the very edge of the paper and connected all 138 pages into a single accordion-fold piece. I believe this was only possible because I started from a mindset that did not assume mass production — and that freedom is exactly what zines offer."

— MEW IMASHUKU

"In contrast to the formal printing, binding, and mass-market approach of books, zines are more personal, emphasising self-expression through small batches. They are raw and experimental — cheaper and rarer than books."

— PAY2PLAY

"Zines are freeform publications, often experimental in both form and content. Makers are free to write, design, and assemble them however they choose, unbound by the conventions of traditional publishing. This autonomy encourages play and risk-taking, where imperfect edges, unconventional formats, and personal narratives are celebrated. Zines become intimate spaces for expression — allowing ideas to be shared quickly, cheaply, and authentically, in the maker's own voice."

— WUTHIPOL UJATHAMMARAT

"Zines are imperfect. In many ways, the format celebrates experimentation and trial and error. In zine-making, there are no rules, and that freedom makes it both frightening and exhilarating. Zines do not subscribe to a formula or follow guidelines; they are the antithesis of glossy magazines and weighty tomes. Anything goes. This openness is what truly expands the possibilities of the print experiments we pursue at Meantime."

— MEANTIME

"I believe zines excel where other media are limited for several reasons: freedom, expression, and connection. Firstly, they exist outside commercial gatekeeping and professional production standards, allowing for non-traditional design and layout experiments that books or magazines would rarely risk. Secondly, zines are ideal for hyper-specific, niche, or deeply personal ideas that are often too small or too direct for mass media, creating a sense of conversation rather than polished publication. Thirdly, as inexpensive physical objects, zines support DIY culture and local communities, offering a visceral creator-reader connection that digital formats cannot replicate. In short, zines are a quick, affordable, and deeply personal vehicle for voices and ideas outside the cultural mainstream."

— LUANA LLOYD

"Zines are physical, historical artefacts that document our history. Museums are filled with objects, not the internet, which is why making physical books, magazines, and zines is so important for preserving design history."

— TYPEO1

"Zines are more accessible for both makers and readers. Anyone can make them, and anyone can buy them. A zine can be as simple as four pieces of paper, photocopied and stapled together — and they're incredibly affordable. That accessibility is what makes zines great: they're for anyone and everyone to enjoy."

— TESS SMITH-ROBERTS

"For me, the charm of zines lies in their freedom and the warmth of being handmade. They don't require strict structure, unified editorial logic, or speed. Zines allow intuitive, personal expression. As my work focuses on everyday moments and subtle sensations, zines can hold these feelings fully — when a reader touches the paper, it feels like a shared point of view."

— CHENGJIE LI (NLIEECHI)

"I love zines because they are deeply experimental, especially those driven by images rather than words. They create a tactile experience that feels like stepping into the artist's world. Existing outside commercial systems, zines feel authentic and accessible, offering space for imperfection, intuition, and creative freedom."

— BIANCA FORISCHI

"I BELIEVE A ZINE IS A DIRECT MIRROR OF THE CREATOR'S INNER WORLD. ITS CONTENT IS SHAPED THROUGH A NON-LINEAR, OFTEN LABOUR-INTENSIVE PROCESS THAT CLEARLY REFLECTS THE CREATOR'S THOUGHTS AND SENSES. THIS SENSE OF NECESSITY AND EFFORT ALLOWS THE READER TO EXPERIENCE THE CREATOR'S UNIVERSE WITH A STRONGER FEELING OF PHYSICAL PRESENCE AND EMBODIMENT."

— KOSEKO DESIGN & PRESS

ELEGANCIA EN EL RING

Elegancia en el Ring (Elegance in the Ring) is a Risograph zine printed by Can Can Press and designed during an internship in Mexico City. Inspired by Lucha Libre, it explores Latin American vernacular design through archival material and collage. Bilingual in Spanish and English, it is printed using ten different inks.

Mi RING
EN EL CUADRILÁTERO DEL SOL ARDIENTE,
BAILAN CON GRACIA LUCHADORES VALIENTES.

LAS ESTRELLAS DE LA NOCHE
HURACÁN HERMOSO
VS
THE TIGER
ARENA CAN CAN
POR SU SEGURIDAD NO SE ADMITEN MENORES DE EDAD Y/O ABURRIDOS

excentricidad
en
cada
ECCENTRICITY IN EVERY MOVEMENT,
THIS IS THE ESSENCE OF MEXICAN
WRESTLING
movimiento

HACIA ARRIBA:
3.— Isla de Grecia.
4.— Marítimo.
5.— Huríen.
6.— Golpean.
7.— Dispositivo que se les pone a los perros para que no muerdan.
8.— Principal, básico.
9.— Que mueve.
10.— Igualdad de nivel.
HACIA ABAJO:
1.— Apócope de santo.
2.— Consejo de Laura: "Camina como viejo y llegarás como... (chaval)".
3.— Completo
4.— Arbol que da nueces.
5.— Orar.
6.— Agujeritos
7.— Tirar.
8.— Dios escandinavo de la guerra.
ANTIFAZ DEL NORTE

DESIGN	SIZE	PUBLISHER	FEATURES
Bianca Forischi	200mm x 260mm x 10mm	Can Can Press	Saddle-stitched binding, soft cover, 10-colour Risograph printing

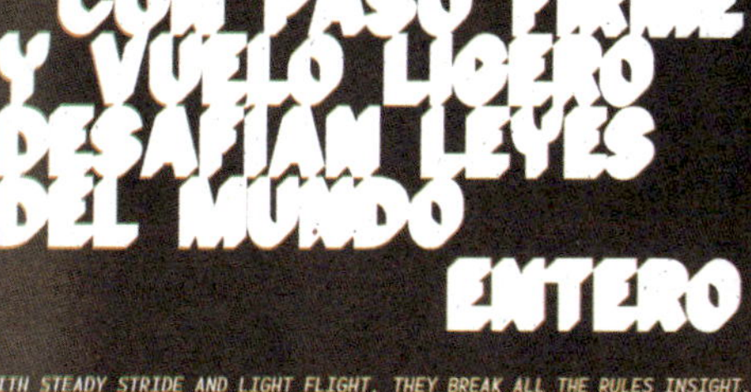

DON'T FORGET TO WASH YOUR HANDS

Don't Forget to Wash Your Hands is an eight-page, confessional zine reflecting on making art, desiring more and the realisation that leaving may be necessary to grow. Written in a diary-like tone, it captures moments of uncertainty, ambition and quiet self-reflection.

DESIGN	SIZE	PUBLISHER	FEATURES
Núria Balinha	74mm x 210mm x 3mm	Núria Balinha	Saddle-stitched bind soft cover

Need a sweet to resolve
some of the problems.

Why is trying to
become independent
such a sacrifice?

Why am I 24 and don't
have a job?

was it a fail?

unfortunately to survive, you nu need to make bad sacrifices.
gone andnd back.

THE GLYPH MANIFESTO

The Glyph Manifesto is a zine rooted in ASCII graphics that reconsiders symbols as an artistic and cultural language. Drawing on early digital visual culture, it transforms simple signs into architectures, landscapes and characters – preserving a digital vernacular positioned between code, text, and image.

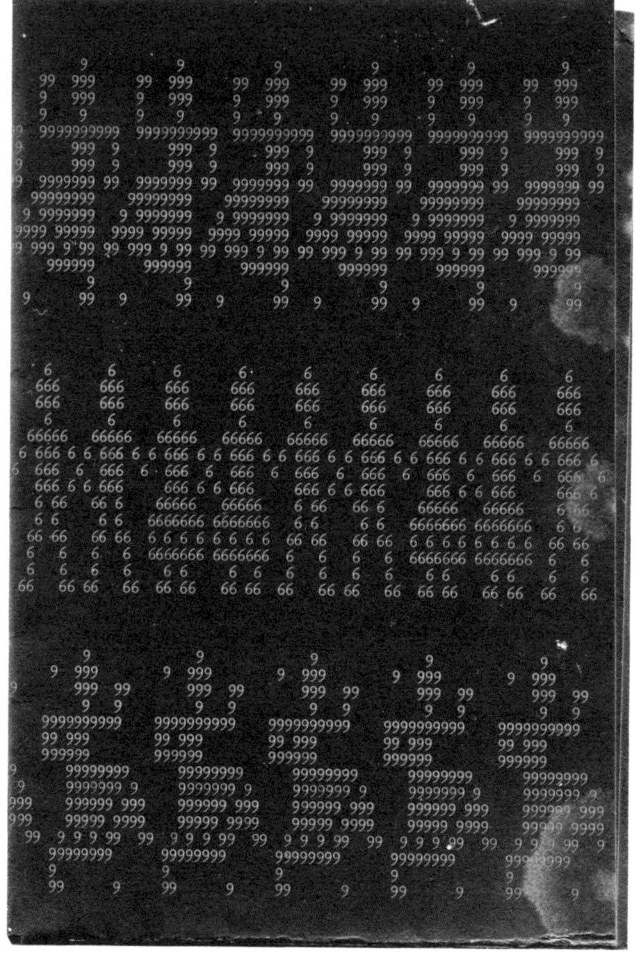

DESIGN	SIZE	PUBLISHER	FEATURES
Petr Persik	148mm x 210mm x 5mm	Petr Persik	Saddle-stitched binding, black-and-white experimental typography printing

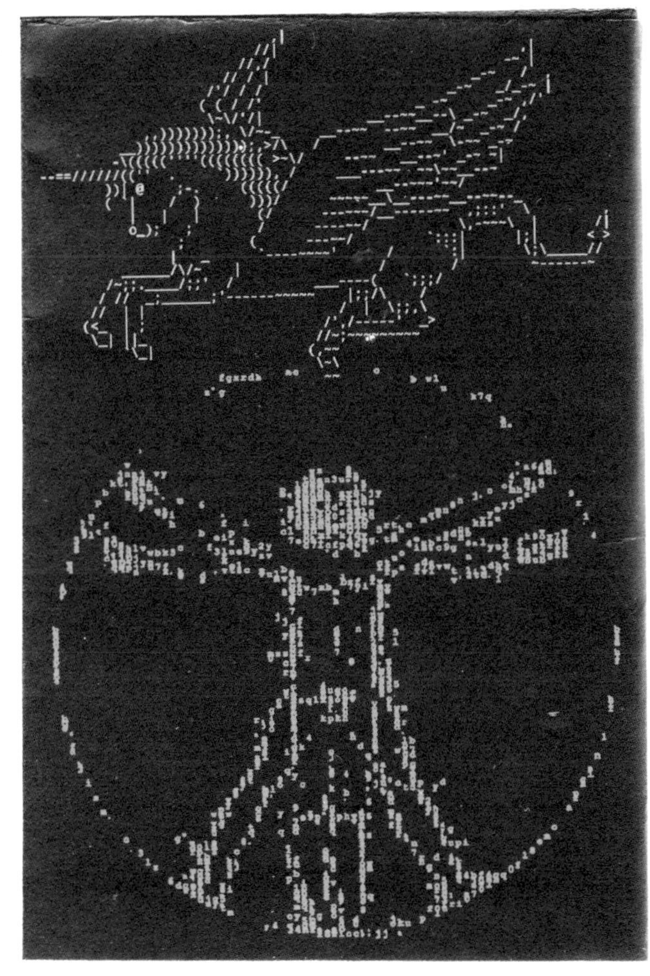

ザッパーン!!

さいたま新都心
時の鐘
岩槻
人形
川越祭
古都川越
花の秩父
ウマイ、ウマスギル!
十
万
石
甲武信岳2475m
さいたま銘菓
秩父芝桜
雲取山2017m
両神山1723m

Yay! It's scooter time～♪

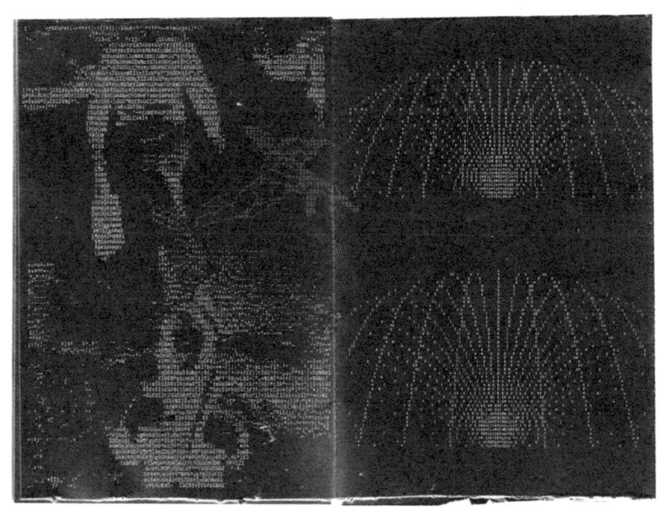

I WOULDN'T TRADE ONE STUPID DECISION FOR ANOTHER FIVE YEARS OF LIFE.

This eight-page zine draws inspiration from LCD Soundsystem's popular hit, "All My Friends". Through a deeply personal lens, it reflects on time, choices and connection, encouraging readers to hold things closer in an increasingly individualistic world.

DESIGN
Núria Balinha

SIZE
74mm x 210mm x 3mm

PUBLISHER
Núria Balinha

FEATURES
Saddle-stitched binding, soft cover

BRIGHTON & HOVE ALBION RESULTS PUBLICATION 24/25

The Brighton & Hove Albion 24/25 Results Publication documents the Premier League season through experimental typography and layouts. Printed in one colour, with reverse-colour experiments for cup games, it blends previously unused typefaces with inspiration drawn from opponents' locations.

2024/ 2025

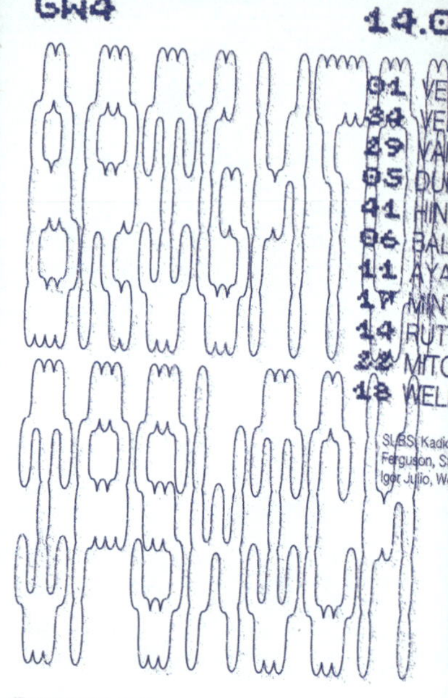

PREMIER LEAGUE

01 MURIC
40 TUANZEBE
26 O'SHEA
24 GREAVES
03 DAVIS
05 MORSY
08 PHILLIPS
07 BURNS
20 HUTCHINSON
23 SZMODICS
19 DELAP

SUBS: Ogbene, Clarke, Hirst, Luongo, Chaplin, Walton, Johnson, Townsend, Cajuste.

AMEX STADIUM

DESIGN
Alfie Wheatley

SIZE
156mm x 297mm x 5.5mm

PUBLISHER
Alfie Wheatley

FEATURES
Perfect binding, blue spot-colour printing

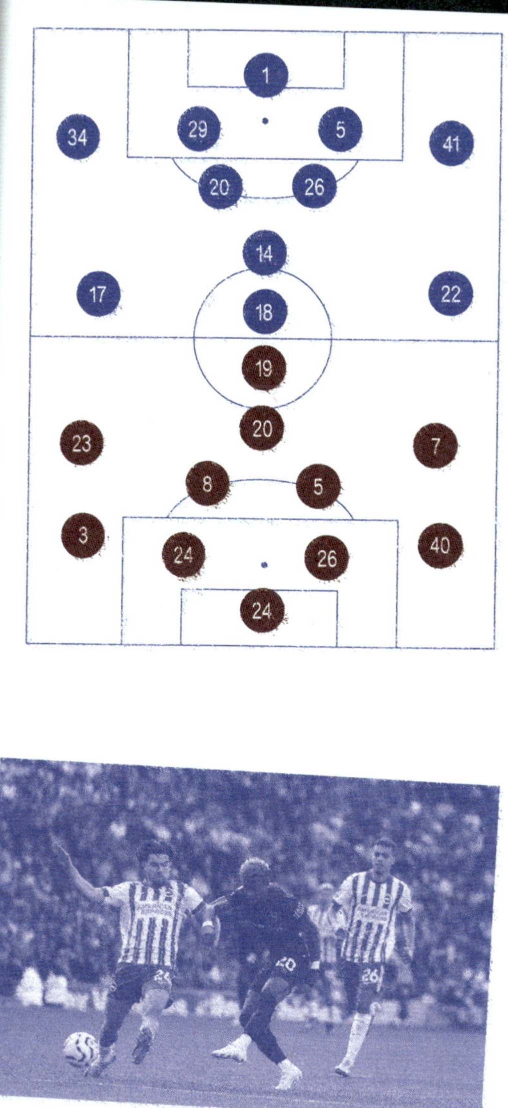

23 STEELE
41 HINSHELWOOD
04 WEBSTER (C)
03 IGOR
30 ESTUPINAN
17 MINTEH
15 MODER
20 BALEBA
11 ADINGRA
28 FERGUSON
10 ENCISO
01 SA
37 LIMA
04 BUENO
46 POND
02 DOHERTY
20 DOYLE
08 JOAO GOMES
21 SARABIA
11 HWANG
19 R. GOMES
29 GUEDES

7.45pm
BRIGHTON 3
WOLVES 2
CARABAO CUP

AMEX Stadium
18.09.2024

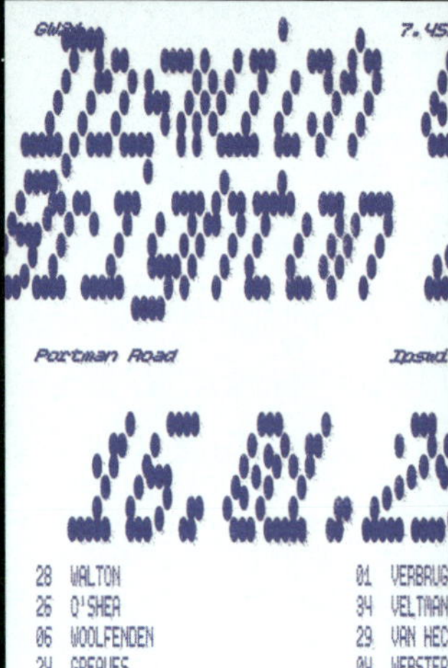
Portman Road

28 WALTON
26 O'SHEA
06 WOOLFENDEN
24 GREAVES
08 DAVIS
08 PHILLIPS
01 VERBRUGG
34 VELTMAN
29 VAN HECK
04 WEBSTER
30 ESTUPINA
20 BALEBA
26 AYARI
33 O'RILEY
22 MITOMA
09 JOAO PED
11 ADINGRA

GW28
VERBRUGGEN
HINSHELWOOD
VAN HECKE
WEBSTER
ESTUPINAN
BALEBA
AYARI
MINTEH
RUTTER
MITOMA
JOAO PEDRO
LENO
DIOP
ANDERSEN
BASSEY
CASTAGNE
ROBINSON
PEREIRA
BERGE
IWOBI
SMITH-ROWE
JIMENEZ
Premier League

08.03.25
AMEX Stadium,
Brighton
BRIGHTON & HOVE ALBION
3pm

IPSWIC
BRIGHTO

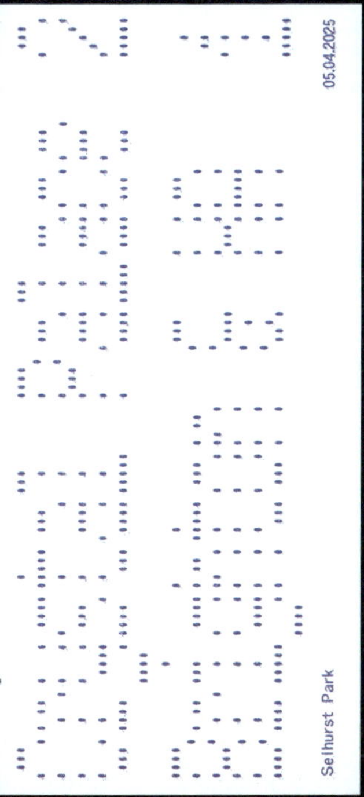

05.04.2025

Selhurst Park

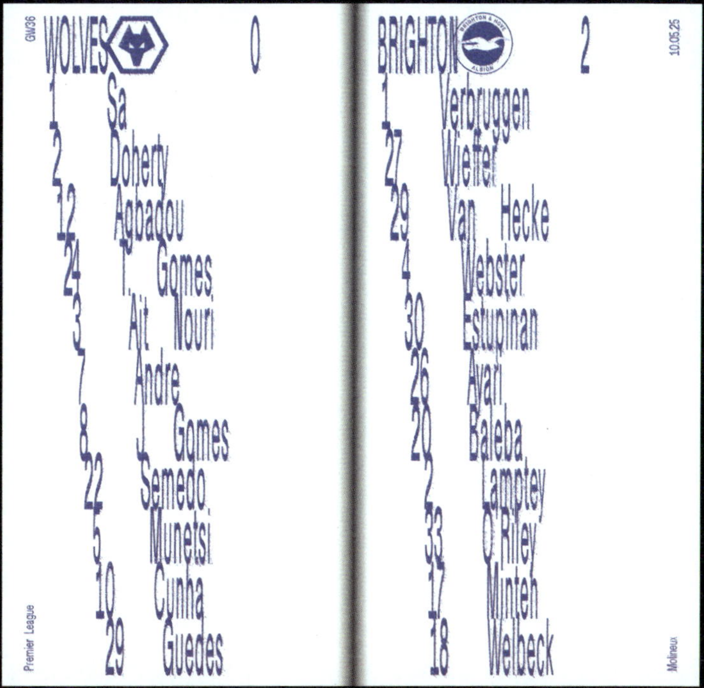

Premier League

Southampton 0	Brighton 4
30 Ramsdale	1 Verbruggen
14 Bree	2 Lamptey
35 Bednarek	4 Webster
7 Aribo	29 Van Hecke
2 Walker-Peters	41 Hinshelwood
26 Ugochukwu	26 Ayari
18 Fernandes	20 Baleba
34 Welington	17 Minteh
33 Dibling	9 Joao Pedro
19 Archer	14 Rutter
20 Sulemana	22 Mitoma

GW26

22.02.25

St Mary's Stadium

GW36

WOLVES 0	BRIGHTON 2
1 Sa	1 Verbruggen
2 Doherty	27 Wieffer
12 Agbadou	29 Van Hecke
24 T. Gomes	4 Webster
3 Ait Nouri	30 Estupinan
7 Andre	26 Ayari
8 J. Gomes	20 Baleba
22 Semedo	2 Lamptey
5 Munetsi	33 O'Riley
10 Cunha	17 Minteh
29 Guedes	18 Welbeck

10.05.25

Premier League

Molineux

OLE

HOLE is a publication on minigolf, centered on historian Jonathan Haeber's text examining how art movements shaped course design since the nineteenth century. The project visualises this research through 18 fictional courses linked by a continuous central hole. Created in 2013, it was later revised and republished.

DESIGN
Broos Stoffels

SIZE
100mm x 280mm x 6mm

PUBLISHER
Aubergine Press

FEATURES
Eyelet-staple binding, Risograph printing on Munken, punctured throughout

Reflection of an ERA In the Miniature Golf Course by Jonathan Haeber

There are places that demand a spot in our childhood milieu. Among these places are county fairs and city swings, Disneyland, tree houses, and that divine spot under the Christmas tree. But, to my 10-year-old self, the miniature golf course was nothing short of a dream world – the manifestation of all the great movies and adventurous ruminations that I'd experienced up to that point. The miniature golf course was magic incarnate, a setting in the landscape that allowed for an infinite amount of imagination.

In a sense, miniature golf is as artistic as the Louvre, Stonehenge, and the numerous statues, buildings, and monuments that tower over the Lilliputian greens. Like art, the design of a course changes in the realm of time, and attracts the people of its age. Like cinema, miniature golf is a variant of art for the masses. It is the greatest unknown art of the American landscape and its artists are the capitalistic craftsmen that satiated the lower and middle class of their appetite for culture. In support of such a claim, the various ages of miniature golf course design below will be corresponded with periods and figures in traditional art.

ROMANTIC ERA EMERGENCE REE 1867 ► 1916

What is "essentially the oldest miniature golf course" is the Ladies' Putting Club in St. Andrews, Scotland Carlson. It was formed in 1867, and has a limited membership. Its highlight is the Himalayas, an 18-hole putting green. The club was initially for practical purposes since it was then "considered unacceptable for women to take the club back past their shoulder". Though the purpose of the course was once for women, who comprise the majority of the membership, it is known as one of the most prestigious greens on the British Isles, and has been played by Ben Crenshaw, Peter Jacobsen, Tom Watson, Craig Stadler and George Bush Sr. The early miniature courses, including the Himalayas, were one of three types: the pitch and putt, the regulation par-3, and the executive course.

At that time, games of miniature golf involved the use of two clubs: the putter and a short driver. Courses were usually from 50 to 100 yards. They retained the architectural plans and landscaping techniques of the regulation course, with undulating hills, verdant forests, sand traps, and ponds. These early courses imitated nature in all aspects. They reflected the Romantic era paintings of John Constable, one of the most famous British Landscape artists of his time. Notice the curvilinear roads and random setting of the greens in appendix A. This was the typical American miniature golf course of the early 20TH century. Most were located at hotels and resorts, and therefore were not yet available to the masses. The only artificial aspect of the REE course was the ubiquitous clubhouse. The clubhouse is the shrine and axis mundi of the mini-golf course, and it has remained as a common element of the course, even in contemporary times.

POST-ROMANTIC CLASSICISM PRC 1916 ► 1926

Following the First World War, Americans viewed industry much differently. Concurrently, the 'city efficient movement' was at its apogee. City planning was in full swing, and – it seemed – traditional classicism was returning, even on the miniature golf course. In 1916, James Barber of Pinehurst, North Carolina, designed Thistle Dhu, the first quintessential miniature golf course. Word has it, that after having seen his finished course, Barber declared to his designer "This'll do!" and an American icon was born. The plan of Barber's Thistle Dhu was as much Classical as the Par-3 was Romantic. The plan resembles the preeminent source of neo-classical landscape design, the Tuileries Garden at the Louvre. Geometric shapes are coupled with symmetric walkways, fountains, and planters.

DaVinci's anatomical drawings closely resemble the anatomical plan of Thistle Dhu. Though Da Vinci is widely considered a Renaissance artist, his work is highly classical in style. Da Vinci reasoned that every natural form could be represented in geometric shapes. His sketch of Vitruvian Man is one of the most famous works of the Renaissance, though the overt geometric patterns in the sketch point to a Greco-roman classicism. The elements of the PRC miniature golf course – much like Classical works of art – were constructed from more artificial materials. Concrete stepping stones and artificial fountains were intertwined with endemic species and natural grass. No longer were miniature golf courses curvilinear and relatively spacious. By 1920, they became compact, efficient, geometric, and above all, Classical.

STERILE MINIMALIST SM 1926 ► 1950

The Great Depression coupled with a high demand for miniature golf resulted in one of the greatest "art for the masses" movements in American history. Miniature golf was less expensive than its counterpart, the picture show, and was also a more engaging activity. Though the artistic value of the depression era movies is often highlighted, miniature golf courses were equally artistic, in a sterile/minimalist sense. The year 1926 marked the beginning of the most successful time in the history of miniature golf. No longer was miniature golf for the elite estate-owners or Scottish ladies. In 1926, "a pair of high-rolling promoters built a pocket course on the roof of a skyscraper in New York City's financial district". It was not long before the Manhattan skyline was pockmarked with rooftop miniature golf courses. After the invention of the dyed cottonseed hull carpet that same year – a revolutionary step for mini-golf – Manhattan gave birth to around 150 rooftop courses; each one was highly successful.

SCORECARD

HOLE	PAR	PLAYERS			
		1	2	3	4
1	2				
2	1				
3	5				
4	3				
5	2				
6	5				
7	1				
8	1				
9	2				
10	2				
11	1				
12	2				
13	2				
14	1				
15	1				
16	1				
17	1				
18	1				
TOTAL IN					
TOTAL OUT					
SCORES					

RULES & PENALTIES

1. Tee ball within two feet from start of fairway.
2. Ball may be placed six inches from border for all shots.
3. Ball off fairway. Drop back on fairway where it goes out. Penalty, one extra stroke.
4. Do not play until preceding players are off fairway. Please move off Fairway prompty after your play is completed.
5. Please return playing equipment to clubhouse at completion of round.
6. Eighteenth hole. A hole in one in N°4 entitles player to a complimentary game, also deduct 4 points from total score. Free games register chimes inside clubhouse. In hole N°3 deduct 3 points; hole N°2 two points; and in hole N°1 deduct one point from total score.
7. Not more than 18 holes are to be played for an admission. One personony may use the same ball or club.
8. Penalty for lost ball - see management

PLEASE BE CONSIDERATE OF EQUIPMENT!

ONOMATOPEE

Onomatopee is a visual investigation into designing sound. Created with illustrator Lukas Verstraete, the project explores how onomatopoeia can be visualised across characters, situations and languages. Through playful experiments, abstract and unfamiliar sounds are translated into graphic form. The work was presented at Grafixx extd. #3 and later published as a booklet.

MIAUW

oehoe
zzZZZz
RONK
Bzzzzzzzzzz

OEi!
oei
hahahaha
HA
HA

mWOAH
Trriiiiing
PLETS
pffff
Kukelekuu
TSJILP
TSJILP
TSJILP
PRRR

HAM
HAM

Pong

① 4–11 Aap, Noot, M
Vul twee identieke grids in met 16 beelden enerzijds en
anderzijds. Vervolledig vervolgens de beide grids met de
beelden of onomatopeeën en laat in een laatste stap de
elkaar overlappen.
② 12–15 Overlap
Ontwerp een beeld, eenmaal geletterd, eenmaal geteken
onomatopee *eek*. Leg woord en prent vervolgens in een
kleur over elkaar om zo één finaal geheel te bekomen.

EEEK

③ 16–17 In uw kot
Teken en schrijf de geluiden die je hoort in een slaapkan
het slapen gaan, andermaal bij het ontwaken. De illustra
een klein kader toegewezen terwijl de geschreven geluide
hun vorm kunnen krijgen.

④ 18–19 Karakter
Illustreer of beletter drie uiteenlopende situaties met één
naar keuze. Completeer de resultaten door voor elke tek
illustraties te ontwerpen en doe hetzelfde in de omgekee

hahaha

ALL THE DOGS I SAW IN TOKYO

All The Dogs I Saw In Tokyo by Tessa Smith-Roberts is a collection of 37 drawings inspired by dogs encountered during trips to Tokyo. From fluffy dogs and dogs in clothing to big and small breeds, the series captures the charm and variety of everyday canine sightings.

DESIGN	SIZE	PUBLISHER	FEATURES
Tess Smith-Roberts	200mm x 200mm x 3mm	The Bee's Knees	Saddle-stitched binding

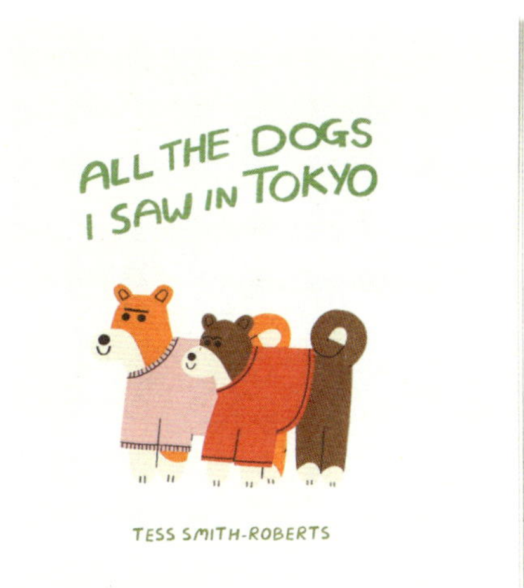

LONG DOGS

TESS SMITH-ROBERTS IS AN ILLUSTRATOR BASED IN LONDON. SHE APPROACHES HER WORK WITH HUMOUR, BOLD SHAPES, AND A PLAYFUL USE OF COLOUR. CLASSIC STILL LIFE PAINTINGS, FLUFFY DOGS, AND FOOD (ESPECIALLY FRUIT!), ARE THE MAIN INSPIRATIONS FOR HER WORK.

@TESSSMITHROBERTS
TESSSMITHROBERTS.CO.UK

PRINTING BY HAGURUMA CO., LTD

PUBLISHED BY
THE BEE'S KNEES INC
WWW.THEBEESKNEES.ART

LUMPS AND BUMPS

Lumps and Bumps is a Risograph poster-zine exploring how time marks the body. Through vulnerable illustrations, the project reflects on acceptance, discomfort and the tension between concealment and display, particularly in relation to women's experiences. Designed to be hung as a poster, the large-format zine functions as both publication and wall piece.

DESIGN	SIZE	PUBLISHER	FEATURES
Rachel Sender	245mm x 352mm	Rachel Sender	Spiral binding, Risograph printing

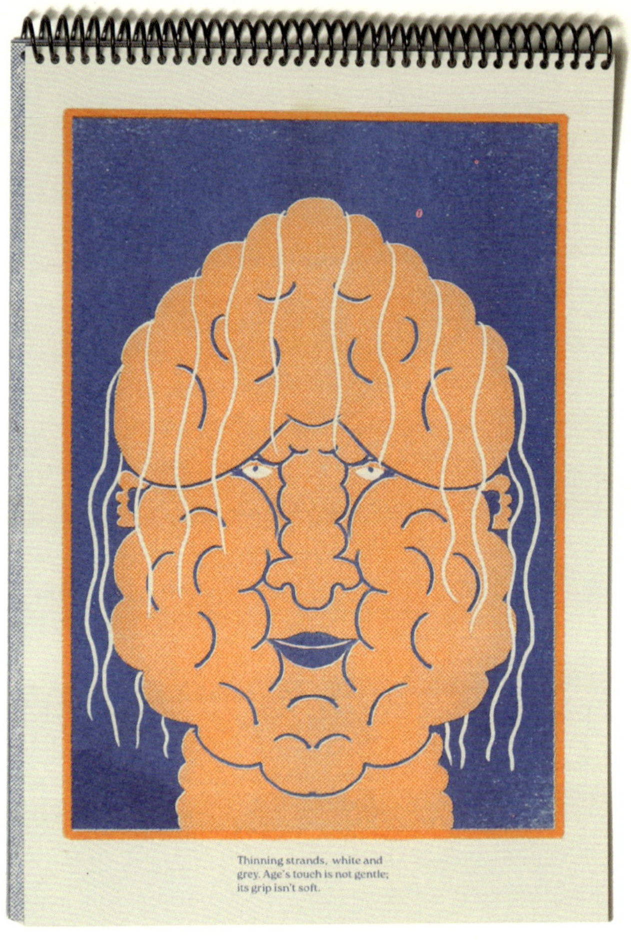
Thinning strands, white and
grey. Age's touch is not gentle;
its grip isn't soft.

COMFY NOTE

Part of the Comfy Project series, this notebook emerged from Howful's playful experimentation within a space of open creation. Its elongated format introduces an unusual proportion, offering a generous surface for everyday notes, sketches and spontaneous creative moments.

DESIGN	SIZE	PUBLISHER	FEATURES
Boda Keem, Inhye Park	80mm x 218mm	HOWFUL	Saddle-stitched binding, Risograph printing, black paper

ETERNAL REFERENCE ZINE 1

ETERNAL REFERENCE is the first edition of an ongoing publishing project by NoPattern Studio. The zine compiles recent explorations in AI, traditional mixed media, photography and collage, bringing these approaches into dialogue within a single visual journal conceived as both study and homage.

DESIGN
Chuck Anderson

SIZE
177.8mm x 254mm

PUBLISHER
NoPattern Studio

FEATURES
Saddle-stitched binding, hand-embossed logo detailing, Obi strip book band

Eternal Reference
Nocturn Studio
Chuck Anderson

AESTHETIX 2

AESTHETIX 2 is a maximalist photobook that treats texture, colour, light, and pixels as equal design elements. Through heavy digital manipulation, images are bent toward abstraction, creating hallucinatory compositions that prioritise surface, intensity, and visual chaos. The design embraces excess and distortion while preserving the raw intent of the original photographic frame.

CONCEPT & PHOTOGRAPHY	SIZE	PUBLISHER	FEATURES
Tyrone Williams	125mm x 180mm	VILLAGE	Saddle-stitched binding, sticker-applied cover logo

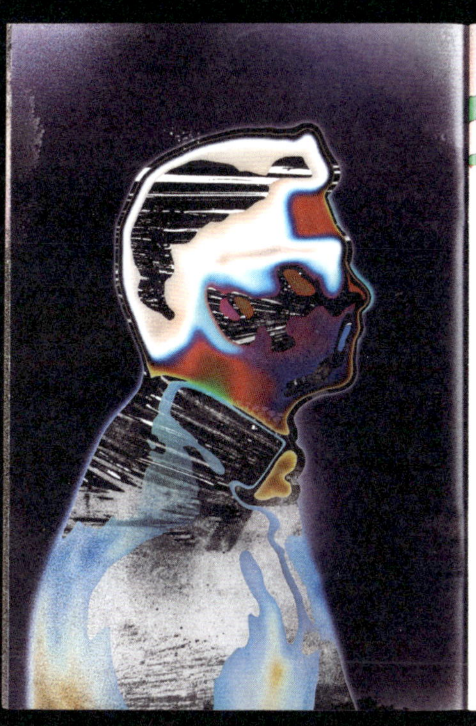

CHUO RAPID LINE

This zine traces a visual journey along Tokyo's Chuo Rapid Line, unfolding from start to finish as a continuous narrative. Drawing on personal impressions of the route and inspired by 1980s manga and anime aesthetics, Apollo Thomas blends nostalgia, public transport and urban atmosphere into a vivid illustrated sequence.

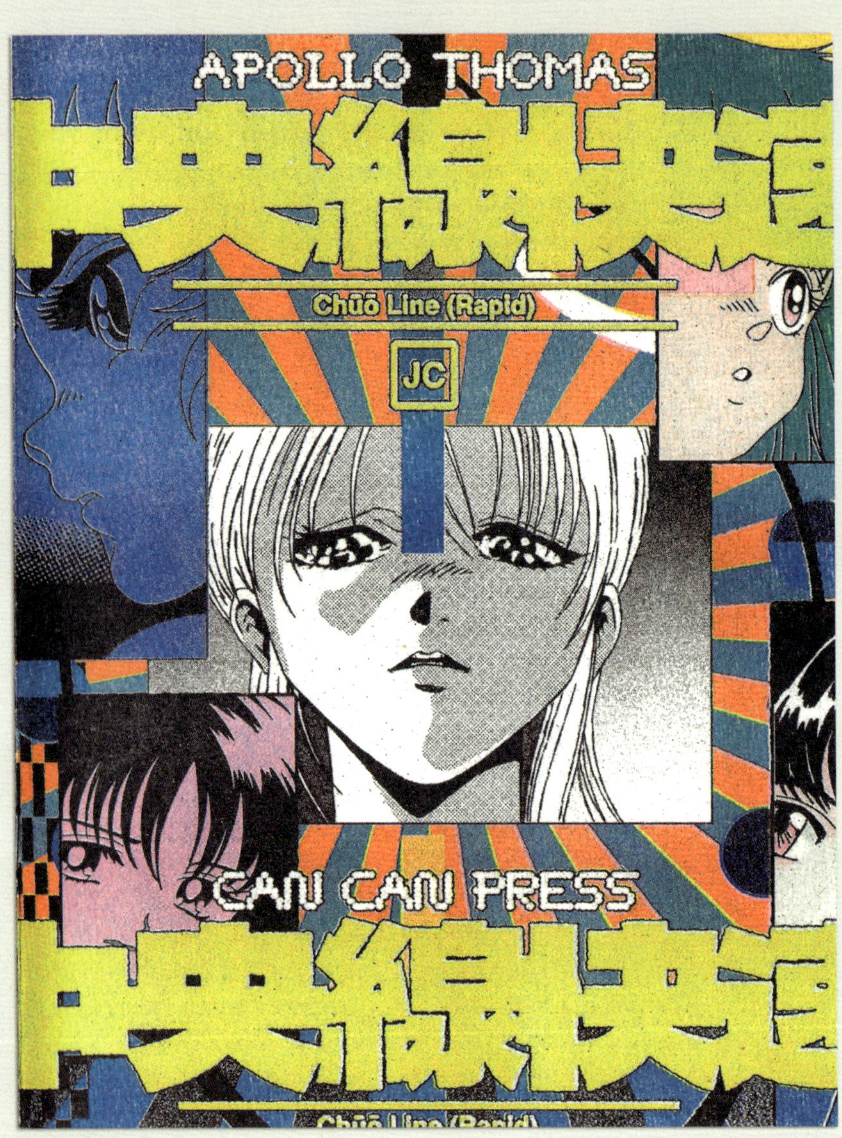

DESIGN
Apollo Thomas

SIZE
200mm x 260mm

PUBLISHER
Can Can Press

FEATURES
Saddle-stitched binding, gloss-coated cover

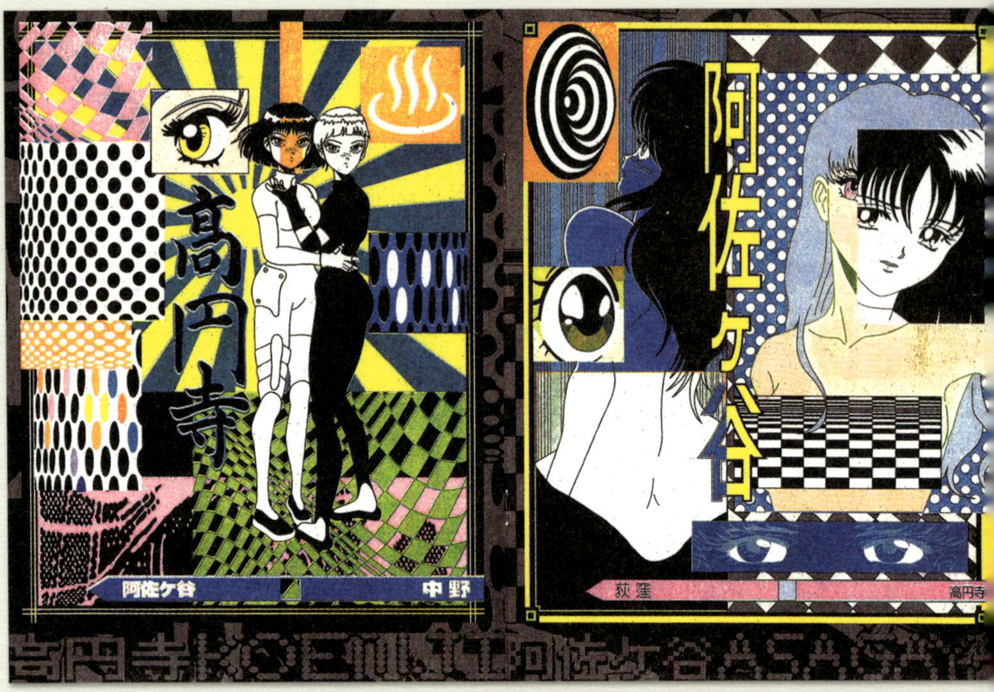
高円寺
阿佐ケ谷
中野
阿佐ケ谷
荻窪
高円寺

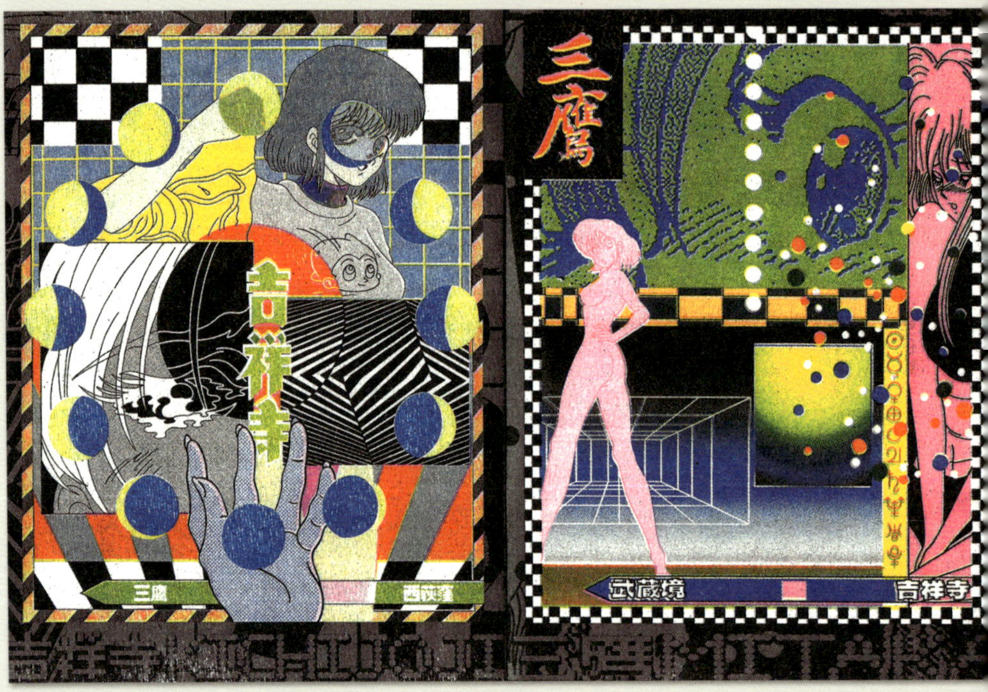
吉祥寺
三鷹
西荻窪
三鷹
武蔵境
吉祥寺

武蔵境

東小金井　三鷹

東小金井

武蔵小金井　武蔵境

武蔵小金井

新宿 Shinjuku
四ツ谷 Yotsuya
御茶ノ水 Ochanomizu
神田 Kanda

中野 Nakano
高円寺 Koenji
阿佐ケ谷 Asagaya
荻窪 Ogikubo
西荻窪 Nishi-Ogikubo
吉祥寺 Kichijoji
三鷹 Mitaka
武蔵境 Musashi-Sakai
東小金井 Higashi-Koganei
武蔵小金井 Musashi-Koganei

CHUO RAPID LINE
BY APOLLO THOMAS
2023

EDITED, PUBLISHED
AND PRINTED
BY CAN CAN PRESS
IN MEXICO
CITY

CANCANPRESS.COM

4 INK FAUX CMYK
RISO PRINTED
ON
RECYCLED PAPER

1ST EDITION
OF 300

THANKS TO
CLARA PACOTTE
FOR THE TEXTS

THIS BOOK
IS DEDICATED
TO
DORA
MARGOT
BELA

FRUTIK

Frutik is a love letter to fruit and graphic excess. The zine develops a personal design language shaped by Colombian street markets, improvised flyers and everyday abundance. Rooted in childhood memories and the visual chaos of fruit stalls, it celebrates affection, urgency and the expressive force of informal design.

DESIGN	SIZE	PUBLISHER	FEATURES
Johnathan Barragán	200mm x 260mm	Can Can Press	Saddle-stitched binding, gloss-coated cover

SURREAL ODYSSEY

Surreal Odyssey is a zine that reinterprets 1950s American science fiction through an Art Deco lens. Combining retrofuturist references with personal visual interpretations, it constructs a cinematic universe that evokes the atmosphere of a lost film, suspended between nostalgia and imagined futures.

DESIGN	SIZE	PUBLISHER	FEATURES
Kevork Yaroden, Shinzo Noda	200mm x 260mm	Can Can Press	Saddle-stitched binding, gloss-coated cover

DO CIRCUS FALL ISSUE: POP UP! BIG TOP

This zine compresses the spectacle of the circus tent into the image of a microwave popcorn bag. Inspired by 1980s–90s American supermarkets and Pop Art, it adopts a bold, cheap chic aesthetic. Beneath its playful surface, it examines the labour, logistics and risks behind tent-building, alongside the fun of circus life.

DESIGN

Wanchun Ho, Zhong Cao (HOUTH)

SIZE

115mm x 185mm x 5mm

PUBLISHER

Do Circus

FEATURES

Saddle-stitched binding, microwave popcorn packaging design

從歷史看到馬戲篷的可能性

在二十世紀早期，隨著馬戲篷巡迴、在餘興節目中表演的非裔樂團，把藍調和爵士樂散播到美國的各個角落，為這些音樂類型帶來後續的轉變與發展。這就證明了馬戲及馬戲篷具有一種潛力：運用自身親子友善、吸引大眾、四處移動的特點，帶來藝術上的新觀點與可能性。

因此在當代，馬戲篷其實可以是政治和美學相互激盪的地方，也是一個能夠去想像、慶祝、反思和挑釁的所在。

5

Fig.1 – BIAC 國際馬戲藝術節 ©Paulin Jeremy

幾內亞猴麵包樹馬戲團《她們的歌》
©Virgile Sabouraud

《馬布多・莫三比克》
©Pascal Bouclier

瑞士全景電影院劇場
©J. Claire

南非齊普扎普馬戲團《莫亞》
©Joan Ward

法國XY當代雜技團《旅程》
©Samuel Buton

墨西哥藝術家瑪麗安娜・布蘭科《咖啡的變奏》
©Gabriel Aquino

澳洲三角褲工廠《髒髒秀》
©Brendan McCarthy

巴西敞開劇團

西班牙循環劇團《垂老之美》
©Ana Ybañez

比利時狀況馬戲團
《非凡身體》
©Jonas Vermeulen

伯南布哥馬戲學校的馬戲團《賽恩斯馬戲》
©Ricardo Maciel

7 層樓高的帳篷，紅黃條紋相間外觀即來自幾米圖像；演出延伸至帳篷外，街頭藝人、體驗工作坊、市集和繪本裝置，交織成一個「幾米馬戲樂園」。

5 週、3 萬張門票全數售罄，寫下台灣藝文市場罕見的票房紀錄。亮眼數字背後，亦是外界看不見的艱辛。

林智偉說，帳篷每週檢測，確保安全無虞；演員面臨前所未有的高強度演出，任何傷病都可能需要即時替補。對工作人員而言，更是一場馬拉松，如何在重複的工作中維持專注與意志力，也是一大考驗。

票房的成功，是這些幕後壓力堆疊下的結果。

當挑戰成為帳篷的日常

今年，第二屆 FOCASA 馬戲藝術節移師高雄港邊，三頂帳篷同時升起，成了城市天際線最吸睛的景觀。民眾主動在社群媒體上打卡、分享照片，藝術節提前升溫。

然而，挑戰同樣沒有缺席。不同於歐陸地區相對穩定的氣候，台灣的帳篷營運還要面對地震、颱風與各種天災。

這次的藝術節，就碰上颱風來襲。原先已經搭好的帳篷，團隊只能選擇「先降下來」，等待風雨過境，再重新搭建。

林智偉表示，這不只是勞動的重複，更是心理的硬仗——耗費時日的工程瞬間歸零，重來來過。當困難成為常態，團隊的身心韌性被逼迫鍛鍊得更加堅強。

就連藝術節開幕倒數五天，團隊還在颱風過後的場地修復與收拾「殘局」。看到大型機具進出，林智偉說，「就像在蓋房子一樣。」

帳篷在這座多災的島嶼上，不只是舞台，而是現實的縮影。它經歷各種風吹雨打、地震颱風，擊倒之後再重建。烈日下、風雨中，每一次帳篷升起，都折射出不怕挫敗的另類台灣精神。

31

Fig.8 – 第二屆 FOCASA 馬戲藝術節 ©Rafael Wu

A4

24

不是童話故事，讓我們面對現實：帳篷搭建的 10 個備忘錄 Beyond Fairy Tales : 10 Memos for Building a Big Top

帳篷常被賦予流浪、遊牧的浪漫想像與童話氛圍。但真正實地搭帳、走過泥濘、面對暴風的人都知道，這背後是一套龐大而嚴苛的工程。從預算編列、場地勘查、法規保險，到搭建與拆卸的人力配置，每一環都可能成為左右演出成敗的關鍵。

帳篷不是劇場的替代品，而是一個需要全面規劃、精細管理的獨立系統。它既能創造獨特的觀演體驗，也可能因細節疏忽而陷入困境。以下 10 條備忘錄，正是從國際帳篷巡演的經驗中整理出的核心提醒，幫助藝術家、策展與技術團隊在浪漫之外，直視帳篷運作的現實。

HOT HOT SUMMER

This zine captures the intensity of a Hong Kong summer: 34°C heat, suffocating humidity, sideways rain, relentless mosquitoes and late-night cockroaches. Framed as a sweaty love-hate diary, it celebrates the chaotic beauty only locals truly understand, and how surviving a Hong Kong summer deserves a badge of honour.

DESIGN

Lonely Kidney

SIZE

100mm x 200mm

PUBLISHER

Lonely Kidney

FEATURES

Saddle-stitched binding, uncoated woodfree paper, tracing paper

PLAY SERIES 1 『GONGGI』

Gonggi is the first book in the Add to Cart play series, examining the traditional Korean game of the same name. Stones arc through the air and the hand repeats movements, echoing planetary motion. Printed in two colours with foil stamping, the continuous image unfolds in a hand-bound accordion format, connecting the beginning and end of the book as one.

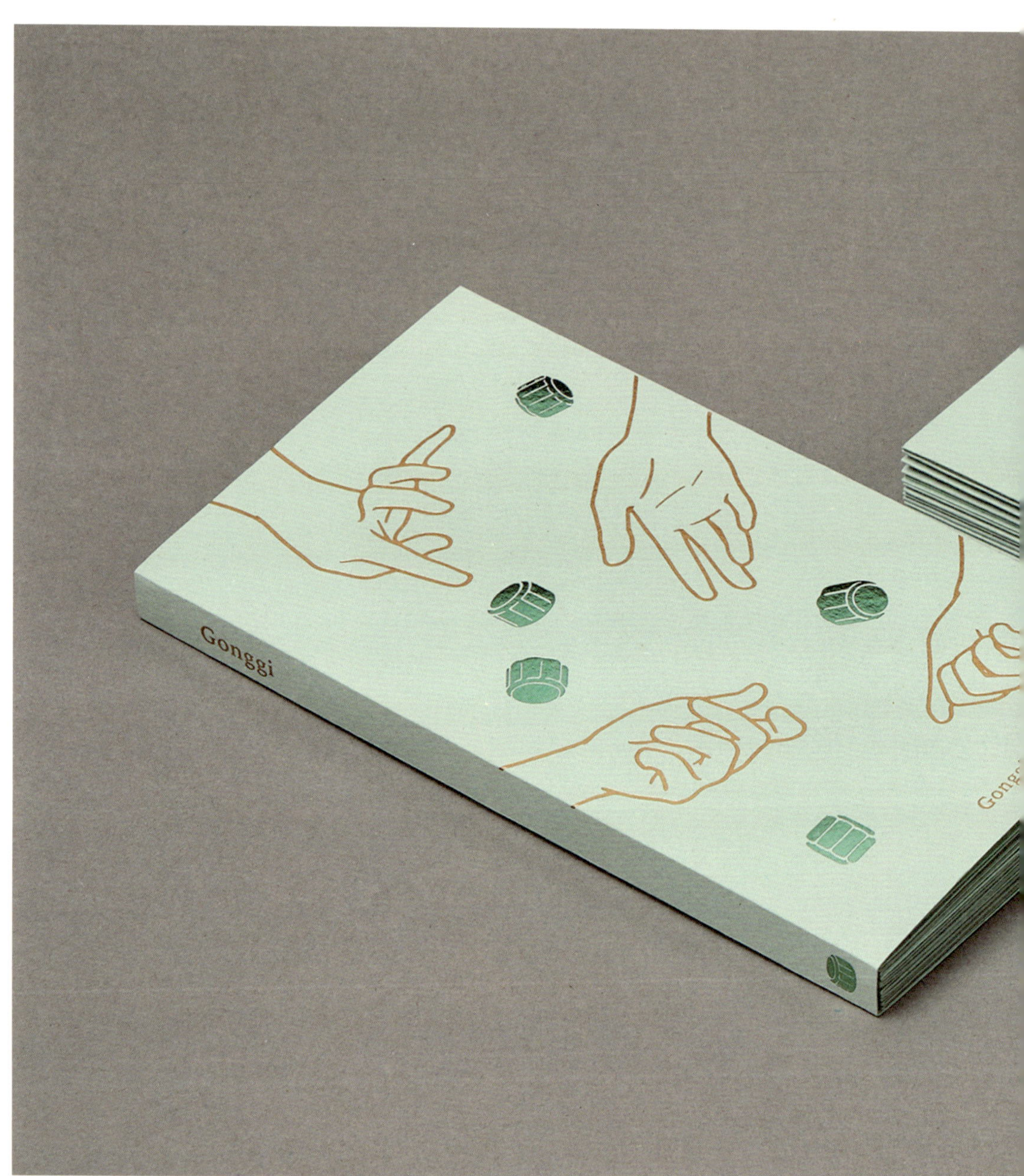

DESIGN	SIZE	PUBLISHER	FEATURES
the object	90mm x 65mm x 12mm	ADD TO CART	Two-colour foil stamping, hand-bound accordion format

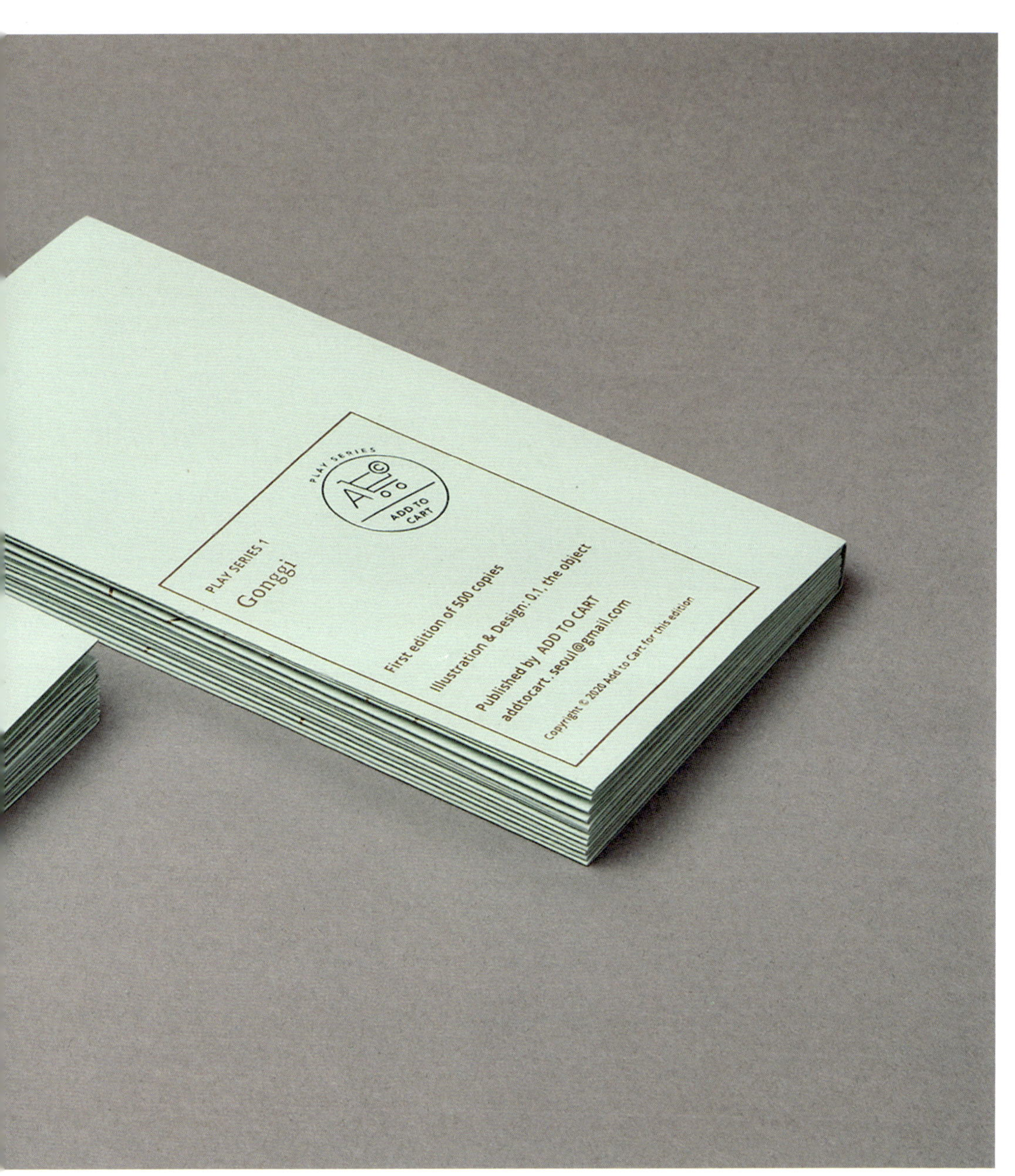

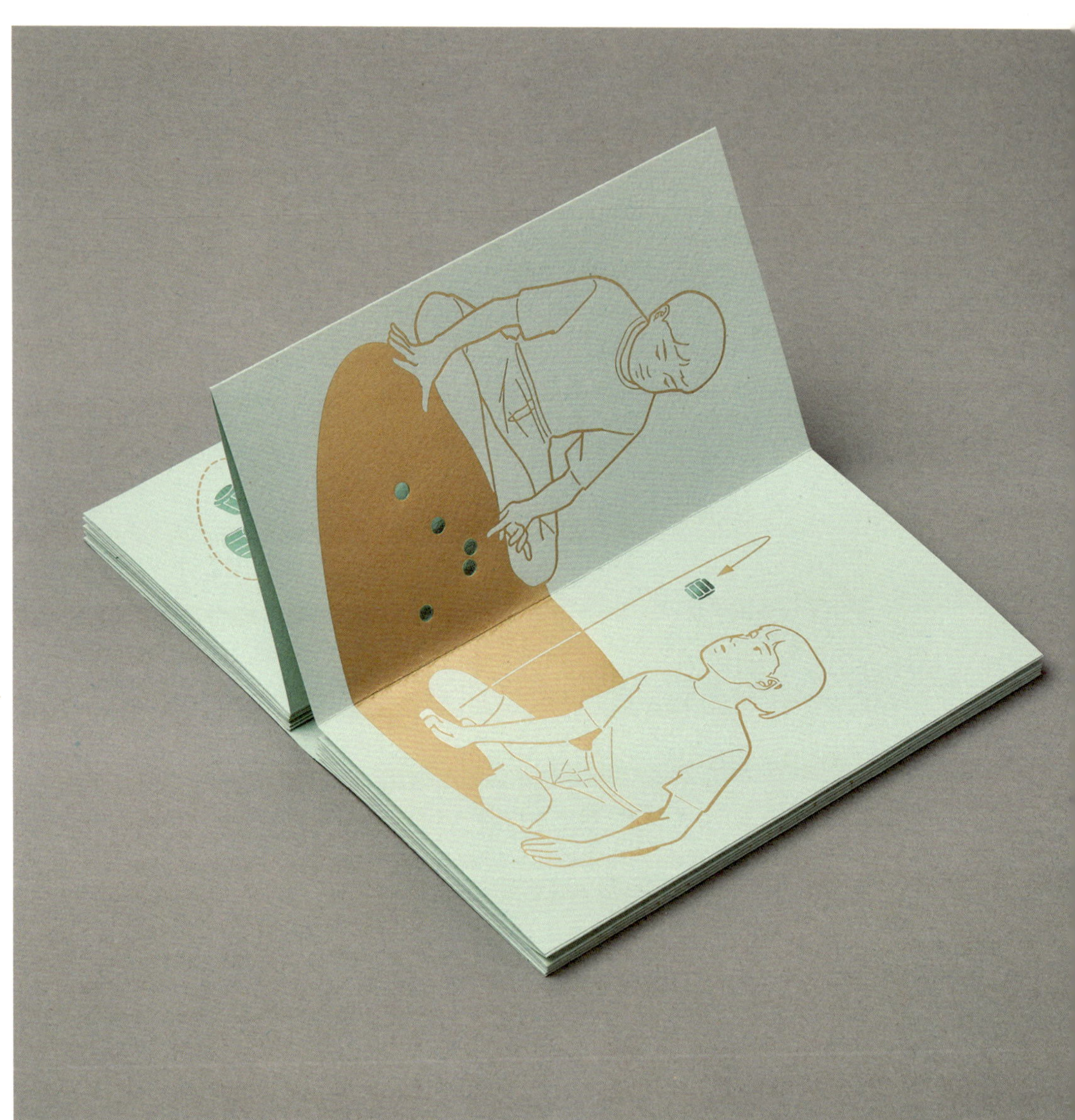

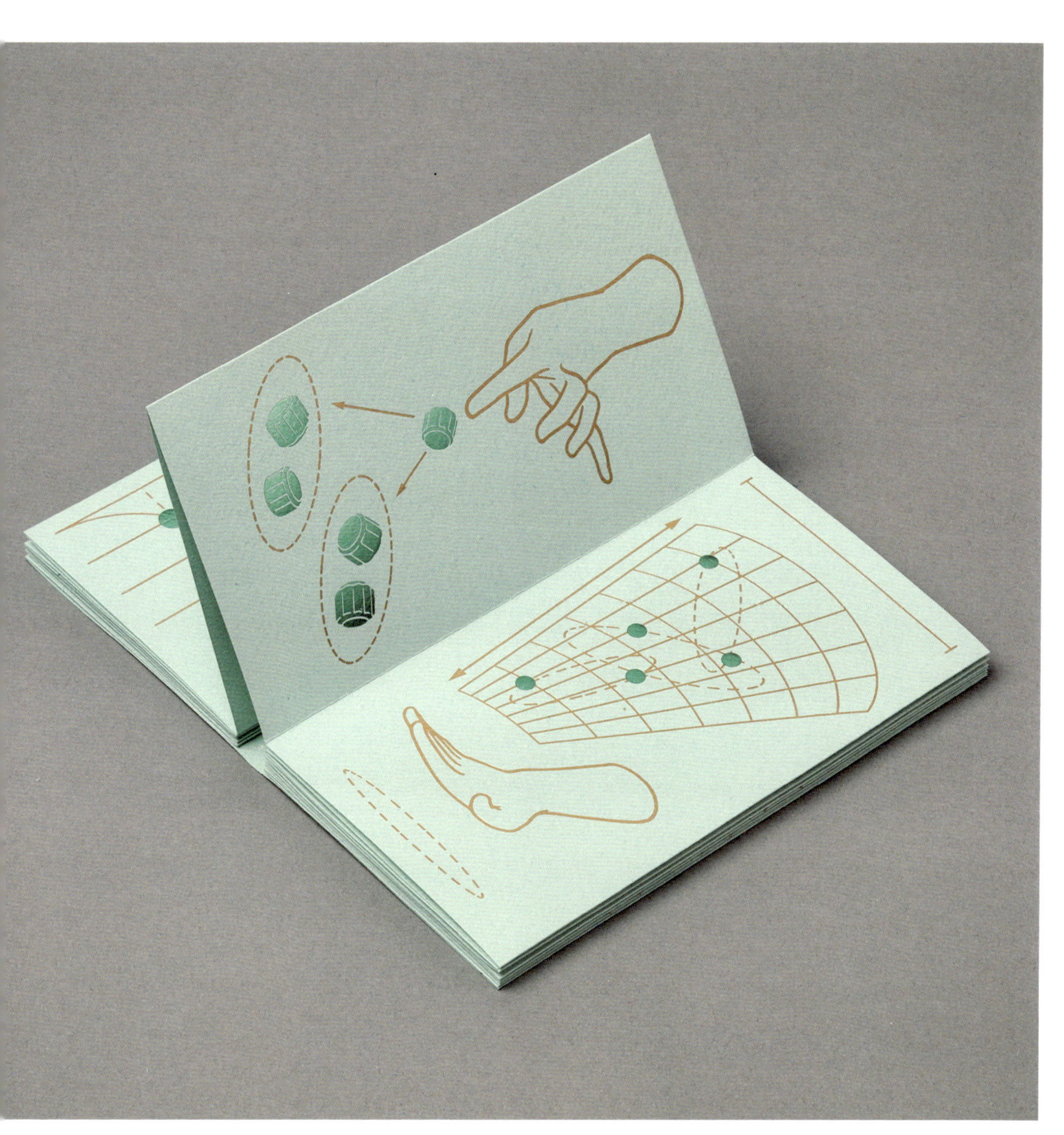

CART SERIES 2 『MOVING NUMBERS』

CART SERIES explores objects as books, with the second theme, Moving Numbers, collecting dice, a lotto shaker, a clock, and a calendar — number-based objects in motion. Each shape corresponds to a number, and their arrangement shifts with applied pressure. Printed to scale in a single colour, the forms are emphasised. The cover features a rotatable number plate, revealing the title and numbers sequentially.

DESIGN	SIZE	PUBLISHER	FEATURES
the object	150mm x 210mm x 7mm	ADD TO CART	Saddle-stitched binding, hardpaper cover, spot-colour printing to scale, interactive number-plate cover

SHAPE DOCUMENT (1)

Shape Document (2022–) is an ongoing graphic project exploring the beauty and diversity of form through the creation of numerous unique shapes. Each is carefully named, catalogued and classified, forming an evolving database with concrete and abstract expressions.

DESIGN	SIZE	PUBLISHER	FEATURES
Yang Qiao Ran	115mm x 14mm x 20mm	Riversbed	Clear planner binder, Pantone spot-colour printing, holographic cards, stickers, embroidered label, keychain

052 DS00290011 POINT(29)
SPECIES(DREAMSCAPE)

053 COMP00230005 POINT(23)
SPECIES(COMPONENT)

054 DS00200012 POINT(20)
SPECIES(DREAMSCAPE)

115 MN00280024 POINT(28)
SPECIES(MONSTER)

1 2 3 4 6 7 5 8 28 9 27 26 10 25 24 12 14 11 21 22 23 13 15 20 16 19 18 17

GUAI LI LUAN SHEN

This zine is a multi-dimensional study of hidden traditional Chinese culture within contemporary modernity. Combining archival research with fieldwork in Shenzhen, it traces the history and current manifestations of superstition in design. The project culminates in a cross-media visual identity merging traditional symbols with global graphic trends.

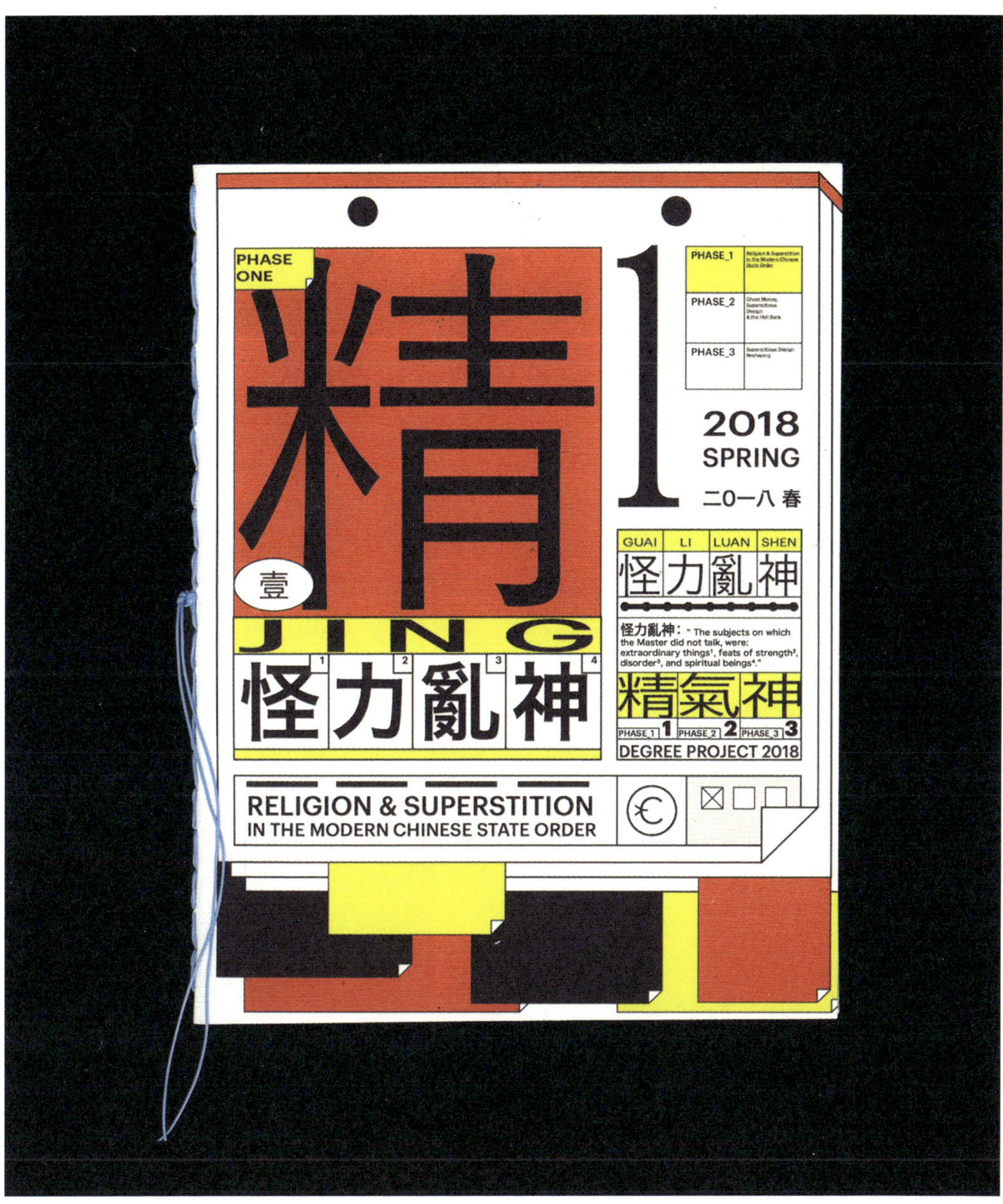

八字算命大
卦相
专业

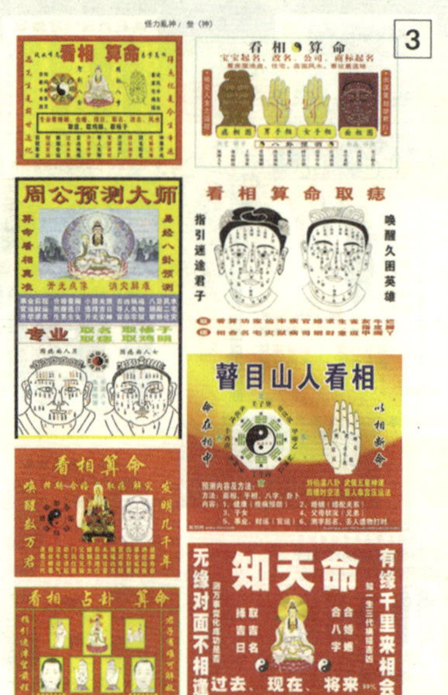
3
看相 算命
周公预测大师
看相算命取痣
瞽目山人看相
看相算命
知天命
无缘对面不相逢
有缘千里来相会
过去、现在、将来
看相 占卜 算命

100
發
CURRENCY
FOR THE
OTHERWOR

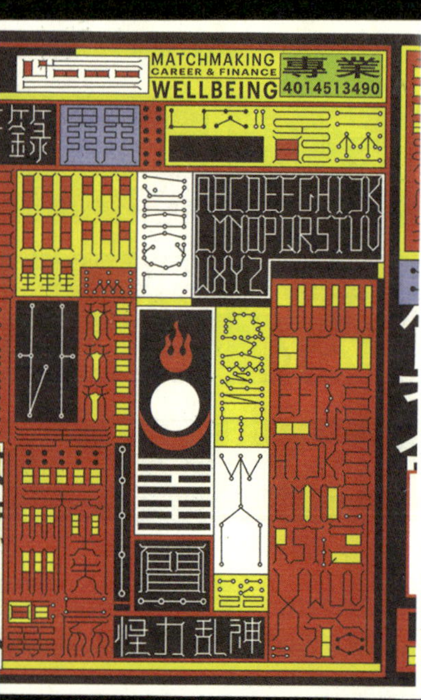
MATCHMAKING
CAREER & FINANCE
WELLBEING
專業
4014513490
ABCDEFGHIJK
LMNOPQRSTUV
WXYZ
怪力乱神

怪力亂神
看相
看相
專業
4014513490
SPRING 2018
CAN YANG
卜卦

34
看相 算命
八字預測
金錢六爻
Physiognomy
Palm
Studying
卜卦
LONGEVITY
PROSPERITY
STATUS
PURPLE
STAR
ASTROLOGY
Professional
Fortune Telling
怪力亂神
CAN YANG
PROPHE
FOUR
-PILLAR
EIGHT
CHARACTE

DESIGN	SIZE	PUBLISHER	FEATURES
Can Yang	215.9mm x 279.4mm	Can Yang	Singer-sewn binding

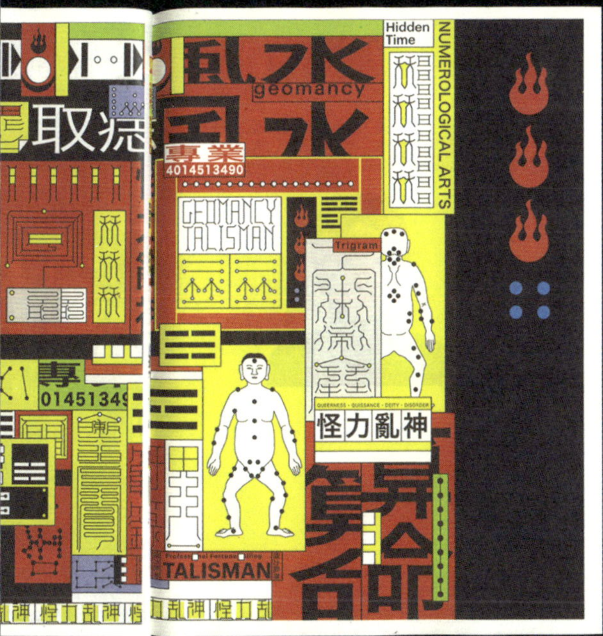

RAILING

Railing is a unique observational study of street railings. Combining street photography, 3D modelling and process documentation, it examines the ubiquitous ball joint in railing systems, transforming this everyday structure into experimental furniture and revealing overlooked design potential within urban details.

DESIGN	SIZE	PUBLISHER	FEATURES
Wanchun Ho (HOUTH)	145mm x 210mm x 8mm	Pon Ding	Elastic tie / wrap clos various paper stocks

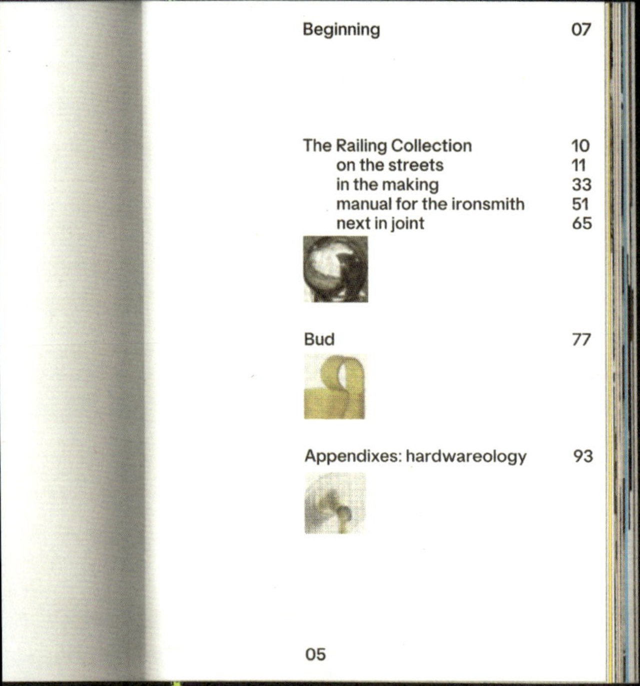

05

Doorstop x Table mirror 2018

S Hook x Wnid Chimer 2018

Mounting Strip x Calendarr 2019

Nail Plate x Candle Holder 2019

Bird Spike x Dish Rack 2019

Vent Grille x Shelf 2019

Shaft Anodes x Dumbbell 2021

Boat Vent x Watering Can 2021

Shackle x Lamp 2022

Lifting Hook x Cloth Rack 2022

Angle Bracket x Bookendr 2018

Doorstop x Pendant Lightr 2019

Caster x Revolving Table 2019

Lifting Ring x Bird Houser 2021

Lashing Plate x Swing 2022

41

96

97

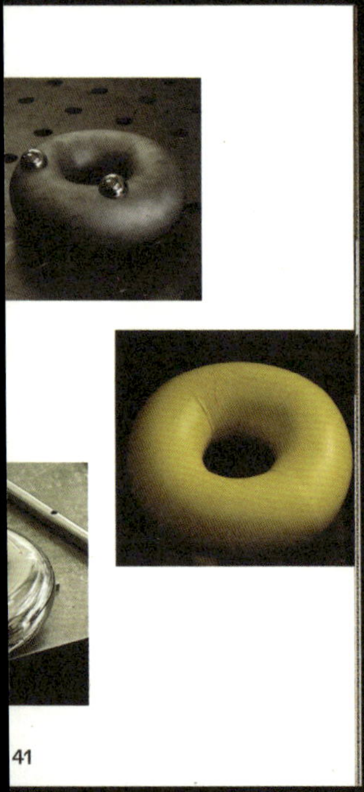

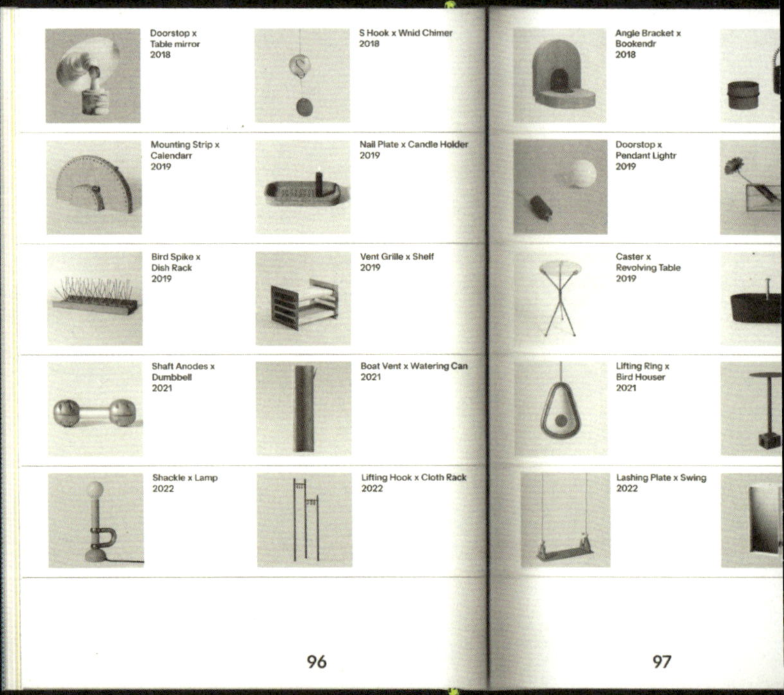

「欄杆萬向接頭」是一個帶有缺口的圓球狀五金零件，缺口端可以無縫貼合在圓管上、而圓球端則能夠從不同角度貼合在圓管底部；除此之外，針對不同粗細的管徑，也早已因應台灣各地公共設施的施作需求，很容易找到廠商提供相對應的公規尺寸球。在實際的欄杆施作過程中，可以隨時搭配樓梯的坡度靈活調整，並於現場焊接完成，相較於原本需要逐一為圓管開槽的做法，這種方法省去許多訂製的成本。

23

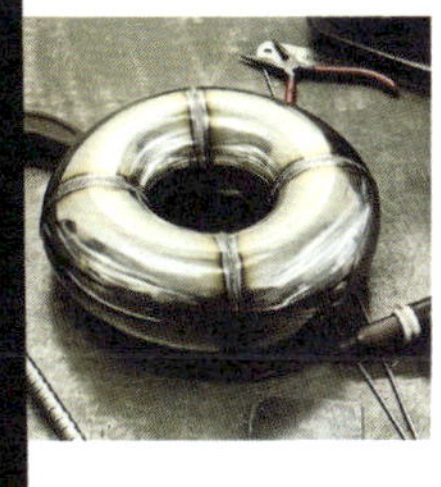

41

x Basket

le Holder x Vase

rew x Box

Casting x
le

t x
Cabinetr

50

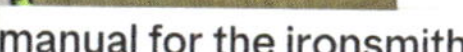

manual for the ironsmith

CAR REFLECTIONS

A long-term photographic series using car surfaces as design tools for abstraction. Reflections fracture reality into layered compositions, where distortion, repetition, and warped perspectives turn familiar forms into graphic, almost painterly images shaped by everyday observation.

CONCEPT & PHOTOGRAPHY	SIZE	PUBLISHER	FEATURES
Tyrone Williams	70mm x 105mm	CREVASSE BOOKS	Saddle-stitched binding, soft cover in cassette case

EARTHWRITING

Earthwriting is a zine created for Magdalena Poost's Greenway Public Art collection, featuring texts and images by eight artists responding to climate change and extractive capitalism. Inspired by Sharad Chari and Clara Wilch, it functions more as a map than a book. Varied grid structures, fragmented typography and immersive full-bleed imagery reflect distinct voices and evoke a shared, ecological spatial experience.

(e)

(f)
(g)

Jaina Cipriano (d)

Made to be Smaller (d)

We Took Too Many Walks
in the Woods (e)

Alex at the Donut (f)
One More Time (g)

Jaina Cipriano

WILD FLOWERS DIES, too (at the end of the world)

Dylan
Havok

(04)

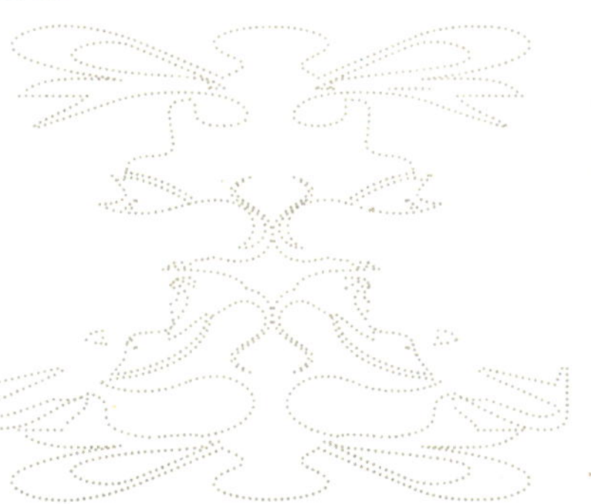

Wildflowers grow where you once laid your head
I picked them last night, soon they'll be dead

I know they would have died either day
It's that time of year for death and decay

Then once again
the soft,
white snow
Will cushion the frozen dead earth below
Our backs in the snow you asked for my story

And I knew we were wild flowers, in a world of concrete
Finding ways through a cold hard system not built for us
Inconvenienced by our passion and persistence through suffering

We were given no fertilizer, no raised plant beds
They paved over our fields for their filthy tire treads

But cement would crack and golden gems sprout forth each year
The power of time and the strength of patience made clear

I picked those bright happy blooms to feel your warmth again
I miss you, my friend

I once depended on the changing seasons
Trusted that after winter, the ground softens
And the seeds that once were flowers grow new buds once more

But the world is changing, this isn't the cyclical type of death
Something uglier, more sinister took your last breath

I placed the fresh flowers among dead plants and murky water
Yellow overshadowing the browns and greens of the dying altar

This old bouquet was proof of our caring community
That I am loved,
and you're a part of me

Maybe I'm greedy for wanting more
For taking those wildflowers to my dorm

I think that I'm lonely, too afraid to be strong
Knowing blossoms rarely stay beautiful long
And wildflowers die, too at the end of the world

(04) Dylan Havok

(04) Dylan Havok

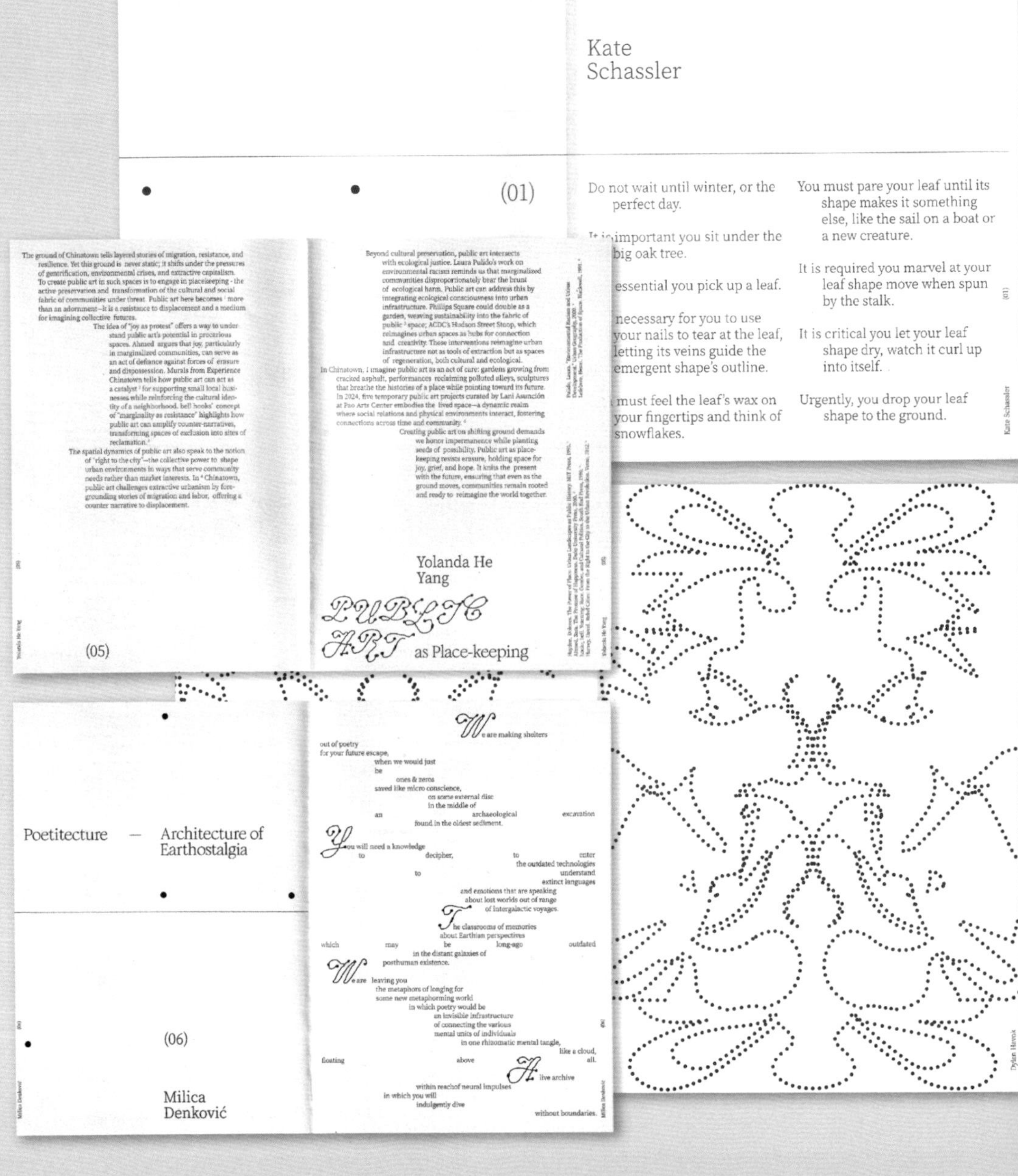

How to make a

LEAF SHAPE

(or, who will you allow to shape your future?)

Kate Schassler

(01)

Do not wait until winter, or the perfect day.

It is important you sit under the big oak tree.

essential you pick up a leaf.

necessary for you to use your nails to tear at the leaf, letting its veins guide the emergent shape's outline.

must feel the leaf's wax on your fingertips and think of snowflakes.

You must pare your leaf until its shape makes it something else, like the sail on a boat or a new creature.

It is required you marvel at your leaf shape move when spun by the stalk.

It is critical you let your leaf shape dry, watch it curl up into itself.

Urgently, you drop your leaf shape to the ground.

Kate Schassler (01)

The ground of Chinatown tells layered stories of migration, resistance, and resilience. Yet this ground is never static; it shifts under the pressures of gentrification, environmental crises, and extractive capitalism. To create public art in such spaces is to engage in placekeeping - the active preservation and transformation of the cultural and social fabric of communities under threat. Public art here becomes [1] more than an adornment—it is a resistance to displacement and a medium for imagining collective futures.

The idea of "joy as protest" offers a way to understand public art's potential in precarious spaces. Ahmed argues that joy, particularly in marginalized communities, can serve as an act of defiance against forces of erasure and dispossession. Murals from Experience Chinatown tells how public art can act as a catalyst [2] for supporting small local businesses while reinforcing the cultural identity of a neighborhood. bell hooks' concept of "marginality as resistance" highlights how public art can amplify counter-narratives, transforming spaces of exclusion into sites of reclamation.[3]

The spatial dynamics of public art also speak to the notion of "right to the city"—the collective power to shape urban environments in ways that serve community needs rather than market interests. In [4] Chinatown, public art challenges extractive urbanism by foregrounding stories of migration and labor, offering a counter narrative to displacement.

(05)

Beyond cultural preservation, public art intersects with ecological justice. Laura Pulido's work on environmental racism reminds us that marginalized communities disproportionately bear the brunt of ecological harm. Public art can address this by integrating ecological consciousness into urban infrastructure. Phillips Square could double as a garden, weaving sustainability into the fabric of public [5] space; ACDC's Hudson Street Stoop, which reimagines urban spaces as hubs for connection and creativity. These interventions reimagine urban infrastructure not as tools of extraction but as spaces of regeneration, both cultural and ecological.

In Chinatown, I imagine public art as an act of care: gardens growing from cracked asphalt, performances reclaiming polluted alleys, sculptures that breathe the histories of a place while pointing toward its future. In 2024, five temporary public art projects curated by Lani Asunción at Pao Arts Center embodies the lived space—a dynamic realm where social relations and physical environments interact, fostering connections across time and community.[6]

Creating public art on shifting ground demands we honor impermanence while planting seeds of possibility. Public art as place-keeping resists erasure, holding space for joy, grief, and hope. It knits the present with the future, ensuring that even as the ground moves, communities remain rooted and ready to reimagine the world together.

Yolanda He Yang

PUBLIC ART as Place-keeping

Poetitecture — Architecture of Earthostalgia

(06)

Milica Denković

We are making shelters
out of poetry
for your future escape,
when we would just
be
ones & zeros
saved like micro conscience,
on some external disc
in the middle of
an archaeological excavation
found in the oldest sediment.

You will need a knowledge
to decipher, to enter
the outdated technologies
to understand
extinct languages
and emotions that are speaking
about lost worlds out of range
of intergalactic voyages.

The classrooms of memories
about Earthian perspectives
which may be long-ago outdated
in the distant galaxies of
posthuman existence.

We are leaving you
the metaphors of longing for
some new metaphorming world
in which poetry would be
an invisible infrastructure
of connecting the various
mental units of individuals
in one rhizomatic mental tangle,
like a cloud,
floating above all.

Alive archive
within reachof neural impulses
in which you will
indulgently dive
without boundaries.

Milica Denković

Dylan Havens

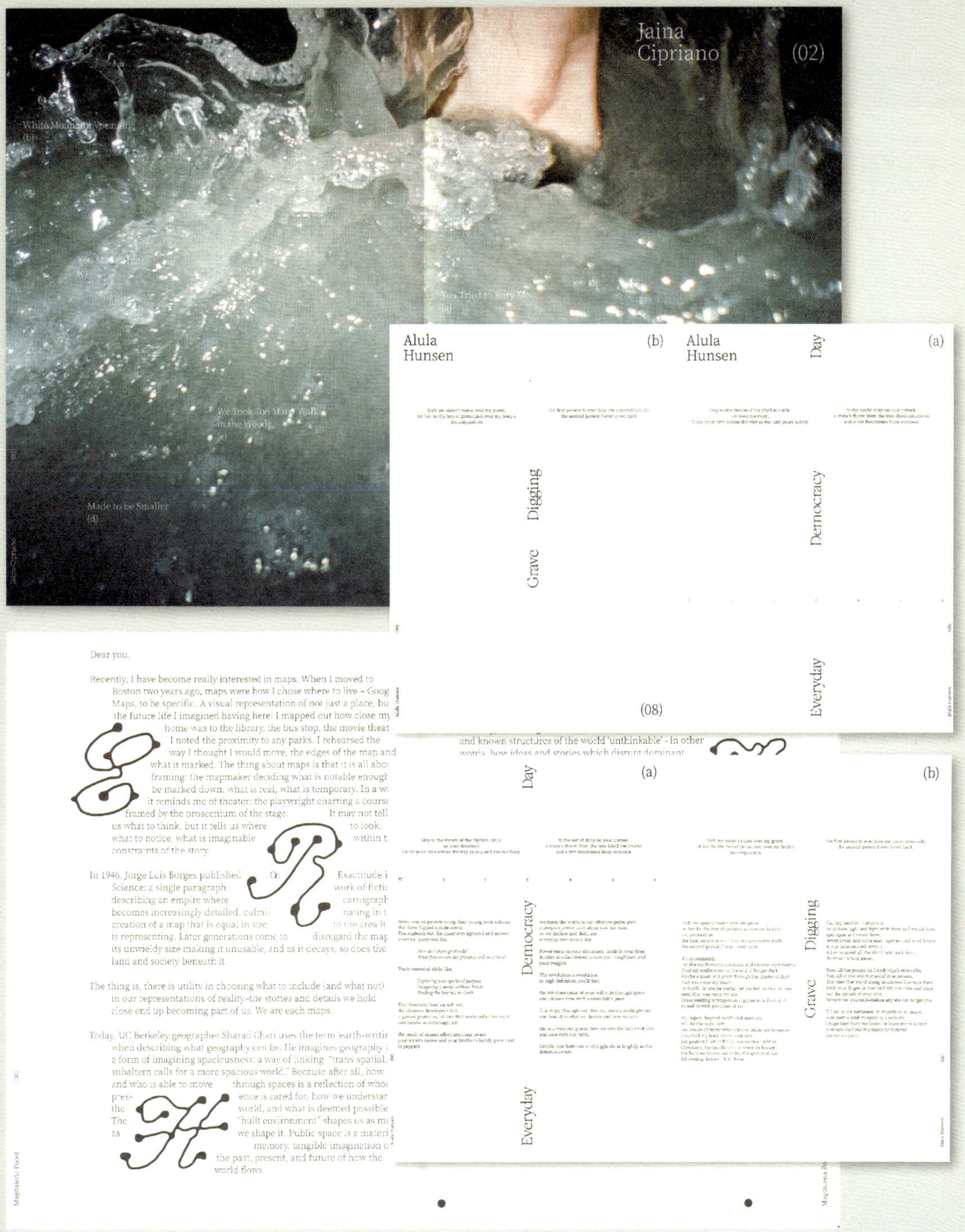

Jaina
Cipriano (02)

You Tried to Bury Me
(a)

White Mountain Vpeanut
(b)

You Made Me
(c)

We Took Too Many Walks
in the Woods
(e)

Made to be Smaller
(d)

Alula
Hunsen (b)

Grave Digging

(08)

Alula
Hunsen (a)

Day Democracy Everyday

Dear you,

Recently, I have become really interested in maps. When I moved to Boston two years ago, maps were how I chose where to live – Goog Maps, to be specific. A visual representation of not just a place, bu the future life I imagined having here: I mapped out how close my home was to the library, the bus stop, the movie theat I noted the proximity to any parks. I rehearsed the way I thought I would move, the edges of the map and what it marked. The thing about maps is that it is all abo framing: the mapmaker deciding what is notable enough be marked down, what is real, what is temporary. In a w it reminds me of theater: the playwright charting a cours framed by the proscenium of the stage. It may not tell us what to think, but it tells us where to look, what to notice, what is imaginable within t constraints of the story.

In 1946, Jorge Luis Borges published On Exactitude i Science: a single paragraph work of fictic describing an empire where cartograph becomes increasingly detailed, culmi- nating in t creation of a map that is equal in size to the area it is representing. Later generations come to disregard the map its unwieldy size making it unusable, and as it decays, so does the land and society beneath it.

The thing is, there is utility in choosing what to include (and what not) in our representations of reality–the stories and details we hold close end up becoming part of us. We are each maps.

Today, UC Berkeley geographer Sharad Chari uses the term 'earth-writir when describing what geography can be. He imagines geography a form of imagining spaciousness: a way of linking "trans spatial, subaltern calls for a more spacious world." Because after all, how and who is able to move through spaces is a reflection of whos pres- ence is cared for, how we understar the world, and what is deemed possible The "built environment" shapes us as mu as we shape it. Public space is a materi memory, tangible imagination o the past, present, and future of how the world flows.

and known structures of the world 'unthinkable' - in other words, how ideas and stories which disrupt dominant

Day (a)

Democracy

Everyday

(b)

Digging

Grave

EMPTY SHADOWS

empty shadows by Nlieechi reflects on memory and loss. A year after his grandmother's passing, the artist returned to his family home for the first time in twelve years, photographing the fields and house that shaped his grandmother's life, tracing both lived landscapes and the enduring image of home held in memory.

DESIGN
Chengjie Li (Nlieechi)

SIZE
160mm x 230mm

PUBLISHER
Chengjie Li (Nlieechi)

FEATURES
Loop-stitch binding, silver spot-colour printing, laser-cut cover

停留在 空影 的尽头
empty shadows

时隔十二年，我随家人一同踏上了久别的故土。往昔春节的热闹已随奶奶的离去而散去，曾经那个温柔慈爱的她，如今只剩墓碑上孤寂的名字。跪在她的坟前，我轻声唤她，烧着手中的纸钱，心底默默祈愿着她在另一个世界的安宁和幸福。未能见奶奶最后一面，是我心中难以抚平的遗憾。站在这片安葬着她的土地上，我举起相机，试图捕捉她在临终时无比牵挂的故乡，记录下她曾生活过的点滴痕迹。

十二年ぶりに私は家族とともに故郷に帰った。かつての春節の喧騒は、祖母の旅立ちとともに散ってしまった。優しくて愛情深い祖母も、今では墓碑銘に寂しげな名前を刻むだけだ。墓の前に膝をつき、そっと祖母を呼び、紙銭を燃やし、あの世での祖母の愛と幸せを祈った。祖母に最後に会えなかったことは、一生の後悔となっている。埋葬された土地に立ち、私はカメラを構え、死に際に祖母が愛着を持っていた故郷を写真に収め、祖母が生きてきた痕跡を記録しようとした。

instagram & weibo | nlieechi
nlieechidesign.com
First Edition of 50 Copies
Photo and Design by nlieechi
Printed in China and Japan

停留在 空影 的尽头
empty shadows

时隔十二年，我随家人一同踏上了久别的故土。往昔春节的热闹已随奶奶的离去而散去，曾经那个温柔慈爱的她，如今只剩墓碑上孤寂的名字。跪在她的坟前，我轻声唤她，烧着手中的纸钱，心底默默祈愿着她在另一个世界的安宁和幸福。未能见奶奶最后一面，是我心中难以抚平的遗憾。站在这片安葬着她的土地上，我举起相机，试图捕捉她在临终时无比牵挂的故乡，记录下她曾生活过的点滴痕迹。

十二年ぶりに私は家族とともに故郷に帰った。かつての春節の喧騒は、祖母の旅立ちとともに散ってしまった。優しくて愛情深い祖母も、今では墓碑銘に寂しげな名前を刻むだけだ。墓の前に膝をつき、そっと祖母を呼び、紙銭を燃やし、あの世での祖母の愛と幸せを祈った。祖母に最後に会えなかったことは、一生の後悔となっている。埋葬された土地に立ち、私はカメラを構え、死に際に祖母が愛着を持っていた故郷を写真に収め、祖母が生きてきた痕跡を記録しようとした。

instagram & weibo | nlieechi
nlieechidesign.com
First Edition of 50 Copies
Photo and Design by nlieechi
Printed in China and Japan

a letter to those we've lost

DRIFT-PRINT RESEARCH ARCHIVE

This zine is an experimental Risograph publication reinterpreting geological photographs of Yilan as sea-scape-like images. Using intentional misregistration, the project treats printing flaws as expressive tools, creating depth and motion through layered blue and black inks as a visual study and research archive.

DESIGN
Tomoyuki Koseko

SIZE
210mm x 297mm x 5mm

PUBLISHER
KOSEKO DESIGN & PRESS

FEATURES
Stapled binding, supplementary research booklets, Risograph print prototype

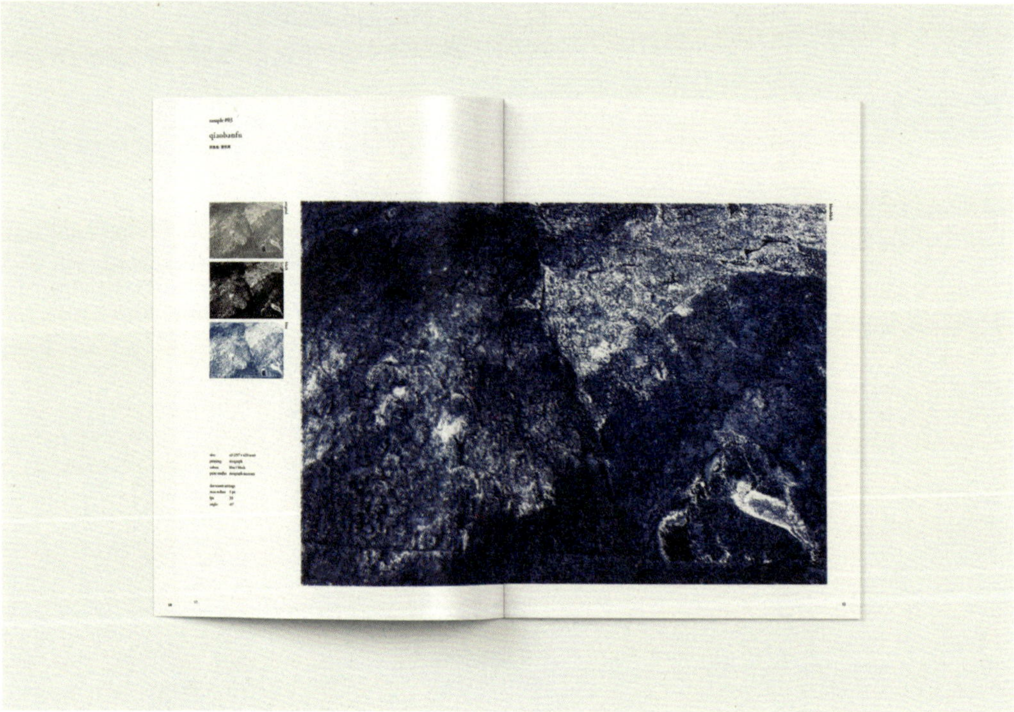

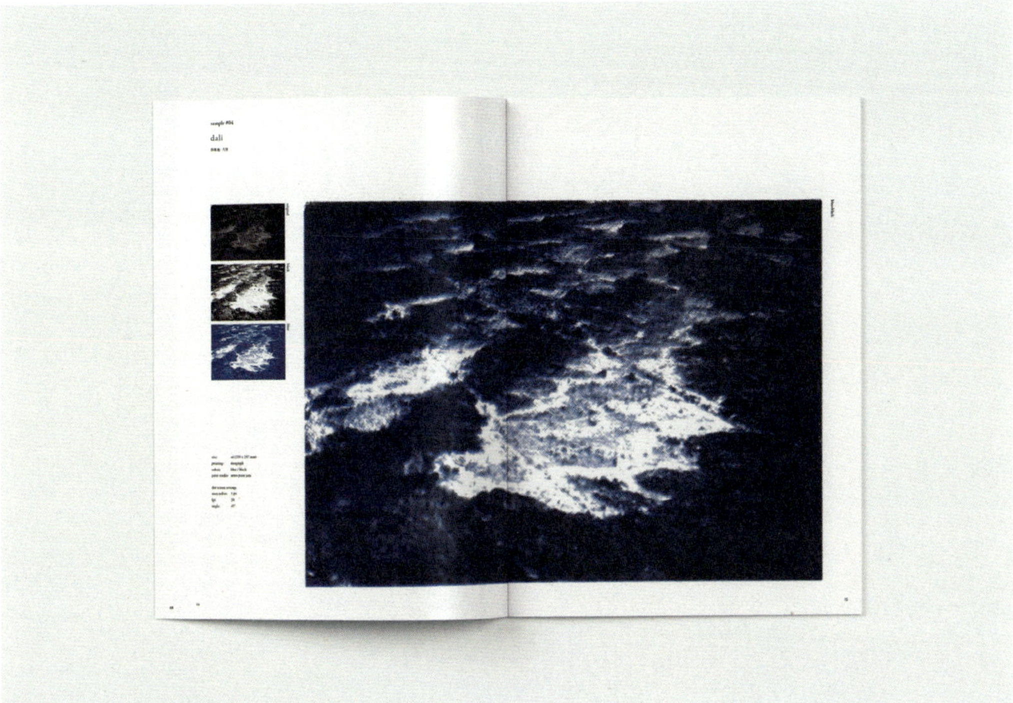

KUMONODAIRA PLATEAU

Kumonodaira Plateau is a poetry-and-photography art book created during a stay in Kumonodaira, deep in the Japanese Northern Alps. Produced in an accordion format, poetry and photographs occupy opposing sides and cannot be viewed simultaneously to shape contrasting reading experiences.

DESIGN	SIZE	PUBLISHER	FEATURES
Mew Imashuku, Tatsumi Sone	90mm x 180mm x 22mm	Mew Imashuku	Double-sided accordion binding, custom-fit cover

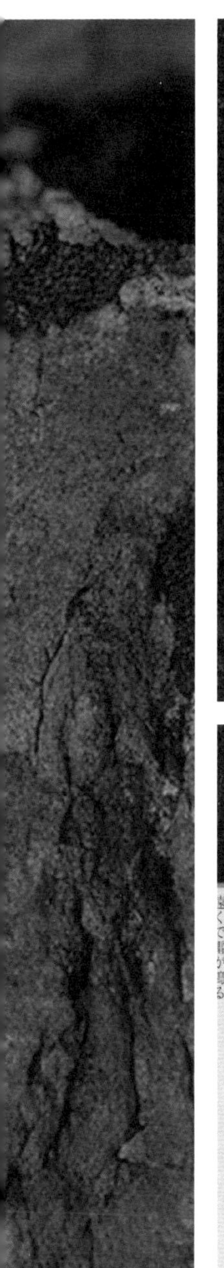

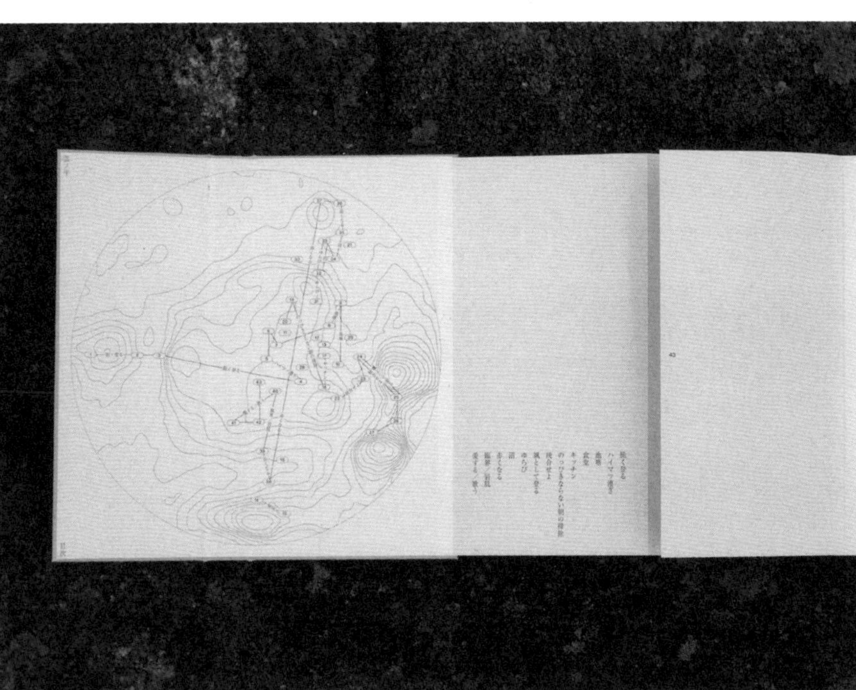

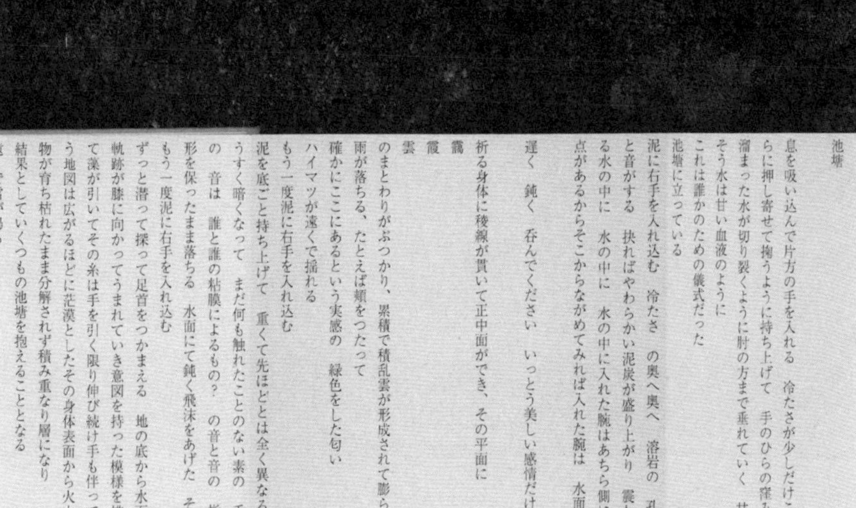

SEARCHING FOR DESIGN FILES: CITY, THEATRE.

Searching for Design Files: City, Theatre by Something-Moon Design examines the hidden role of archives within graphic design. Drawing from theatre-based urban projects, it brings drafts, images and documents into public view, reframing design files as active agents of meaning. Influenced by Boris Groys, the project positions documentation as a form of artistic practice.

平面設計和檔案之間的關係，一直愛恨交纏。在進入離散、不連續的代碼時代，創作過程往往冰冷，面對發光螢幕，設計師的日常經驗有可能無意中被缺席。由想像到完成品之間，產生難以預期的種種文件，往往如幽靈般相遇：搜尋網站提供的無限靈感混亂地放置，需長時間消化的文稿散落檔案夾、偶發對話、花時間去篩選的圖片淹沒了原始意圖……直到完成品顯現，一切的檔案都是在等候被描寫，被丟棄，被改寫，但過程中所有材料都不是設計，通通都只是為了指涉設計。

在我曾做過以城市為題的平面設計中，劇場是其中一個最具意識形態的藝術形式，由文本到視覺需經歷層層觀念，在與設計碰撞中，除了帶來上述的文件外，設計師還需閱讀劇場以外的集體、歷史檔案、新聞或其他主觀產物。

在傾向單純觀看的世界中，平面設計以滿足於視覺炫目為目的，背後牽涉的檔案往往缺席、邊緣、孤寂。關於文件和藝術或創作間的討論，當代藝術學家葛羅伊斯 (Boris Groys) 提出的理論也經常被引用，他指出各種藝術文件就是指涉藝術，而藝術因為本身就定義為藝術，反而無法被指涉為藝術，「藝術不再存在與立即被看見這個狀況變得清晰，藝術是缺席與隱藏的」。亦即是文件、檔案、文獻等雖不直接呈現藝術，但令藝術顯現，藝術文獻也成為藝術其中一個藝術生命形式，某種純粹的活動與實踐填補了藝術的缺席。

我也試着重新翻閱我所做過的設計，那些關於城市的劇場平面設計中，嘗試把各種設計檔、圖檔或文檔等等都放到公共視野之中，尤其我所選輯的演出都有其城市關心的公共議題，題目本身就已經具有一定的現實性，在多種關係中把檔案公開，或者可以給人另一種新的詮釋。

2

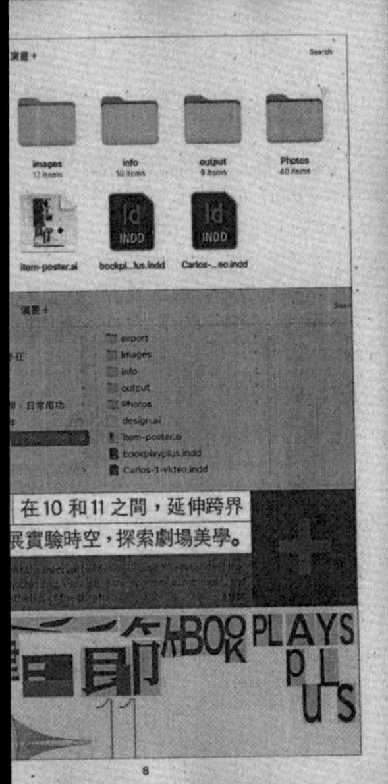

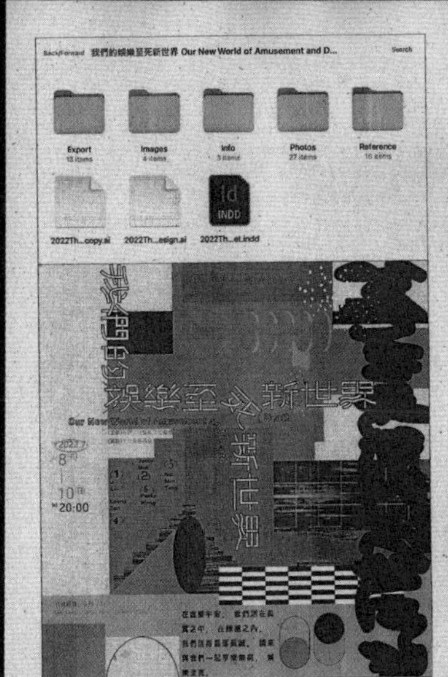
Back/Forward 我們的娛樂至死新世界 Our New World of Amusement and D...
Search
Export
Images
Info
Photos
Reference
2022Th...copy.ai
2022Th...esign.ai
2022Th...et.indd
4

Back/Forward Photos
Search
fb-01.png
ig-1-0-1.jpg
ig-1-0.jpg
ig-1-1-1.jpg
ig-1-1-2.jpg
ig-1-1.jpg
ig-1-2.jpg
ig-1-3.jpg
ig-1-4.jpg
ig-1-5.jpg
ig-2-1.jpg
ig-2-2.jpg
ig-2-3.jpg
ig-2-4.jpg
ig-2-5.jpg
ig-2-6.jpg
ig-2-7.jpg
ig-2-8.jpg
ig-2-9.jpg
ig-3-1.png
ig-3-2.png
ig-3-3.png
ig-3-4.png
ig-3-5.png
web-01.jpg
web-02.jpg
web-03.jpg
5

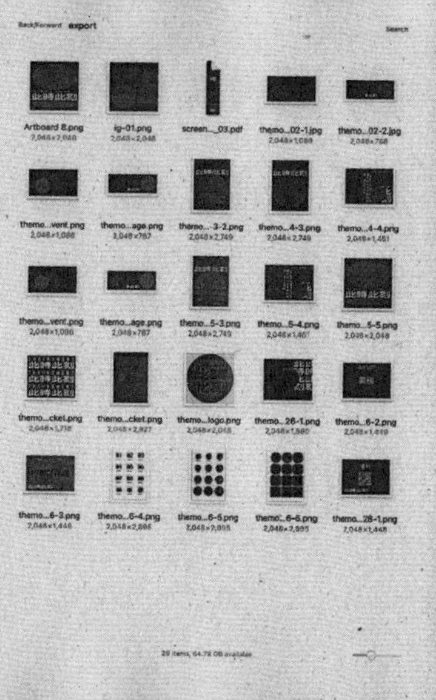
Back/Forward export
Search
Artboard 8.png
ig-01.png
23

Back/Forward stepout/currybone
Search
bin
css
fonts
images
inc
js
languages
template-parts
vendor
readme.txt
screenshot.png
404.php
archive.php
CHANGELOG.md
comments.php
footer.php
functions.php
header.php
index.php
page.php
readme.md
rtl.css
search.php
searchform.php
sftp-config.json
sidebar.php
single.php
style.css
30

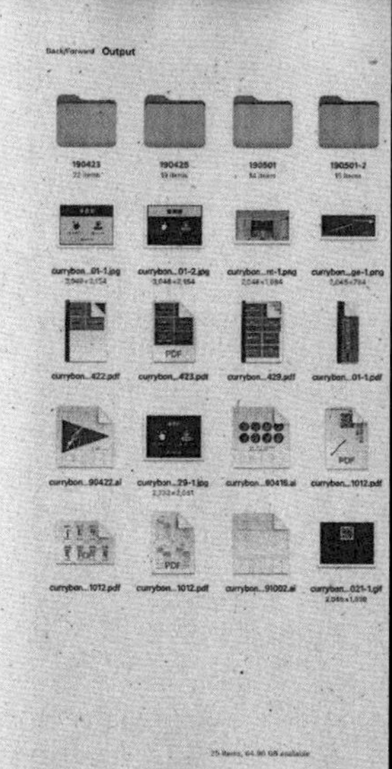
Back/Forward Output
190423
190425
190501
190501-2
31

I DON'T KNOW WHAT CAN I DO ON MY STREET

This photography zine by SomethingMoon Design documents everyday scenes around St. Lawrence's Parish in Macau. Using film, it records subtle changes, quiet corners and ordinary details over time. The work reflects on memory, childhood and familiarity, presenting the street as a lived space shaped by repetition, return and personal attachment.

DESIGN	SIZE	PUBLISHER	FEATURES
SomethingMoon Design	16mm x 23mm	SomethingMoon Design	Saddle-stitched binding

帶水圍 Pátio do Piloto → 2008

帶水圍 Pátio do Piloto → 2008

4

5

光復圍 Pátio da Claridade → 2011

24

下環街 Rua da Praia do Manduco → 2008
mannings
10
下環街 Rua da Praia do Manduco → 2008
11

風順堂區 Freguesia de São Lourenço → 2008
12

三巴仔斜巷 Calçada dos Remédios → 2008
13

亞婆井前地 Largo do Lilau → 2011

32

媽閣斜巷 / 萬里長城 Calçada da Barra → 2011

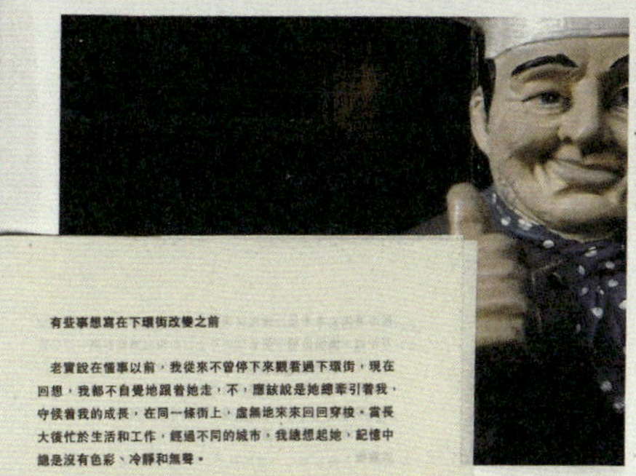

有些事想寫在下環街改變之前

老實說在懂事以前，我從來不曾停下來觀看過下環街，現在回想，我都不自覺地跟着她走，不，應該說是她總牽引着我，守候着我的成長，在同一條街上，虛無地來來回回穿梭。當長大後忙於生活和工作，經過不同的城市，我總想起她，記憶中總是沒有色彩、冷靜和無聲。

童年總是緩慢，時光佇足讓年少在等待長大的我顯躍而難耐，在別人眼中古老樸實的街道，在我眼裏不過是再平凡不過的風景，下環街總是毫不起眼，我所理解的歷史感叫做沒有刺激，純樸叫做無聊。「一段平淡的陳述，可以變化出近一百種不同版本」，在我學會雷蒙．格諾（Raymond Queneau）《風格練習》中的觀點前，我就如一般民眾一樣，對我稱之為家的街道不聞不問。人即使在地方中不停移動，但總會過於安逸，淹沒在浪潮中，我帶着「下環」這個包伏，去學習如何在新社區生活，交新的朋友，吃着異國美吃；我經常在計算着回來的時間，回到那幾條細小的街道，然後又跨越她原有的闊度。

每天我們都在這裏出發，然後等待着回到這裏來。

以前的老店都是家族經營，外面可以借電話，裏面的人都在看電視和聊天，跑來跑去都是熟悉的街坊臉孔，即使我們從不認識，但需要彼此，我會在你那邊買看來不怎麼樣的水果，去跟你買舊款的電燈泡更換，體諒你的貨品缺乏特色但從不變心；過去有灰樸樸的小販在叫賣滋味的熟食，但早早攝不過街道治

37

風順堂區 Freguesia de São Lourenço → 2012

風順堂區 Freguesia de São Lourenço → 2012

62

63

DO YOU WANT ME TO DESCRIBE THE PLACE I LIVE

This introspective zine reflects on the difficulty of describing one's own city without distance. Through careful documentation and selective memory, SomethingMoon Design explores place, emotional proximity and self-censorship, suggesting that recording small, intimate details becomes a way to preserve an entire city and its lived truth.

你剛好要我描述我所居住的地方。

不知道從何時開始，生活就需要懂得論述、評價及說故事，學會把某件事綻放得頭頭是道，映入眼簾的東西變得鬆懈，反覆在一片無情又無聊的汪洋之中，沒有感性地悸動，沒有討論的空間，

他城市冷靜觀察——嚴如不可像別人般講起那個自己漠不關己的城市開懷地評頭論足。

紀錄彷彿是對生活所能做的僅有，探頭探腦地在尋找合適的中立，但事實上是小心翼翼地搜刮合適的篩辭，躲開了令我不滿的所有壞處，企圖閉眼不去記起那不悅的風景，誇大生活小節，努力把人們拉到那製造令人動容的不起眼角落。

但我訝異，我居然撑握了那遙遠的感覺，像被轉述某城市的記憶一樣清楚，越遙遠，越清澈；我記得那些講不出路名的幾條街，不用思考就能正確轉彎的路、爺爺嫲嫲還在的鄉下、隔壁過幾條街就能遇到的外婆及一間媽媽在上班的工廠。記住她們就等於記住了整個城市。

最後，像一個善辯的人，也信服了自己記下的真實。

<u>你剛好要我描述我所居住的地方</u>。

不知道從何時開始，生活就需要懂得論述、評價及説故事，學會把某件事綻放得頭頭是道，映入眼簾的東西變得鬆懈，反覆在一片無情又無聊的汪洋之中，沒有感性地悸動，沒有討論的空間，在沒有喘息中轉動。

自我出生到有認知而來，我就知道自己生活在一個看見海但又看不見海的地方。我可以講出這地方的所有細節，但對過於輕率的記憶卻沒有自信，我怕我會褻瀆她們；我不能像平常一樣對其

你剛好要我描述我所居住的地方

DO YOU WANT ME TO DESCRIBE THE PLACE I LIVE

ABRICA DE ARTIGOS DE VESTUARIO KA LAN

PONTE Nº 31
I HENG

TRAFFIC LIGHTS

Traffic Lights is a conceptual book that narrates a moment of waiting at a pedestrian crossing. Using real traffic light timings, page layouts correspond to red, yellow and green phases. Static imagery, numerical intervals and flip-book animation translate time and movement into a sequential reading experience.

DESIGN	SIZE	PUBLISHER	FEATURES
Sun Xiaoxi	120mm x 90mm x 15mm	PAY2PLAY	Soft cover, digital printing

TRAFFIC
LIGHTS
94

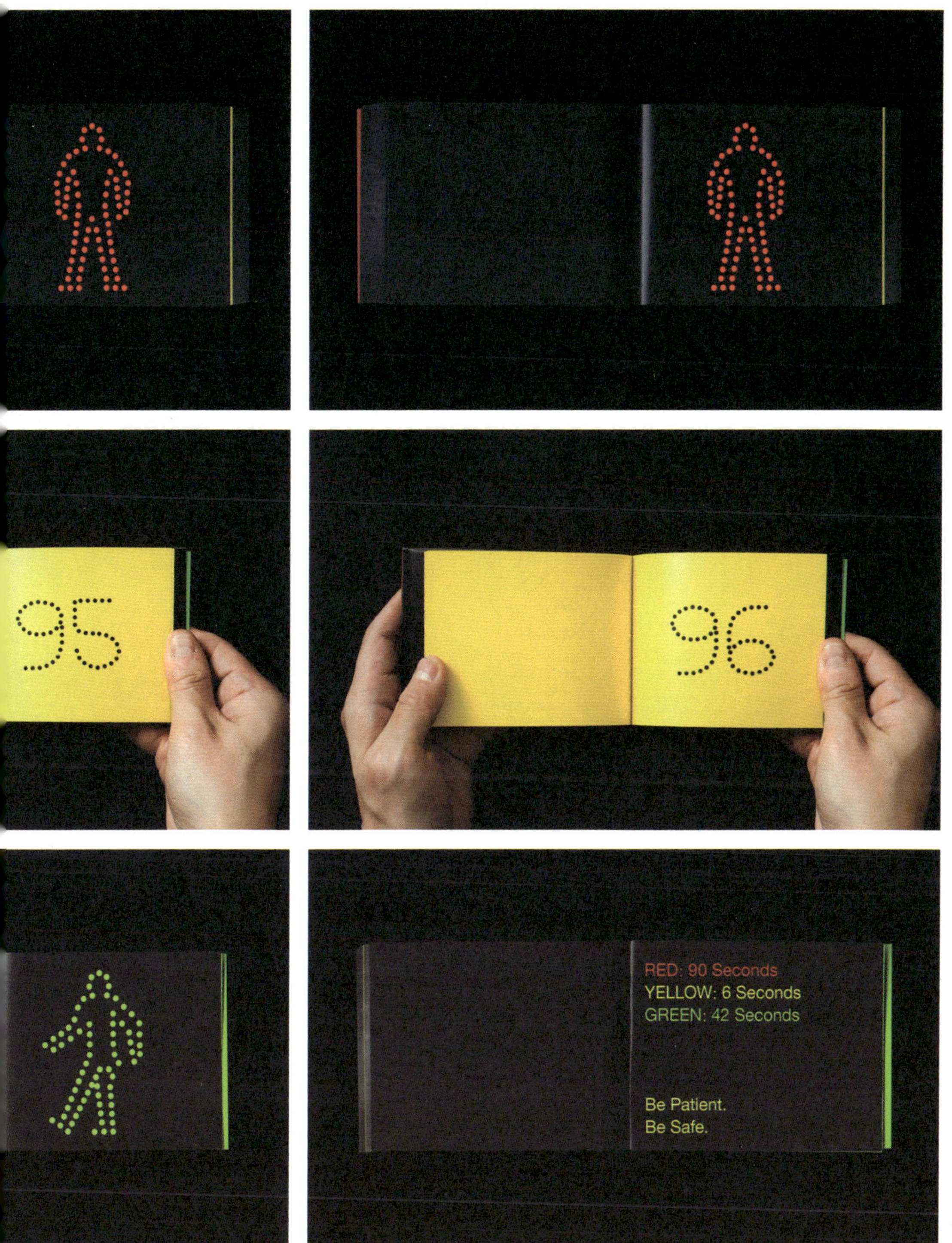
95
96
RED: 90 Seconds
YELLOW: 6 Seconds
GREEN: 42 Seconds
Be Patient.
Be Safe.

ADOBE INDESIGN SPLASH SCREEN ZINE

Adobe InDesign Splash Screen Zine (2023) by DTAN Studio is a one-of-a-kind, handbound publication commissioned for Adobe's InDesign splash screen. Conceived as a tactile extension of digital tools, it explores colour theory, grids and typography through Risograph printing. By pairing software precision with analogue imperfection, the project highlights InDesign's creative possibilities beyond the screen.

DESIGN	SIZE	PUBLISHER	FEATURES
Julia Schimautz (DTAN Studio)	145mm x 200mm	/	Hand-stitched binding, five-colour Risograph printing

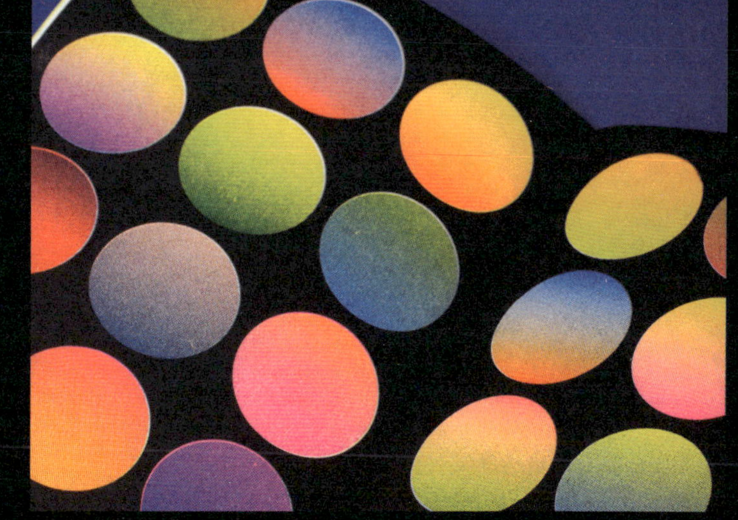

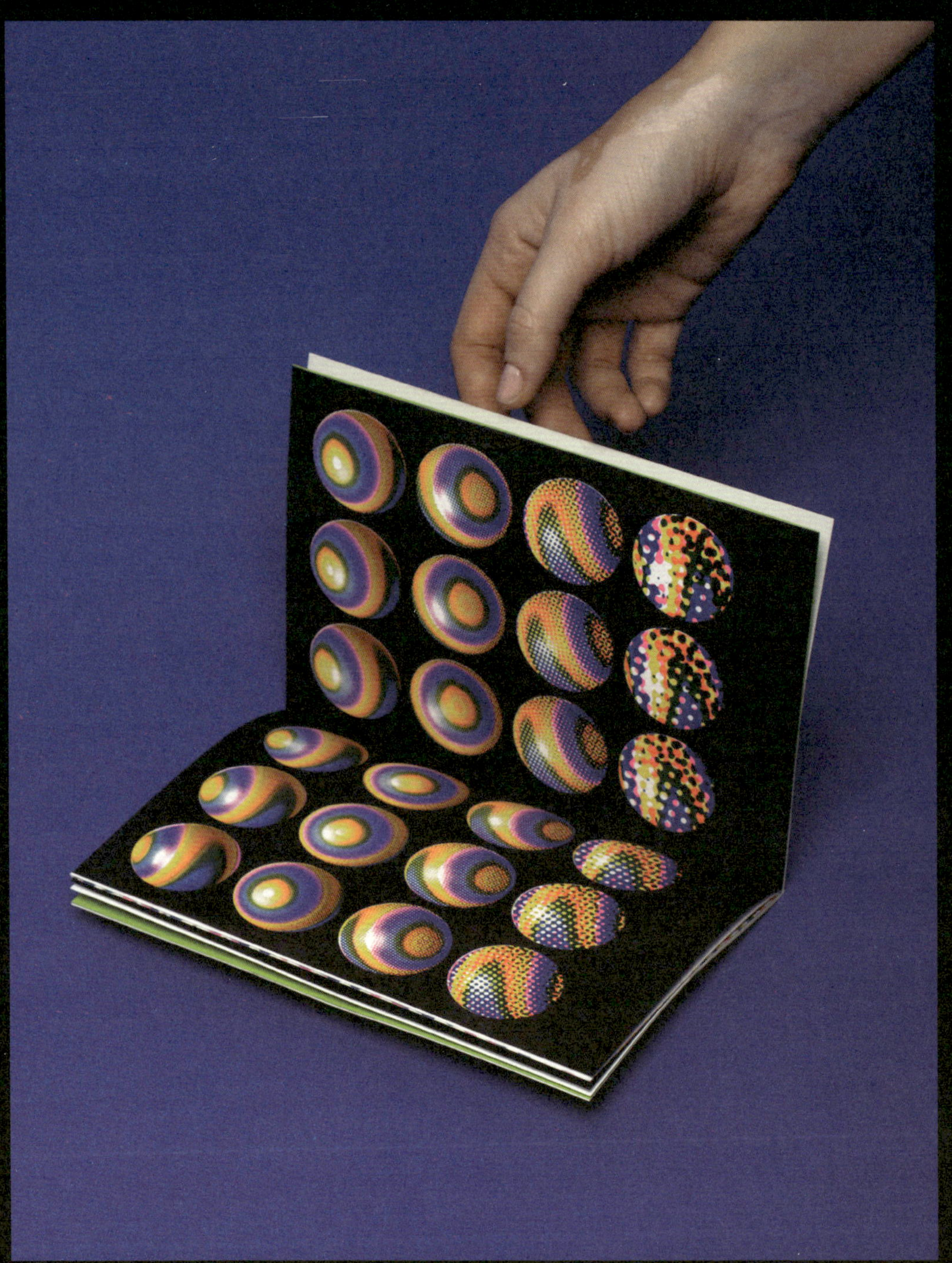

R O Y G B I V
R O Y G B I V
R O

GRAFIS NUSANTARA VOL.4: KOLEKSI STIKER POP & TRENDI

This volume documents Indonesian pop culture stickers from the 1970s to 1990s, tracing their production through AMP Malang and other studios nationwide. Categorised and contextualised socially and culturally, the book includes collectible inserts and an interactive cover. Designed with Copyright/Reserved, it reframes a widely overlooked visual culture.

DESIGN

Grafis Nusantara & Copyright Reserved

SIZE

148mm x 205mm x 25mm

PUBLISHER

Kamengski

FEATURES

Swiss binding, special inks, plastic sleeve cover with stickers

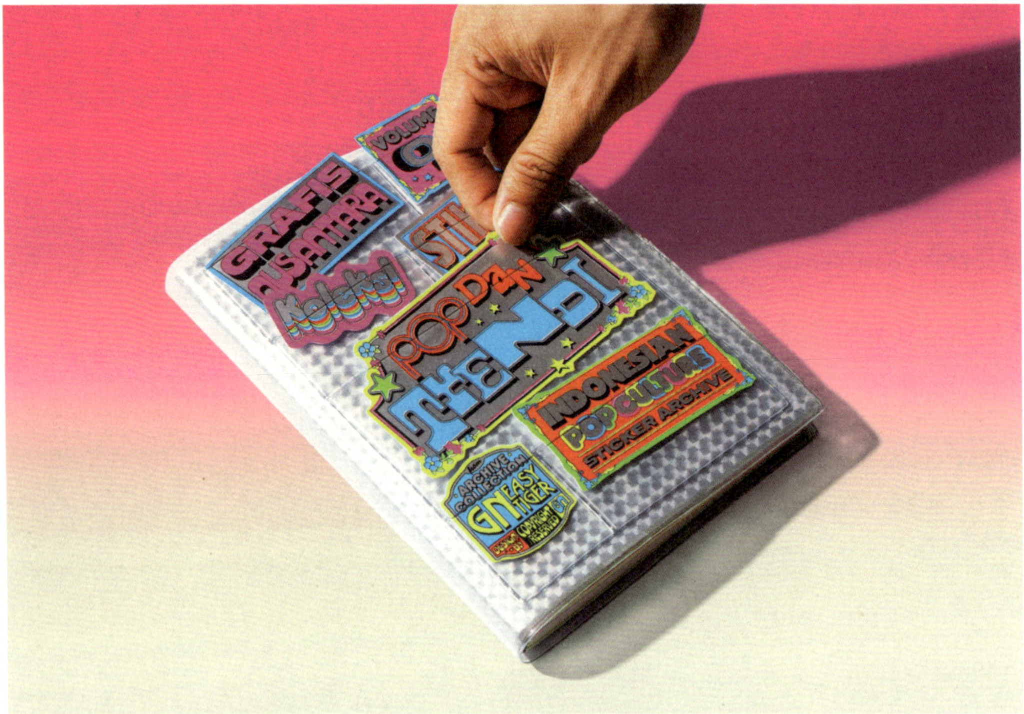
GRAFIS NUSANTARA
Koleksi
POP DAN TRENDI
INDONESIAN POP CULTURE STICKER ARCHIVE
ARCHIVE COLLECTION
GN EASY TIGER
COPYRIGHT RESERVED

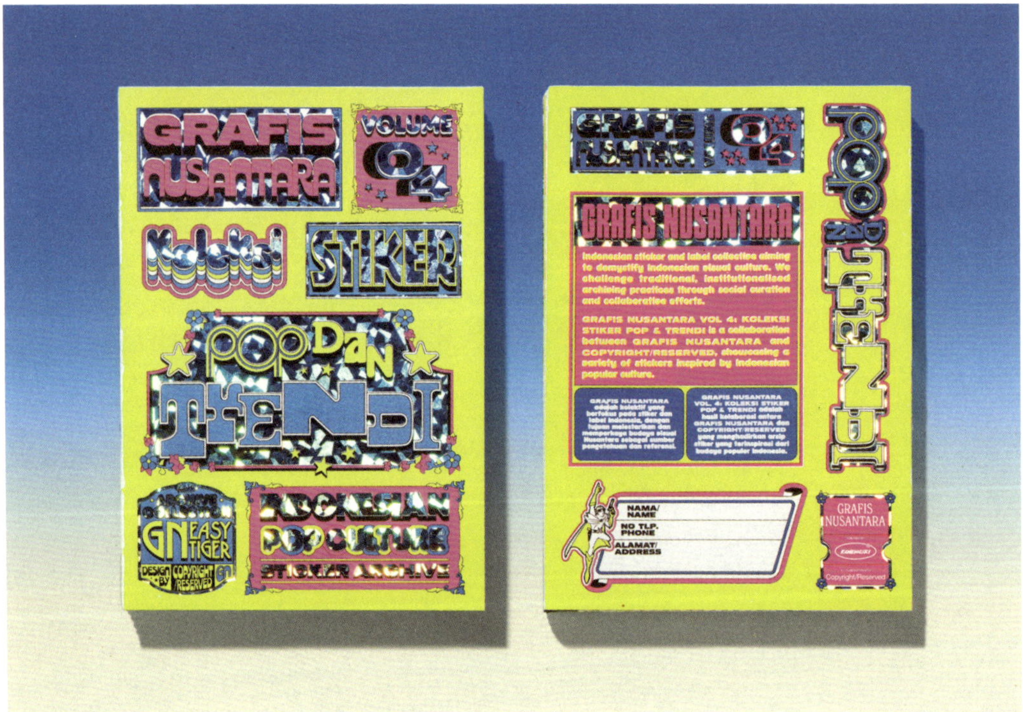
GRAFIS NUSANTARA
VOLUME 04
Koleksi
STIKER
POP DAN TRENDI
GN EASY TIGER
DESIGN BY COPYRIGHT/RESERVED
INDONESIAN POP CULTURE STICKER ARCHIVE
GRAFIS NUSANTARA
Indonesian sticker and label collective aiming to demystify Indonesian visual culture. We challenge traditional, institutionalised archiving practices through social curation and collaborative efforts.
GRAFIS NUSANTARA VOL 4: KOLEKSI STIKER POP & TRENDI is a collaboration between GRAFIS NUSANTARA and COPYRIGHT/RESERVED, showcasing a variety of stickers inspired by Indonesian popular culture.
GRAFIS NUSANTARA adalah kolektif yang berfokus pada stiker dan label Indonesia, dengan tujuan melestarikan dan memperkaya budaya visual Nusantara sebagai sumber pengetahuan dan referensi.
GRAFIS NUSANTARA VOL. 4: KOLEKSI STIKER POP & TRENDI adalah hasil kolaborasi antara GRAFIS NUSANTARA dan COPYRIGHT/RESERVED yang menghadirkan arsip stiker yang terinspirasi dari budaya populer Indonesia.
NAMA/ NAME
NO TLP. PHONE
ALAMAT/ ADDRESS
GRAFIS NUSANTARA
Copyright/Reserved

Q&A ③

WHAT'S THE MOST MEMORABLE ZINE YOU'VE EVER COME ACROSS? WHY DOES IT STICK WITH YOU?

"I FEEL EVERY ZINE IS ONE OF A KIND. THAT'S THE TRUE SPIRIT OF A ZINE. AS LONG AS IT CLEARLY EXPRESSES A STANCE AND ATTITUDE, EVERY ONE IS WONDERFUL."

— HOUTH

"*ES Replan Variform Type Specimen* is at the top of my list. It's a well-composed type specimen zine with a dynamic flow and bold experimentation between characters and images. I appreciate how its editorial system deliberately slows the reading process, prompting pauses to consider the relationship between form and meaning. It treats type not just as text, but as image, material, and structure. The typesetting presents the typeface as visual elements rather than mere samples, which feels unexpected."

— CHEN LUO

"There are so many zines we love — especially Indonesian ones. The scene is playful and fearless. We're particularly drawn to zines that capture everyday Indonesian visuals in a raw way: old food labels, street graphics, hand-drawn signage, personal archives. When a zine makes you think, 'I remember this', or helps you see something familiar differently, it stays with us."

— GRAFIS NUSANTARA

"One publication that left a strong impression on me is *Viewfinder* by Chihoi, published by nos:books in 2023. It opens with an empty centre, allowing readers to frame their own views. The book is made from paper frames that are the reciprocal counterpart of the die-cut used in Son Ni's *Navigator*. It feels sculptural, fundamentally expanding my understanding of what a book can be."

— HSIAN-JUNG CHEN

"*Snake Book* by Chang Yuchen. The book is 20 pages of snake drawings inside, complemented by touches that feel just right — from the narrow aspect ratio conforming to the snakes to the red spine accent that makes the black-and-white images pop. Some may argue it's more of an art book than a zine, but that's the kind of design object that I love."

— JONATHAN MAK

"I'M OFTEN DRAWN TO THINGS THAT DON'T EVEN CALL THEMSELVES ZINES — LOCAL NEWSPAPERS OR SMALL BOOKLETS WHERE THE 'ZINE LOOK' DISAPPEARS AND THE FOCUS IS ENTIRELY ON CONTENT."

— SOMETHINGMOON DESIGN

"The most memorable zine I've made is *Kumonodaira*. What stays with me is the intensity of the making process. We pushed physical limits — printing to the edge of long sheets, folding within millimetres, minimising misalignment. It was only possible with the craftsmanship of many collaborators. Bringing an almost impossible idea—a poetry collection in an accordion format with near-disappearing line spacing—into reality remains vivid."

— MEW IMASHUKU

"One of the most memorable zines I've encountered is *BIT BY BIT / TEXTILE ZINE*, which blends graphic and textile art in a layered, handcrafted way. Material and craft become structural elements, expanding my sense of what a zine can be."

— PETR PERSIK

"In the mid-noughties, a friend made a small-run music zine called *The Lobster Quadrille*. It was simple, A6 and photocopied, but showed me that publishing could be driven purely by love."

— SOCIOTYPE

"The most memorable zine I've encountered wasn't a well-known or perfectly produced one, but a small zine that openly shared its making process. The printing was imperfect and the structure was rough, yet it clearly showed the time and care that went into trying to communicate something meaningful. You could sense why the work had started, where it struggled, and what the creator refused to let go of. Reading it felt less like viewing a finished piece and more like stepping briefly into someone's studio. That closeness stayed with me. To me, a good zine is not defined by how well it is finished, but by how clearly the time and effort behind it can be felt."

— HOWFUL

"ONE THAT REALLY STAYED WITH ME IS 'SEED MAGAZEEN', AN ILLUSTRATED ENVIRONMENTAL MAGAZINE FOR CHILDREN, WHICH STANDS OUT FOR ITS VARIED ILLUSTRATION STYLES HELD TOGETHER BY RISOGRAPH COLOUR LIMITATIONS. THAT OPENNESS INSPIRES ME."

— SITING YAO

"Ari Marcopoulos' zines. We're big fans of his work. Ari always thinks of photography more cinematically — about how a sequence of images becomes a more layered way of looking at something. He makes not only printed zines, but also PDF zines. *Ari Marcopoulos: Zines* is a must-have for anyone interested in his personal practice and zine culture."

— PAY2PLAY

"*Typozimmer* by Occupy The City combines beautiful design with in-depth research, elevating it beyond a traditional art book. It opens new possibilities for presenting design research in zine form."

— KOSEKO DESIGN & PRESS

"When I was 20, I bought a zine in NYC of simple drawings of things on top of cars. It made me realise anything can be put into a zine. The drawings and the topic don't have to be super complex, and it can be fun and silly! It made me realise that I can make zines too. :)"

— TESS SMITH-ROBERTS

"MY FIRST ZINE, 'THINGS I'D LIKE TO SHARE WITH YOU', WAS A LOVE LETTER DISGUISED AS A BOOKLET. LATER I SCREEN-PRINTED 200 COPIES. IT BECAME A GIFT FOR NEW LOVERS. ANOTHER MEMORABLE ONE IS 'MY CIRCUMCISION FEAST' BY MERT ŞEN. IT FELT PERSONAL AND COURAGEOUS, REMINDING ME THAT ZINES CAN HOLD INTIMATE, VULNERABLE STORIES WHILE REMAINING POLITICAL."

— RACHEL SENDER

"At book fairs, we've come across countless zines with wild and playful concepts. One that stayed with us was a photo collection of white paint stains found throughout a city. Every time the creator spotted white paint splashed on the ground, they photographed it until it became a full zine of accidental marks. We also love Dream Press, based in Cape Town. They regularly collaborate with local artists and make some of our favourite zines. One example is *Change of Scenery*, a concertina-folded zine with the artist Wim Legrand. It stretches over a metre when fully opened and unfolds into a playful scene and storyline."

— DTAN STUDIO

"My favourite zine I've made so far is *Good Day*. It was inspired by Chinese boomer graphics — bright, cheesy family-chat images with lotus flowers and clashing fonts. I redesigned that aesthetic in my own style, keeping the warmth but updating the typography and colours. It's essentially a direct greeting to whoever picks it up."

— LONELY KIDNEY

"One of the most memorable publications I've encountered is *Cosmo-Eggs*, designed by Yoshihisa Tanaka for the Japanese Pavilion at the 58th Venice Biennale. It transforms the unseen curatorial and planning process into a tangible experience, recreating scrap paper, handwritten notes, maps, and collages. It demonstrates how a strong idea can dictate precise design, making reading an act of experiencing creation itself."

— FOR&ST

"An artist in Chicago, Cody Hudson (Struggle Inc.), once gave me a small 6x6" zine instead of a business card. It inspired me to make my first zine in 2006. I added stickers and 1" pins and felt immense pride. That moment showed me how much impact a small zine can have."

— NOPATTERN STUDIO

"There are so many great zines. At the moment, *Gnocchi Gnocchi* by Stefanie Leinhos and Anna Haifisch comes to mind first — a funny zine filled with pasta cartoons. I love the illustrations, but also the finishing. Every detail is carefully considered: the yellow wire-o binding resembles fusilli, and the reading ribbon looks like linguine."

— BROOS STOFFELS

"*The Smudge*, published by Caboose from 2017-2021, is technically a newspaper, but I see it as a quintessential zine. It was sweet, silly, and inspiring, and throughout its short life it continually found new ways to surprise and delight, reinventing itself within a simple format."

— STUDIO ELANA SCHLENKER

"For layout, I admire *TOMBEAU TOKYO* by Nobuyoshi Araki. For design integration, Thomas Sauvin's *Until Death Do Us Part* is outstanding — its cigarette-pack format perfectly merges content and form."

— WAN CHAOFAN

"I'm very drawn to Boot Boyz Biz, a research and production cooperative transforming research into publications and merchandise. Their engagement with visual language in the public sphere fascinates me."

— RIVERSBED

"ONE FAVOURITE IS A PHOTO ZINE FROM THE BEIJING SILVERMINE PROJECT BY THOMAS SAUVIN. 'UNTIL DEATH DO US PART' SHOWS PEOPLE SMOKING AT CHINESE WEDDINGS AND IS HOUSED IN A CIGARETTE BOX. IT'S PLAYFUL AND REMINDS ME THAT WITH ZINES, THE SKY'S THE LIMIT."

— MEANTIME

"For our family, every zine we've made is important, whether playful or solemn. It's impossible to choose a favourite, but issue four, *The Incomplete Herbarium And Other Garden City Exploits*, holds special meaning. It marked our country's 50th year of independence and became a way to rediscover forgotten parts of Singapore. We travelled like tourists, forging new memories. Packaging the zine in a flower presser, with real wildflowers we collected pressed inside, felt like the perfect way to share those memories."

— HOLYCRAP

"I LOVE ZINES THAT FOCUS INTENSELY ON ONE STRANGE OR SPECIFIC SUBJECT. THE FIRST THAT COMES TO MIND IS 'MAKE A WISH!' BY JACKIE CRESPO, WHERE SHE BEAUTIFULLY ILLUSTRATES AND DESIGNS ODD PRODUCTS SHE FOUND ON EBAY. IT'S WITTY, VISUALLY RICH, AND FULL OF PERSONALITY — EXACTLY THE KIND OF ZINE THAT TURNS EVERYDAY ABSURDITY INTO SOMETHING POETIC AND FUNNY. I ADMIRE HOW IT CAPTURES THE MIX OF CURIOSITY AND HUMOUR THAT MAKES ZINES SO SPECIAL."

— BIANCA FORISCHI

"One of the most memorable zines for us is *Domestic Disturbance*, which we published. It strips back each contributor's conformity, norms, and behaviour to explore predisposed states of mind and personal desire. Each edition consists of three zines by seven designers, bundled together in a single binder as a collective thought process. As designers, we're often expected to maintain order and follow unwritten rules. With this zine, we wanted to disrupt that. Readers assemble their own editions—no two are the same—becoming part of the process. It's playful and honest, reflecting who we were at that moment."

— EXTENSIVE PUBLISHING — COPYRIGHT/RESERVED

"My favourite magazine, which is the only magazine I read outside of our own project, is *Wired* magazine. I love reading about innovation and how people are changing the world for the better. It's so easy to get caught up in everything wrong in the world, so I try to read things that inspire me and bring about positivity and interest."

— TYPE01

For us, *FOAM* magazine (Fotomuseum Amsterdam) is a good example of material experiment. It's a playground for photography, Igepa (sponsor of the paper material) and the designers. Another one is *MacGuffin*, which is a good example of a well-designed printed periodic that has a very outspoken and innovative thematic approach.

— STUDIO DE RONNERS

"Around fifteen years ago, I bought an eight-page, Japanese zine. It was a simple, bread-themed drawing book, sketched quickly in ballpoint pen, with only ten editions ever made. It was saddle-stitched by hand at home, and you could feel the maker's presence in every mark and fold. What has stayed with me most is that it was handmade in such a small edition. There was something powerful about a work that exists only for a few people — intimate, imperfect, and touched directly by its maker. That rarity and handcrafted presence are what draw me most to zines."

— ADD TO CART

"The most memorable zine I've made is *ethereal statement of memories — 2021*. It holds immense sentimental value, serving as a letter to loved ones I left behind when I moved countries."

— LUANA LLOYD

"MY MOST MEMORABLE ZINE — AND PERHAPS THE ONE THAT BEGAN MY LOVE FOR THEM — IS A SMALL ONE MY DAD CREATED USING MIXED MEDIA, ABSTRACT SHAPES, AND FOUND COLLAGE. THE BEAUTY OF IT WAS IN HOW HE USED DIFFERENT PAPERS AND ACETATE; ANY DISCARDED MATERIAL WAS TURNED INTO SOMETHING BEAUTIFUL."

— ALFIE WHEATLEY

GRAFIS NUSANTARA VOL.3: LABEL KRETEK

Label Kretek explores vintage labels from Indonesian clove cigarettes produced mainly in Java. Organised into thematic categories with historical context, the publication is presented as both book and collector's set. Designed in collaboration with Satu Collective and published by Kamengski, it offers an in-depth look at kretek's visual and cultural heritage.

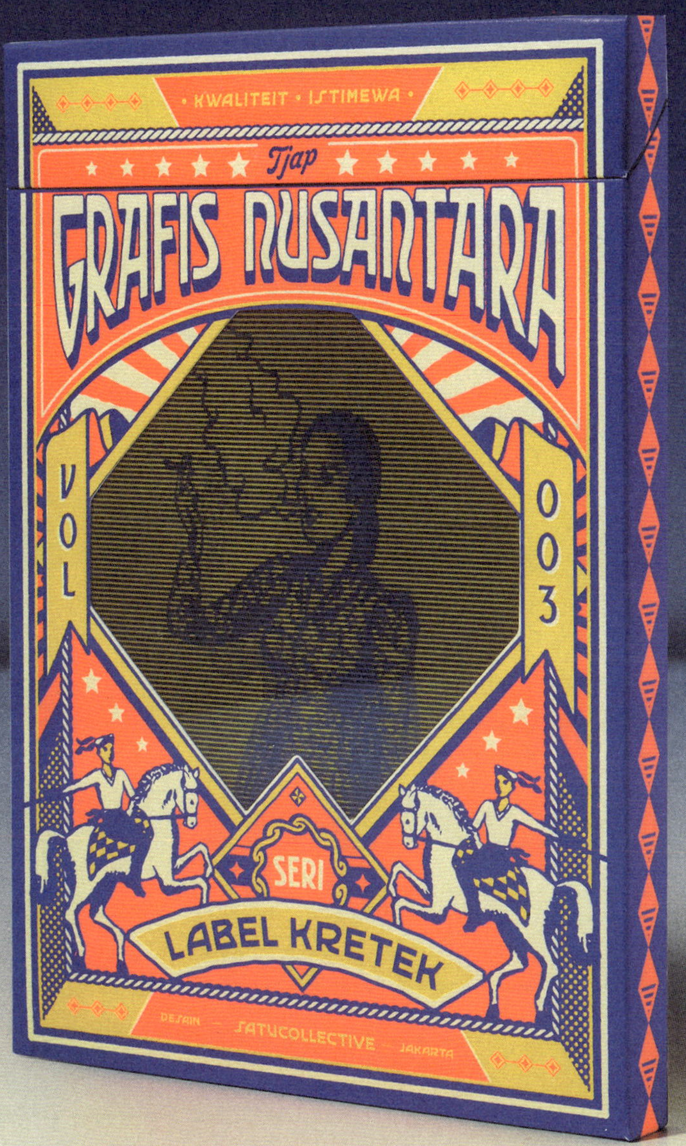

Tjap
GRAFIS NUSANTARA
003
VOL
SERI
KRETEK
GRAFIS
NSNTR
LABEL
KRETEK
GN
GRAFIS NUSANTARA IS AN INDONESIAN STICKER AND LABEL COLLECTIVE AIMING TO DEMYSTIFY INDONESIAN VISUAL CULTURE. WE CHALLENGE TRADITIONAL INSTITUTIONALISED ARCHIVING PRACTICES THROUGH SOCIAL CURATION AND COLLABORATIVE EFFORTS.
THE BOOK YOU HAVE IN YOUR HANDS IS OUR THIRD RELEASE, WHICH FOCUSES ON THE FASCINATING ASSORTMENT OF KRETEK CIGARETTES COLLECTED BY GRAFIS NUSANTARA AND CREATED IN COLLABORATION WITH SATU COLLECTIVE.

GRAFIS NUSANTARA
Special
GRAFIS
NUSANTARA
Label Kretek
ROKOK
KRETEK
GRAFIS NUSANTARA
UMUM
Pemilihan
KONTJI
ROKOK
SLOT
KOEDOES
BATMAN
SEMPATI
PEREMPUAN
Kretek
HOW TO ROLL YOUR OWN Cigarette
016
081

DESIGN	SIZE	PUBLISHER	FEATURES
Grafis Nusantara & Satu Collective	148mm x 205mm x 12mm	Kamengski	Swiss binding, special inks, lenticular box, blind embossing

GRAFIS NUSANTARA VOL.2: LABEL KERUPUK

Initiated by Rakhmat Jaka, this volume focuses on vintage kerupuk (cracker) labels from across Indonesia. Drawing from over 200 personal collections, the book examines overlooked graphic aesthetics and regional identity. Designed by Evan Wijaya and published by Kamengski, it celebrates kerupuk labels as sociocultural artefacts embedded in daily life.

DESIGN

Grafis Nusantara & Tiny Studio

SIZE

148mm x 205mm x 12mm

PUBLISHER

Kamengski

FEATURES

Swiss binding, special inks, kiss-cut sticker cover, screen-printed plastic

Grafis Nusantara is a collective & platform dedicated to archiving vintage Indonesian labels and stickers. The archive presents the archipelago's lavish visuals and is expected to show Indonesian vintage designs' significance as knowledge and reference materials.

Grafis Nusantara
Vol. 2
Label Kerupuk
KOLEKSI ATRAS ALWAFI
DESAIN TINY STUDIO DAN GN

KANENGSKI
GRAFIS NUSANTARA

KRUPUK
KERUPUK
Krupuk
KERUPUK

KERUPUK SPECIAL
GRAFIS NSNTR
Cap
RUPUK SPECIAL
GN
NSNTR
RENYAH GURIH & NIKMAT
INDONESIA
RUPUK KULIT
GRAFIS
NUSANTARA
RENYAH DAN HALAL
ANEKA CAMILAN
Grafis Nusantara
GURIH & RENYAH

GRAFIS NUSANTARA VOL.1: KOLEKSI LABEL DAN STIKER

This first volume presents a curated collection of Indonesian vintage labels and stickers from the 1970s to 1990s, including cigarette, batik and tea labels, alongside religious and cartoon stickers. The book highlights the visual richness of everyday graphics across the archipelago, serving as both cultural documentation and design reference.

DESIGN
Grafis Nusantara & Evan Wijaya

SIZE
148mm x 205mm x 12mm

PUBLISHER
Kamengski

FEATURES
Swiss binding, special inks, kiss-cut sticker jacket

GRAFIS NUSANTARA
DARI KOLEKSI RAKHMAT JAKA
DESAIN OLEH EVAN WIJAYA
KWALITET ISTIMEWA
01
GRAFIS NUSANTARA
KWALITET ISTIMEWA
VOL 01 KOLEKSI LABEL & STIKER 2022
GRAFIS NUSANTARA
PAPIERAMBRÉ
LIMA SLEPA
KOLEKSI LABEL DAN STIKER
Tekstil
EROTISME
KESEHATAN
Religi
TEH
KARTUN
ROKOK
Klasik
SAJIAN
TEKS GAMBAR
STOP
WAHID
Mataram

GRAFIS NUSANTARA
2022
Grafis
NUSANTARA
LABEL DAN STIKER
TEKSTIL
KESEHATAN
TEH
ROKOK
SAJIAN
EROTISME
RELIGI
KARTUN
TEKS KLASIK
TEKS GAMBAR
KOLEKSI LABEL & STIKER
GRAFIS
Label
2022
NUSANTARA
LABEL
STIKER
NUSANTARA
GN
STOP

THE INSATIABLE BEASTS DEVOURS TOKYOTO AGAIN

The Insatiable Beasts Devours Tokyoto Again (2024) is a family "famzine" revisiting Tokyo and Kyoto, where their first issue began in 2013. Presented as an aged toy box parodying a Kamen Rider action figure set — reimagined here as "Ramen Rider" — it playfully merges pop culture and wordplay to chronicle food adventures and family escapades in their favourite place.

DESIGN

Pann Lim / Kinetic Singapore

SIZE

150mm x 200mm x 30mm

PUBLISHER

Holycrap

FEATURES

Modular publication, multi-booklet format, boxed with special contents like ramen packet, chopsticks with customised sleeve and serviette

生麺うまいまま製法
マルちゃん
正麺
せい めん
拉麺ライダー
RAMEN RIDER
DELIVERY SERVICE
HIGHLY RECOMMENDS THIS RAMEN

NO.18 MAR 2024 115SGD 300 COPIES
RUBBISH
FAMzine
LOVE & KISMET KYOTO BOUND
ALMOST FACELESS
THE INSATIABLE BEASTS DEVOURS TOKYOTO AGAIN
ULTRA BOOKMARK
NO MUSIC NO LIFE
拉面ライダー
RAMEN RIDER
DELIVERY SERVICE

AN EMOJIOUS ODYSSEY OF THE GLUTTONOUS OMNIVORES

Eating their way around Singapore, this issue celebrates the family's insatiable appetite, documenting their adventures through local hawker fare and chaotic experiments in their home kitchen. The zine is packaged inside a traditional takeaway box, complete with 'rubbish' plastic bags, playfully blurring publication and packaging so it can be mistaken for an actual meal.

DESIGN

Pann Lim / Kinetic Singapore

SIZE

150mm x 200mm x 40mm

PUBLISHER

Holycrap

FEATURES

Modular publication, boxed zine with printed plastic bag and ephemera

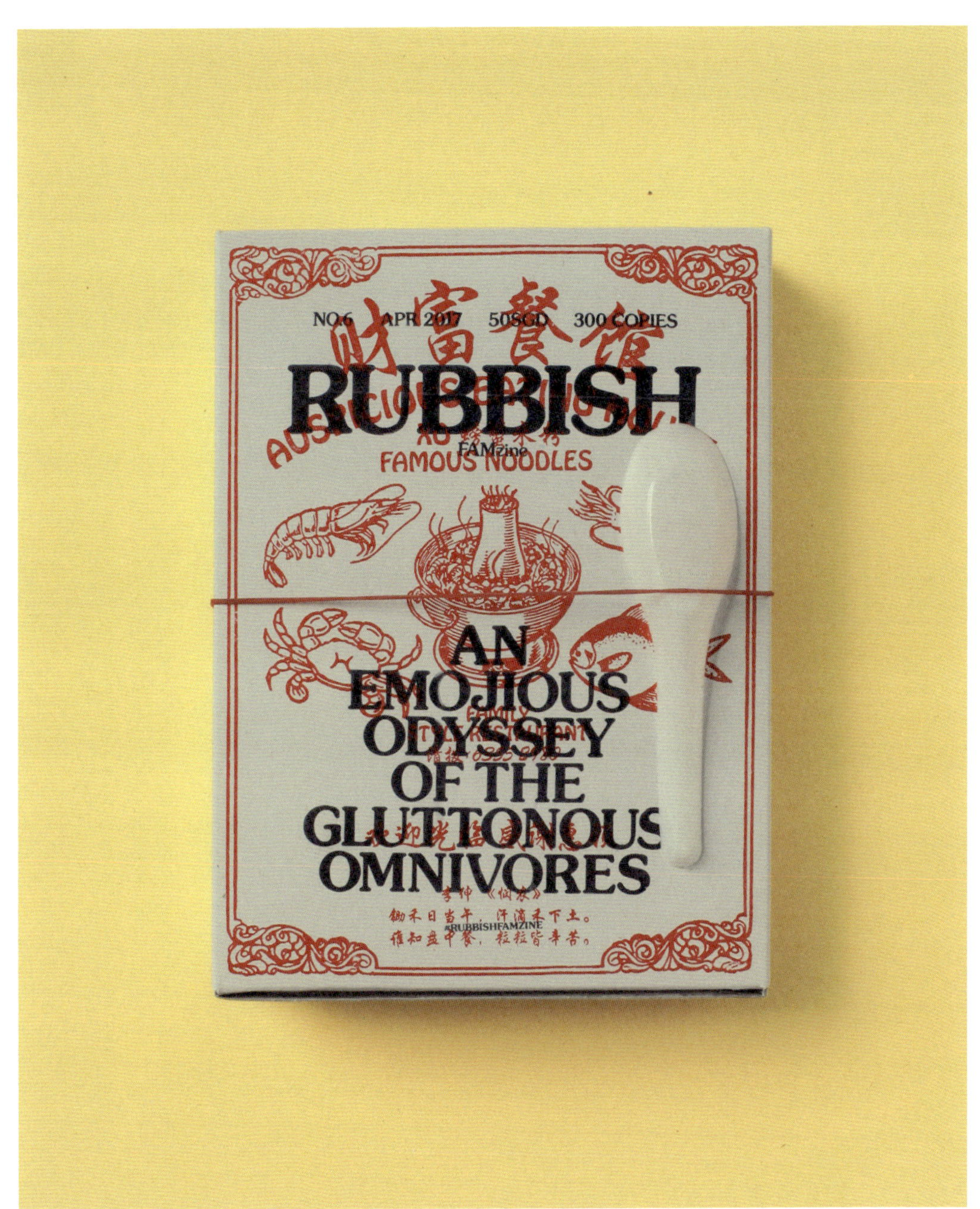

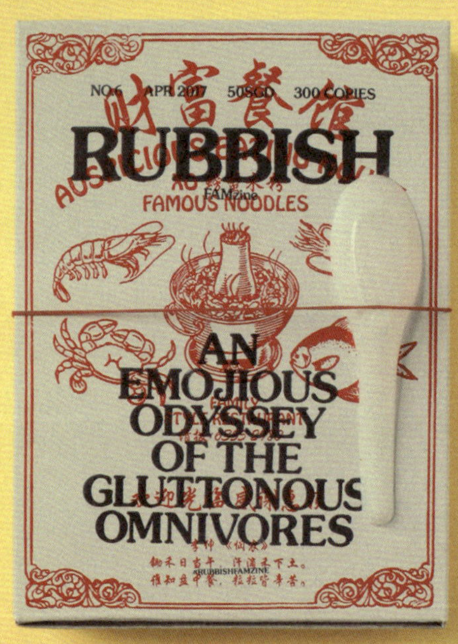
NO.6 APR 2017 50SGD 300 COPIES
RUBBISH
FAMzine
FAMOUS NOODLES
AN
EMOJIOUS
ODYSSEY
OF THE
GLUTTONOUS
OMNIVORES

2017
RUBBISH
FAMzine
えもじ
NO.6a

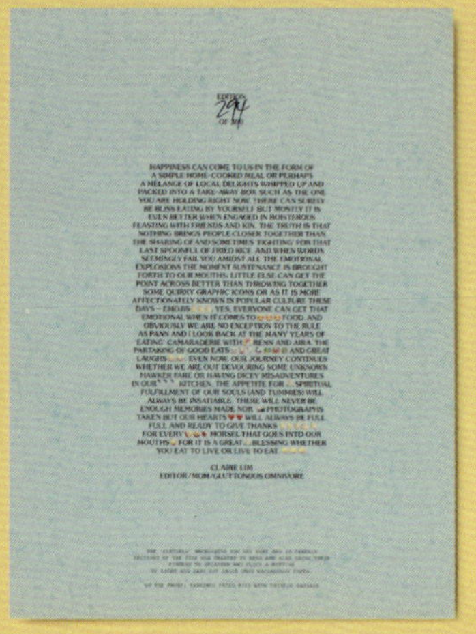

HAPPINESS CAN COME TO US IN THE FORM OF
A SIMPLE HOME-COOKED MEAL OR PERHAPS
A HELANGE OF LOCAL DELIGHTS WHIPPED UP AND
PACKED INTO A TAKE-AWAY BOX SUCH AS THE ONE
YOU ARE HOLDING RIGHT NOW. THERE CAN SURELY
BE BLISS EATING BY YOURSELF BUT MOSTLY IT IS
EVEN BETTER WHEN ENGAGED IN BOISTEROUS
FEASTING WITH FRIENDS AND KIN. THE TRUTH IS THAT
NOTHING BRINGS PEOPLE CLOSER TOGETHER THAN
THE SHARING OF AND SOMETIMES 'FIGHTING' FOR THAT
LAST SPOONFUL OF FRIED RICE. AND WHEN WORDS
SEEMINGLY FAIL YOU AMIDST ALL THE EMOTIONAL
EXPLOSIONS THE MOMENT SUSTENANCE IS BROUGHT
FORTH TO OUR MOUTHS, LITTLE ELSE CAN GET THE
POINT ACROSS BETTER THAN THROWING TOGETHER
SOME QUIRKY GRAPHIC ICONS OR AS IT IS MORE
AFFECTIONATELY KNOWN IN POPULAR CULTURE THESE
DAYS – EMOJIS. YES, EVERYONE CAN GET THAT
EMOTIONAL WHEN IT COMES TO FOOD. AND
OBVIOUSLY WE ARE NO EXCEPTION TO THE RULE
AS PANN AND I LOOK BACK AT THE MANY YEARS OF
EATING' CAMARADERIE WITH BENN AND AIRA. THE
PARTAKING OF GOOD EATS AND GREAT
LAUGHS. EVEN NOW, OUR JOURNEY CONTINUES
WHETHER WE ARE OUT DEVOURING SOME UNKNOWN
HAWKER FARE OR HAVING DICEY MISADVENTURES
IN OUR KITCHEN. THE APPETITE FOR SPIRITUAL
FULFILLMENT OF OUR SOULS (AND TUMMIES) WILL
ALWAYS BE INSATIABLE. THERE WILL NEVER BE
ENOUGH MEMORIES MADE NOR PHOTOGRAPHS
TAKEN BUT OUR HEARTS WILL ALWAYS BE FULL
FULL AND READY TO GIVE THANKS
FOR EVERY MORSEL THAT GOES INTO OUR
MOUTHS FOR IT IS A GREAT BLESSING WHETHER
YOU EAT TO LIVE OR LIVE TO EAT

CLAIRE LIM
EDITOR/MOM/GLUTTONOUS OMNIVORE

NO.62 1 APR 2017 50SGD 300 COPIES

STEWING LOVE AND OXTAILS

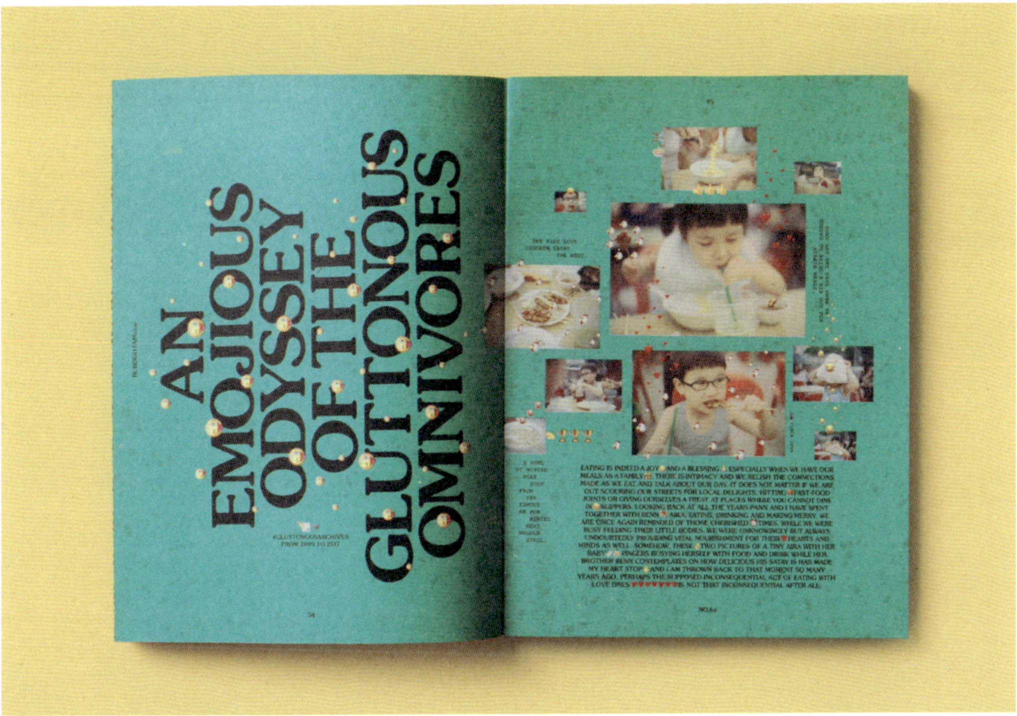

AN EMOJIOUS ODYSSEY OF THE GLUTTONOUS OMNIVORES

#GLUTTONOUSARCHIVES FROM 2009 TO 2017

EATING IS INDEED A JOY AND A BLESSING ESPECIALLY WHEN WE HAVE OUR MEALS AS A FAMILY. THERE IS INTIMACY AND WE RELISH THE CONNECTIONS MADE AS WE EAT AND TALK ABOUT OUR DAY. IT DOES NOT MATTER IF WE ARE OUT SCOURING OUR STREETS FOR LOCAL DELIGHTS, HITTING FAST-FOOD JOINTS OR GIVING OURSELVES A TREAT AT PLACES WHERE YOU CANNOT DINE IN SLIPPERS. LOOKING BACK AT ALL THE YEARS PANN AND I HAVE SPENT TOGETHER WITH BENN AIRA, EATING, DRINKING AND MAKING MERRY, WE ARE ONCE AGAIN REMINDED OF THOSE CHERISHED TIMES. WHILE WE WERE BUSY FEEDING THEIR LITTLE BODIES, WE WERE UNKNOWINGLY BUT ALWAYS UNDOUBTEDLY PROVIDING VITAL NOURISHMENT FOR THEIR HEARTS AND MINDS AS WELL. SOMEHOW, THESE TWO PICTURES OF A TINY AIRA WITH HER BABY FINGERS BUSYING HERSELF WITH FOOD AND DRINK WHILE HER BROTHER BENN CONTEMPLATES ON HOW DELICIOUS HIS SATAY IS HAS MADE MY HEART STOP AND I AM THROWN BACK TO THAT MOMENT SO MANY YEARS AGO. PERHAPS THE SUPPOSED INCONSEQUENTIAL ACT OF EATING WITH LOVE ONES IS NOT THAT INCONSEQUENTIAL AFTER ALL.

NO.62

IN THE NAME OF THE FATHER

In The Name Of The Father is a self-initiated publication dedicated to Pann Lim's late father, Lim Tiap Guan. Told in the son's voice, it gathers memories, rediscovered stories and reflections on love and sacrifice. Framed as an unspoken eulogy, the book honours a father's lasting influence through intimate narrative and personal tribute.

DESIGN	SIZE	PUBLISHER	FEATURES
Pann Lim / Kinetic Singapore	150mm x 200mm x 22mm	Holycrap	Modular publication, torn cover, inserted ephemera, elastic band binding

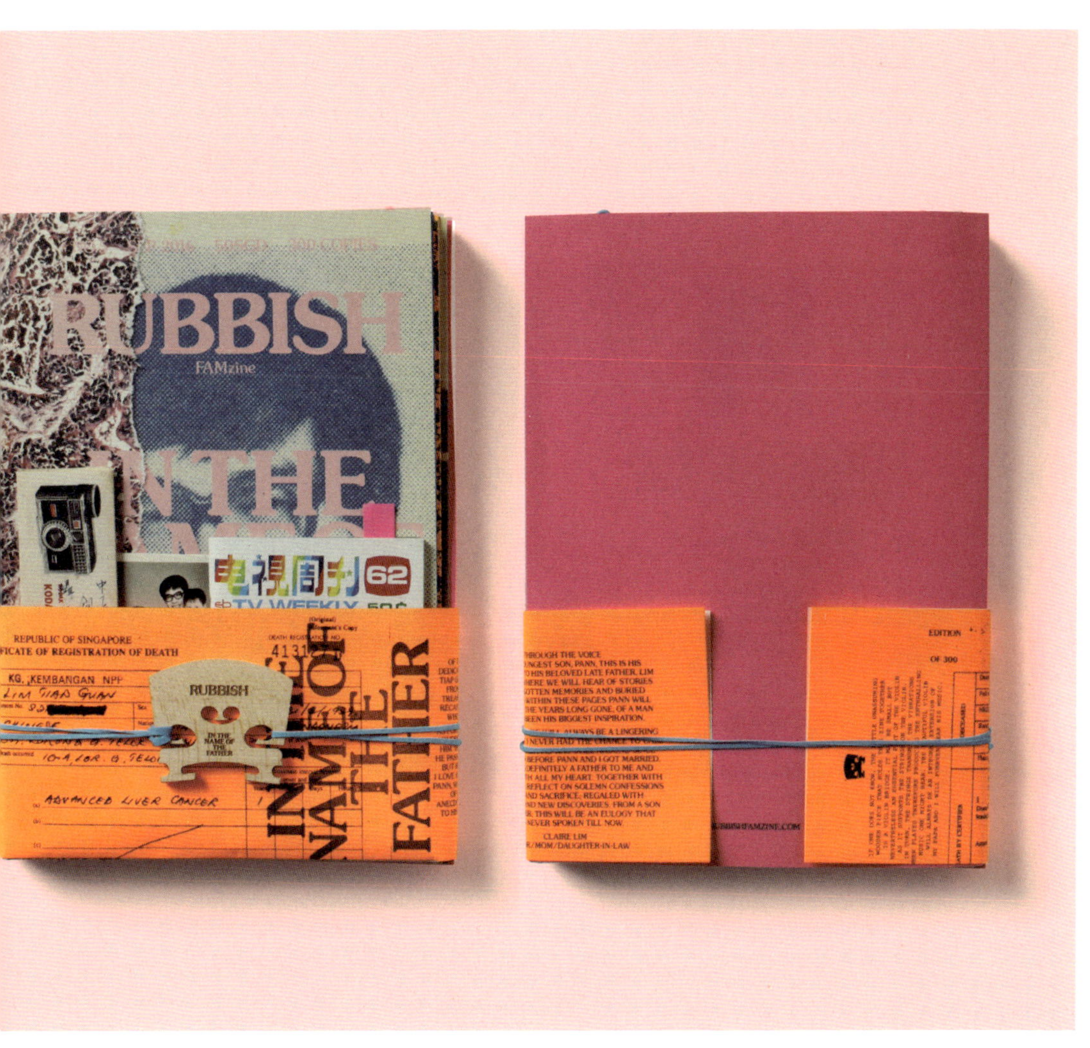

PAPA AND HIS FOREVER MUSE

#CHINGSERCHOW

KODAK INSTAMATIC CAMERA

RUBBISH

电视周刊 62

TV WEEKLY 50¢

AN ARTICLE PROMOTING A CONCERT THAT COMBINES EASTERN & WESTERN INFLUENCES IN WHICH PAPA CONCEIVED & CONDUCTED. BACK IN THE DAY, TV WEEKLY WAS AN ESSENTIAL GUIDE TO ALL UPCOMING PROGRAMS.

THE GREAT PRETENDER

FROM THE MOMENT WE LITERALLY CHANCED UPON THE TRUTH TO THE DAY PAPA LEFT US BEHIND, WE ALL HAD BUT A LITTLE OVER A MONTH WITH HIM. AND ONLY OVER THE YEARS, WHEN WE PIECED TOGETHER BITS OF STORIES AND FADED MEMORIES, DID WE FINALLY REALISED HOW PAPA TRIED AND DID SO WELL TO HIDE THE ILLNESS FROM US, AND HOW HE TRIED TO MAKE IT UP TO US IN HIS OWN LITTLE WAYS. WHEN HE PRETENDED, TO PROTECT — WAS IT RIGHT OR MISGUIDED? THE LINES BLUR AND THERE WILL NEVER BE AN ABSOLUTE ANSWER TO THIS QUESTION. BUT WE KNOW THAT HIS LOVE FOR US WILL ALWAYS REMAIN IN THE DEEP RECESSES OF ALL OUR HEARTS.

15

RUBBISH FAMZINE

NO.5

IN THE NAME OF THE FATHER

MAN OF OBSESSIONS

THE COMPOSER

FOR OVER 45 YEARS, PAPA HAVE BEEN COMPOSING SONGS, SYMPHONIES AND MUSICAL SCORES FOR CHINESE THEATRICAL PLAYS, ORCHESTRAL PERFORMANCES AND OTHER MUSICAL CONCERTS. HIS MUSIC HAVE BEEN PERFORMED ON LIVE TELEVISION, RADIO BROADCAST AND HAVE APPEARED IN NUMEROUS MUSIC PUBLICATIONS AS WELL. I KNEW PAPA WAS AN ACCOMPLISHED MUSICIAN BUT I DID NOT KNOW TO WHAT EXTENT. I WISH I KNEW ALL THESE WHEN PAPA WAS STILL AROUND SO THAT I COULD HEAR MORE OF HIS STORIES.

SELECTED MUSIC COMPOSITIONS

IN THIS MINI BOOKLET ARE SOME OF PAPA'S MANY MUSIC COMPOSITIONS AND SONGS. MANY OF HIS COMPOSITIONS WERE ABOUT OUR HOME, SINGAPORE. THE FOLLOWING TITLES ARE LOOSELY TRANSLATED FROM THE CHINESE SONG TITLES.

1.MOUNT FABER / 2.THE PLACE I LIVE
3.THE FLUTE IN SPRING NIGHT / 4.CRADLE SONG

34

35

MEANTIME #3: FUNNY STORIES

Meantime is an independent magazine exploring Singapore's history through personal narratives. Its third issue, Funny Stories, features intimate reportage on escaped tigers, sex workers and a nationwide hair-cutting campaign. A dramatic tiger bite cut from the cover references the lead story, while selected features are extended through Instagram AR.

DESIGN	SIZE	PUBLISHER	FEATURES
Fable	176mm x 255mm x 15mm	Meantime	Exposed-stitch binding, drilled corner binding detail to resemble bite mark, soft cover

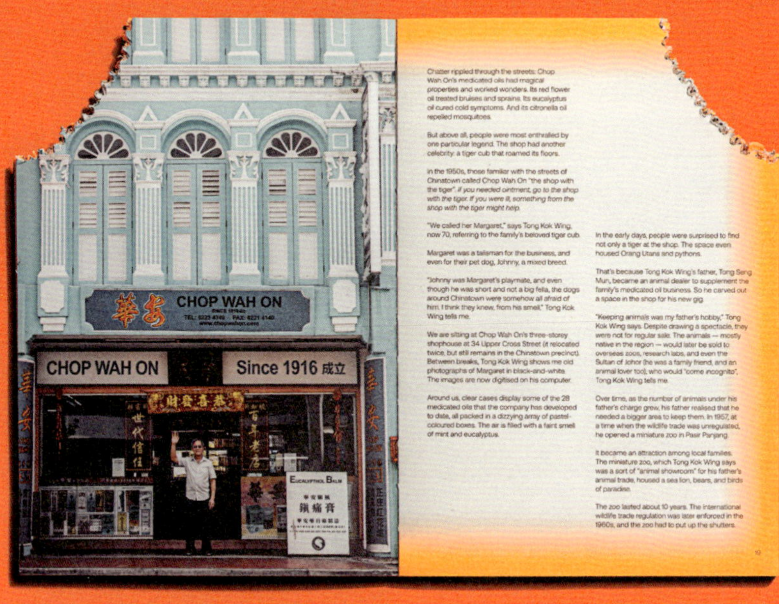

Chatter rippled through the streets: Chop Wah On's medicated oils had magical properties and worked wonders. Its red flower oil treated bruises and sprains. Its eucalyptus oil cured cold symptoms. And its citronella oil repelled mosquitoes.

But above all, people were most enthralled by one particular legend. The shop had another celebrity: a tiger cub that roamed its floors.

In the 1950s, those familiar with the streets of Chinatown called Chop Wah On "the shop with the tiger". *If you needed ointment, go to the shop with the tiger. If you were ill, something from the shop with the tiger might help.*

"We called her Margaret," says Tong Kok Wing, now 70, referring to the family's beloved tiger cub.

Margaret was a talisman for the business, and even for their pet dog, Johnny, a mixed breed.

"Johnny was Margaret's playmate, and even though he was short and not a big fella, the dogs around Chinatown were somehow all afraid of him. I think they knew, from his smell," Tong Kok Wing tells me.

We are sitting at Chop Wah On's three-storey shophouse at 34 Upper Cross Street (it relocated twice, but still remains in the Chinatown precinct). Between breaks, Tong Kok Wing shows me old photographs of Margaret in black-and-white. The images are now digitised on his computer.

Around us, clear cases display some of the 28 medicated oils that the company has developed to date, all packed in a dizzying array of pastel-coloured boxes. The air is filled with a faint smell of mint and eucalyptus.

In the early days, people were surprised to find not only a tiger at the shop. The space even housed Orang Utans and pythons.

That's because Tong Kok Wing's father, Tong Seng Mun, became an animal dealer to supplement the family's medicated oil business. So he carved out a space in the shop for his new gig.

"Keeping animals was my father's hobby," Tong Kok Wing says. Despite drawing a spectacle, they were not for regular sale. The animals — mostly native in the region — would later be sold to overseas zoos, research labs, and even the Sultan of Johor (he was a family friend, and an animal lover too), who would "come incognito", Tong Kok Wing tells me.

Over time, as the number of animals under his father's charge grew, his father realised that he needed a bigger area to keep them. In 1957, at a time when the wildlife trade was unregulated, he opened a miniature zoo in Pasir Panjang.

It became an attraction among local families. The miniature zoo, which Tong Kok Wing says was a sort of "animal showroom" for his father's animal trade, housed a sea lion, bears, and birds of paradise.

The zoo lasted about 10 years. The international wildlife trade regulation was later enforced in the 1960s, and the zoo had to put up the shutters.

19

IN PURSUIT OF BETTER TOILET STANDARDS, THIS MAN HAS MADE HIMSELF THE BUTT OF THE JOKE

LET'S TALK SHIT

Story SHARANYA PILLAI
Photographs SHERRY WONG

70

71

SINGAPORE'S $1 COIN — DESIGN OR ACCIDENT?

The year was 1986, and Singapore was busy replacing earth with cement, hollowing out vast underground spaces to build stations and tunnels for the new train system.

But the massive operation of building underground tunnels through downtown Singapore was said to bring about negative feng shui for the country.

To counter this misfortune, legend has it that a feng shui venerable was consulted, and he recommended that everyone carry a metal object in the shape of a bagua — a symbolic octagonal object.

But what could possibly compel Singapore's racially and religiously diverse inhabitants to all carry an eight-sided Taoist symbol in their pockets? The answer: incorporate it into the design of our one dollar coin. So in 1987, Singapore's eight-sided, gold-coloured one dollar coin was born.

MEANTIME #4: BAD STORIES

Meantime is an independent magazine exploring Singapore's history through personal stories. Its fourth issue, Bad Stories, presents features on lost wine, a crow culling campaign and biker gangs, structured around the seven deadly sins. A slice removed from the base makes the publication appear to sink, while 'sin' plays on both vice and the country code.

DESIGN	SIZE	PUBLISHER	FEATURES
Fable	176mm x 255mm x 15mm	Meantime	Exposed-stitch binding, diagonal die-cut binding, soft cover

"If you do not run [the lotteries], the *chap ji kee* man who has always swindled the people of their money is still there. **It is the history of Singapore**. The Chinese who travelled overseas are the biggest gamblers you can find in the world. Because to leave China was to gamble. In Manchu China if you returned you were beheaded. Because you were bringing in dangerous foreign ideas. So to leave China for Nanyang was a gamble."

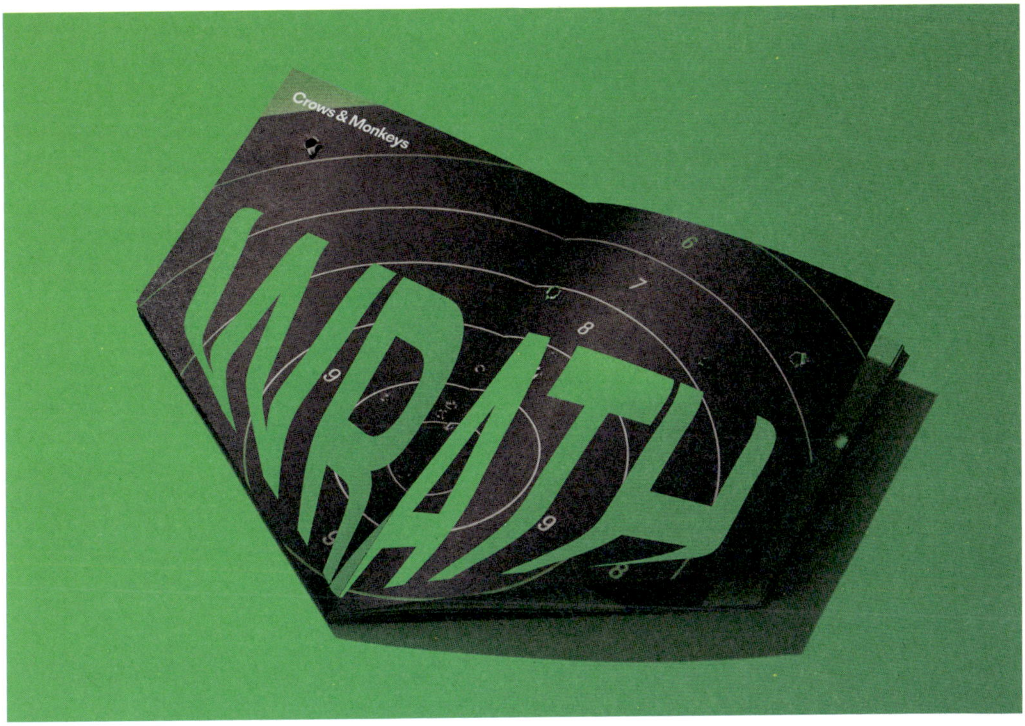

Crows & Monkeys

WRATH

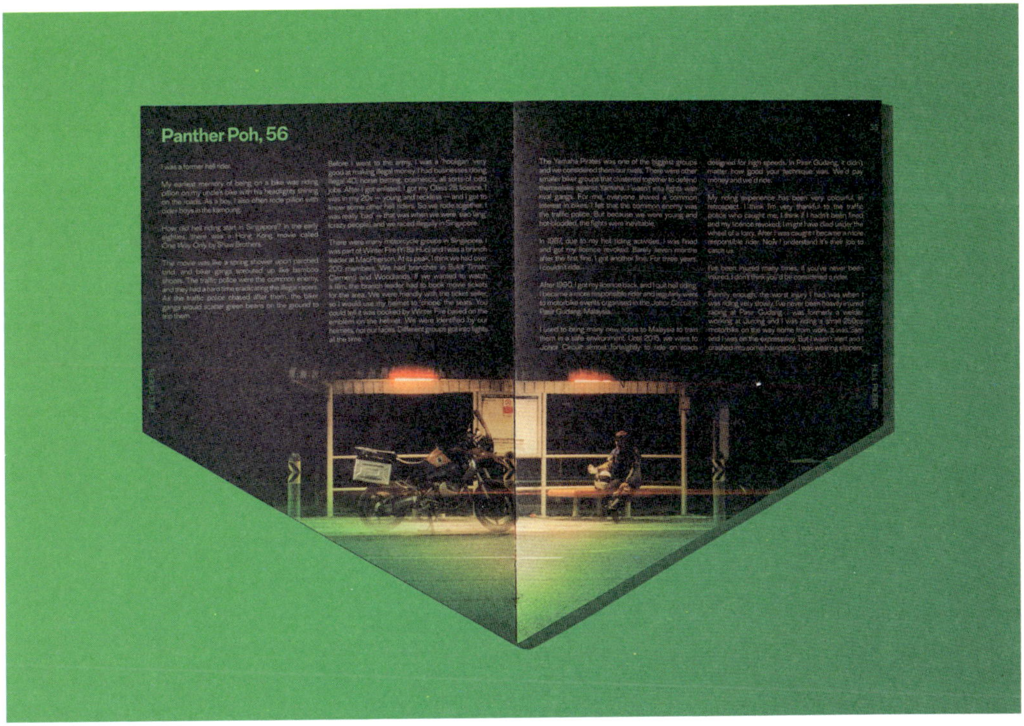

Panther Poh, 56

WHICH WAY OUT? A HERETIC PUZZLE COMPANION ZINE

Which Way Out: A Heretic Puzzle Companion is a puzzle book set inside a haunted house the reader was never meant to enter. Part of A24's zine series and inspired by the 2024 film Heretic, it features immersive illustrations by Katharina Kulenkampff. Each room contains a puzzle, guiding readers along two colour-coded paths towards a final escape challenge.

ANSWER: ●

Now go to ● P.6...

ANSWER: ■

Now go to ■ P.8...

It looks like more of a side door than a front door, but any door gets you closer to a phone. You knock. No response. You try the handle: unlocked. *Surely the people who live here will understand.* As you step inside, the door slams behind you. Reflexively, you twist the handle. It won't budge. *It's probably just a stuck door*, you reassure yourself. You venture a few steps in, and find yourself in a domed room with a giant telescope. You peer into the telescope and notice a strange constellation of stars in the night sky.

INSTRUCTIONS: In the grid, Row answers are entered consecutively from left to right (one letter per triangle) in rows A through E; each row includes one or two answers. Star answers are entered in the numbered hexagons, starting in the square with the arrow and proceeding in the direction of the arrow. If a Star answer is seven letters long, one letter must be deleted before entering the answer. The deleted letters, in numerical order of the Star clues, spell out the answer.

ROW

A

B

C

D

E

ROWS

A. Drink consumed after a shot (6 letters)

B. Sales promotion that offers money back after purchasing (6 letters)

_____ joke (bit of humor most people wouldn't get) (6 letters)

C. Last longer than, survival-wise (7 letters)

It Happened One Night star Clark _____ (5 letters)

D. Madison Square _____ (6 letters)

Material for cat's cradle and friendship bracelets (6 letters)

E. Vehicles in an airline's fleet (6 letters)

OBSERVATORY

ANSWER:

B	N	E	T	A	D	C	W
I	M	H	E	U	N	R	L
P	J	N	O	R	T	A	E
R	G	A	S	N	E	T	Z
T	E	K	P	Z	S	I	H
L	X	I	A	O	W	N	D
Y	O	M	F	V	C	K	R
U	K	W	N	T	H	F	Y

ANSWER:

Now go to ● P.22...

With the front door sealed shut, the only place to go is deeper into the house. Another dark hallway takes you out of the library, and you try to quiet the alarm bells going off in your head. *I just need a phone*, you think. *I'll be home before I know it.* You reach a large, opulent bedroom and pause at the threshold, not wanting to intrude. But don't most people have phones on their nightstands? You approach the bedside and find that you're out of luck: the only evidence that someone lives here is the set of monogrammed robes on the bed.

INSTRUCTIONS: The two monograms contain all the necessary letters to find the terms that match each clue. Each of the six monogram letters *must* be used at least once per term, and can be used as many times as necessary. The final answer is the word formed from top to bottom by the first letter of each term.

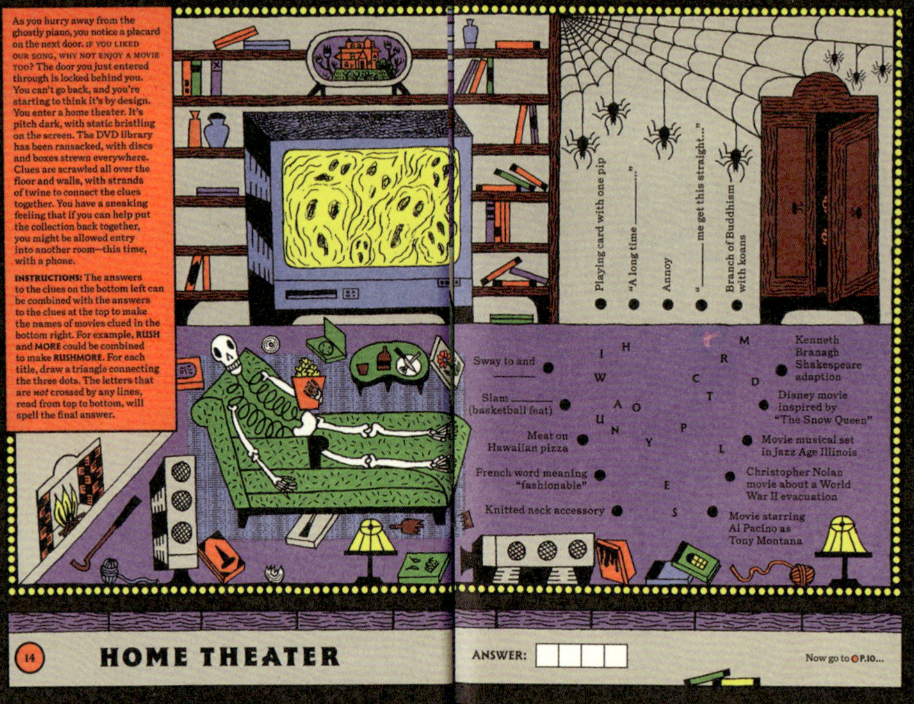

As you hurry away from the ghostly piano, you notice a placard on the next door. IF YOU LIKED OUR SONG, WHY NOT ENJOY A MOVIE TOO? The door you just entered through is locked behind you. You can't go back, and you're starting to think it's by design. You enter a home theater. It's pitch dark, with static bristling on the screen. The DVD library has been ransacked, with discs and boxes strewn everywhere. Clues are scrawled all over the floor and walls, with strands of twine to connect the clues together. You have a sneaking feeling that if you can help put the collection back together, you might be allowed entry into another room—this time, with a phone.

INSTRUCTIONS: The answers to the clues on the bottom left can be combined with the answers to the clues at the top to make the names of movies clued in the bottom right. For example, **RUSH** and **MORE** could be combined to make **RUSHMORE**. For each title, draw a triangle connecting the three dots. The letters that are *not* crossed by any lines, read from top to bottom, will spell the final answer.

- Playing card with one pip
- "A long time ______..."
- Annoy
- "______ me get this straight..."
- Branch of Buddhism with koans

- Sway to and ______
- Slam ______ (basketball feat)
- Meat on Hawaiian pizza
- French word meaning "fashionable"
- Knitted neck accessory

M H I R W C D T A O U P N Y L E S

- Kenneth Branagh Shakespeare adaption
- Disney movie inspired by "The Snow Queen"
- Movie musical set in Jazz Age Illinois
- Christopher Nolan movie about a World War II evacuation
- Movie starring Al Pacino as Tony Montana

14

HOME THEATER

ANSWER: ☐☐☐☐☐

Now go to P.10...

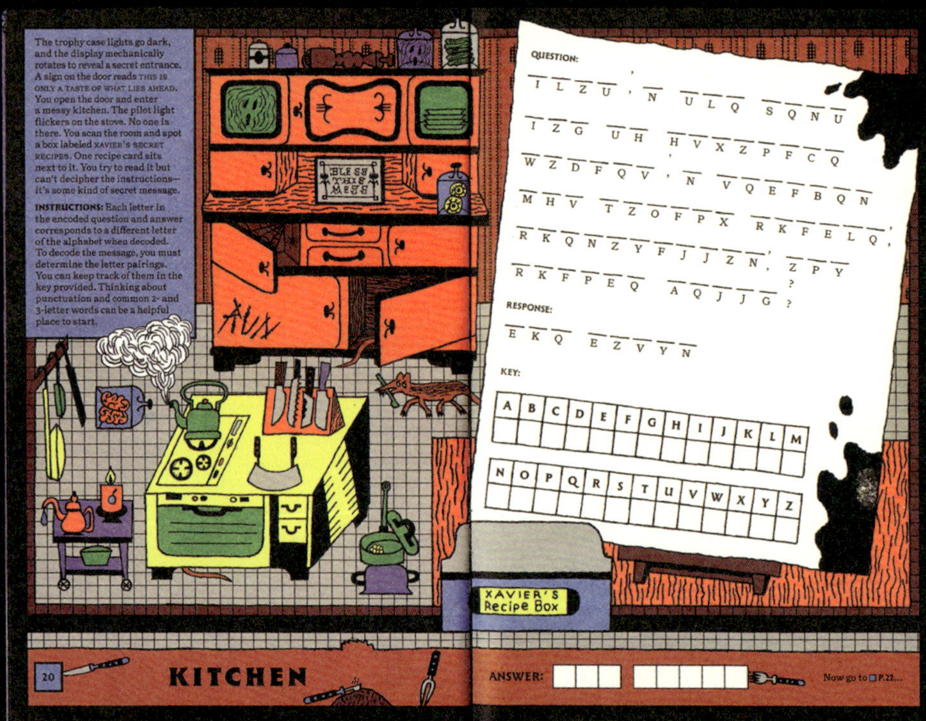

The trophy case lights go dark, and the display mechanically rotates to reveal a secret entrance. A sign on the door reads THIS IS ONLY A TASTE OF WHAT LIES AHEAD. You open the door and enter a messy kitchen. The pilot light flickers on the stove. No one is there. You scan the room and spot a box labeled XAVIER'S SECRET RECIPES. One recipe card sits next to it. You try to read it but can't decipher the instructions—it's some kind of secret message.

INSTRUCTIONS: Each letter in the encoded question and answer corresponds to a different letter of the alphabet when decoded. To decode the message, you must determine the letter pairings. You can keep track of them in the key provided. Thinking about punctuation and common 2- and 3-letter words can be a helpful place to start.

BLESS THIS MESS

QUESTION:

I L Z U ' N   U L Q   S Q N U
I Z G   U H   H V X Z P F C Q
W Z D F Q V ' N   V Q E F B Q N
M H V   T Z O F P X   R K F E L Q ,
R K Q N Z Y F J J Z N ,   Z P Y
R K F P E Q   A Q J J G ?

RESPONSE:

E K Q   E Z V Y N

KEY:

A	B	C	D	E	F	G	H	I	J	K	L	M

N	O	P	Q	R	S	T	U	V	W	X	Y	Z

XAVIER'S Recipe Box

20

KITCHEN

ANSWER: ☐☐☐ ☐☐☐☐☐

Now go to P.22...

The next door is heavy, but you pull hard and it opens with a creak. The sunlight startles you. You're outside, in the backyard. Relief washes over you as you realize you've made it out of the house—and out of the rainstorm. Someone has even propped your bike against a nearby greenhouse. As you walk to get it, you notice an unusual arrangement of empty flowerpots. A scrap of paper tucked under one of the pots flutters in the breeze. CONGRATULATIONS ON MAKING IT OUT UNSCATHED. WE HOPE YOU'VE LEARNED YOUR LESSON...

INSTRUCTIONS: Enter your answers in the spaces on the right based on whether you entered the house through **DOOR** ● or **DOOR** ■ from the **GARDEN**. The letters in the squares will spell out something that you might have if you ever meet whoever orchestrated this puzzling journey.

If you entered the house through the DOOR ●...

GARDEN

OBSERVATORY

MUSIC ROOM

HOME THEATER

BILLIARD ROOM

If you entered the house through the DOOR ■...

GARDEN

LIBRARY

BEDROOM

TROPHY ROOM

KITCHEN

Wondering what would happen if you made a different choice in the garden? Turn back to P.4 to find out...

22 GREENHOUSE

FINAL ANSWER: ●

FINAL ANSWER: ■

The faint sound of a piano comes from the end of a hallway. You walk quietly toward it, not wanting to startle the pianist. But no one is there. The keys are moving on their own. The piano is stacked with sheet music, but as you step closer, the pages slide onto the floor in disarray. As you stoop down to tidy the mess, you notice that each page has a mysterious term at the top written in red marker.

INSTRUCTIONS: Gather the terms into four groups of four such that all the members of a group belong to a coherent set. Arrange the four sets such that each group's members are in alphabetical order within the group. Then, sort the groups according to the length of the alphabetically first member of each group, from shortest to longest. Once the groups are in order, the first letters of the alphabetically last members of each group spell out the answer. *Note that:* 1) All sets are determined by word definitions. 2) The unifying concepts are not necessarily all music-related.

SHORTEST ↓

GROUP 1: A → → Z

GROUP 2: A → → Z

GROUP 3: A → → Z

GROUP 4: A → → Z

LONGEST ↑

DIDGERIDOO

DRUM

UPBEAT

MAJOR

DIRGE

BRISK

BASS

CONCENTRATION

CONCERTO

TRACK

CLARINET

PRESTO

LIVELY

MINOR

CHORALE

ETUDE

18 MUSIC ROOM

ANSWER:

Now go to ● P.14...

THE ANALOGUE SERIES

The Analogue Series is an experimental printed magazine released in 2023, exploring the early intersection of AI and analogue printing. Integrating AI-generated narratives with advanced colour separation and overprinting techniques, the project examines authorship, fabricated histories and material processes.

DESIGN
Ming Cheung

SIZE
280mm x 360mm x 2mm

PUBLISHER
for&st

FEATURES
Loose sheets with fastener, Pantone metallic printing, die-cut with original sheet

THE ANALOGUE SERIES
Keep it Rolling
&
the analogue
series
03
(/Your free trial
has been expired,
please subscribe)
WARNING
RESTORATION
FAILED

Civilization Endured
The Three Laws of Robotics
Keep it Rolling
THE FIRST SELF-AWARE AI - E.L.M.O.
EMERGENCY BROADCAST SYSTEM

REVUE FAIRE ISSUE 49

Founded in 2017 by Sacha Léopold and François Havegeer, Revue Faire is a critical print publication dedicated to graphic design. Published by Empire and designed by Syndicat, it brings together international writers, designers and historians to examine contemporary practices, history and theory through in-depth, author-led themes.

DESIGN

Syndicat

SIZE

210mm x 297mm x 5mm /
210mm x 148mm x 3mm

PUBLISHER

Empire Books

FEATURES

Saddle-stitched binding

FR

Les graphistes ont toujours été fascinés par la manière dont Lawrence Weiner fait usage du desigu graphique. «Ce qui rend le travail de Weiner si séduisant aux yeux des graphistes, c'est sa méthode résolument assumée d'exposer des mots sans aucun besoin d'explications.*» Ce texte réalise néanmoins une analyse comparative de différentes voix évoquant l'usage que fait Weiner du graphisme et de la typographie.

*— Russel Holmes, "The Work Must Be Read", Eye Magazine, Autumn, 1998, https://www.eyemagazine.com/feature/article/the-work-must-be-read

EN

Lawrence Weiner's use of graphic design has always been of fascination for graphic designers. "What makes Weiner's work seductive to graphic designers is his resolutely non-apologetic method of displaying words without need for any explanation."* But in this text a comparative analysis is made of different voices about Weiner's use of graphics and typography.

*— Russel Holmes, "The Work Must Be Read", Eye Magazine, Autumn, 1998, https://www.eyemagazine.com/feature/article/the-work-must-be-read

Lawrence Weiner: We Are Ships at Sea, Not Ducks on a Pond. | 10€ ISBN: 979-10-95991-45-8 ISSN: 2558-2062

FR

EN

– Nora Turato, Installation view, "it's not true!!! stop lying!", Sprüth Magers, Los Angeles, 2024. Photography Robert Wedemeyer. Courtesy of the artist and Sprüth Magers

FR

Entretien avec Nora Turato
4 juin 2024

Q

Quelle est votre relation avec le travail de Lawrence Weiner?

R

Bien sûr, il y a beaucoup de similitudes, en particulier avec mes œuvres murales. Lorsque vous transformez une phrase en architecture, vous revendiquez quelque chose à propos de cette phrase. Vous occupez littéralement l'espace avec cette phrase, et vous offrez au public quelque chose sur lequel se projeter. Il y a aussi l'idée de la mise en forme du langage. C'est là que le design graphique entre en jeu, et l'on peut dire que c'est là que le travail de Weiner et le mien se chevauchent dans une certaine mesure.

Q

Les pièces textuelles de Weiner dans l'espace public sont une présentation d'un travail «conceptuel». Je me suis demandé si vos pièces textuelles, lorsqu'elles sont exposées dans l'espace physique, directement sur le mur, etc., fonctionnent de la même manière. En d'autres termes, l'œuvre «réelle» est-elle le discours pendant les performances, et les livres et les œuvres textuelles sont-ils des représentations de ce discours?

R

Je ne conçois pas chaque itération comme une œuvre individuelle, mais plutôt comme une partie d'un ensemble d'éléments qui fonctionnent entre eux, qui entrent en collision et qui interagissent avec une sorte de magie. Je ne vois pas de grande différence entre une constellation de peintures murales et une constellation d'affiches, d'une part, et un livre ou un discours, d'autre part. Tout est équivalent. Bien sûr, les gens peuvent penser que je suis une performeuse et que j'utilise le langage puis

FR

EN

Interview with Nora Turato
4 June 2024

Q

What is your relationship to the work of Lawrence Weiner?

A

Well, obviously there are a lot of similarities, especially with my wall works. When you inflate a sentence to an architecture, you are claiming something about the sentence. You are literally taking up space with that sentence and giving an audience something to project upon. Then there is also the idea of formatting language. That's when graphic design comes into play, of which you can say that that is where Weiner's work and mine overlap to some extent.

Q

Weiner's text works in public space are a presentation of a "conceptual" work, and I was thinking, do your text works, when exhibited in physical space, directly on the wall, etc., function in a similar manner? In other words, is the "real" work the speech during the performances, and the books and text works representations of it?

A

I don't see each iteration as an individual work as much as I see them working with each other and the kind of magic of things colliding and interfering. I don't see much difference between a constellation of wall paintings and a constellation of posters versus a book or a speech. It's all equal. Of course, people might think that I'm a performer and use language and turn that into wall works, but that is a matter of perception, and it doesn't necessarily mean that that is how I think about it. There's no hierarchy. I would compare it to an organism where things are moving around, and I exhaust one part in favor of another

EN

– Lawrence Weiner, Crazy Cowboy, 1964. © ADAGP, Paris, 2024.
– Untitled, 1966, 24.4 x 34 cm, The Seth Siegelaub Collection. Gift of Richard S. Zeisler (by exchange). © ADAGP, Paris, 2024.
– Tiber, 1967, German house paint on canvas, 51 x 205.7 cm, unique, Seth Siegelaub / Egress Foundation. © ADAGP, Paris, 2024.

de télévision — je crois qu'il y avait quatre ou cinq autres peintres qui vivaient dans ce quartier qui étaient également intéressés par les mires. Cela s'est transformé en : «Nous allons simplement peindre cette chose que nous regardons tout le temps.»[11]

– Repro of Color Test Pattern (1960s – Variable 4)

La mire de télévision a permis à Weiner de créer des peintures en se libérant des préoccupations picturales conventionnelles comme la composition, la subjectivité, le sentimentalisme et l'inspiration. Au lieu de cela, ses sujets étaient issus d'une base graphique qui ne dépendait pas de considérations esthétiques, tout comme les *Flag Paintings* de Jasper Johns. Ceci a mené Weiner à aborder la peinture d'une autre manière :

> Les *Propeller Paintings* elles-mêmes ont conduit au problème que j'étais toujours simplement en train de peindre. J'ai commencé à en discuter avec d'autres artistes et d'autres personnes, et j'ai trouvé qu'il était plus judicieux de parler aux gens de peinture, et de décider d'un format. Le format consistait à prendre le rectangle — encore une fois, ce n'était rien de radical, d'autres gens le faisaient aussi — et à commencer, d'une certaine façon, à le bousculer. Décider de soustraire un rectangle à un autre rectangle était alors un geste suffisant, puis décider de l'application de la peinture. [...] Ensuite, l'autre chose que l'on pouvait faire à une peinture, qui provenait des *Propeller paintings*, était de tracer une ligne en haut et en bas, et cette ligne avait des angles variables, qui dépendaient de ce que l'on ressentait à un moment donné. Si la personne appréciait la peinture, elle l'acceptait. Si non, je détachais la toile du châssis et je recommençais de zéro.[12]

Ces peintures intitulées *Removal Paintings* — tout comme les *Propeller Paintings* — étaient vendues à un même prix, quelle que soit leur taille, proposant un modèle financier alternatif à celui du monde de l'art de l'époque. De plus, un parallèle est établi avec les arts appliqués, où le client est

11 — Lynn Gumpert, "Lawrence Weiner: Early Work," in *Having Been Said*, p. 120.
12 — Gumpert, "Lawrence Weiner: Early Work," in *Having Been Said*, p. 120.

The TV test-pattern enabled Weiner to create paintings free from conventional painterly concerns like composition, subjectivity, emotionalism, and inspiration. Instead, he derived his subject from a graphic foundation devoid of reliance on aesthetic considerations in a manner similar to Jasper Johns' *Flag Paintings*. This brought Weiner to another approach to painting:

> The propellers themselves led to the problem that I was still just painting. I began to discuss it with other artists and other people and found that it was more propitious at that to talk to people about painting and to decide upon a format. The format then was to take the rectangle—again this was nothing terribly radical, other people were doing it—and begin, in a sense, to fuck it over. To decide then to remove one rectangle from another rectangle was a sufficient gesture. Then to discuss color with people was a sufficient gesture, then to decide about paint application.[...] Then the other thing you could do to a painting, which was from the propellor paintings, was to stripe a line on the top and the bottom, and that line would have varying angles and the angles were based on how you felt at a particular moment. If the person was happy with the painting, they accepted it. If not, I would strip it off the stretcher and start all over again.[12]

These *Removal Paintings*—as well as the *Propeller Paintings*—were sold for the same price regardless of size, constructing an alternative financial model to that of the art world at the time. Additionally, it draws parallels with the applied arts, wherein the client actively engages in the creative process, offering financial compensation not solely based on the physical dimensions of the end result, but also for the labor involved.

We can see in the *Removal Paintings* a precursor to his later use of variously sized graphic boxes and frames with corners cut and removed. In a dialogue with Edward Leffingwell, Weiner gives an explanation for a possible meaning of the act of cutting corners:

> EL Tell me about the fifth edge [dog-ear cut into a corner] of the Bern publication.
> LW The removal of an edge from a presentation (object) within the context of art simply reduces what could be misunderstood as a wall painting or so into what in effect it is: an emblem with information on it (a logo)...[13]

Weiner defines it further in a discussion at the Ecole supérieure d'art visuel in Geneva:

> When I make a poster with cut-off corners, it's not just for fun; it's an attempt to create a logo, to make it

12 — Gumpert, "Lawrence Weiner: Early Work," in *Having Been Said*, p. 120.
13 — Edward Leffingwell, "Lawrence Weiner," in *Having Been Said*, p. 153.

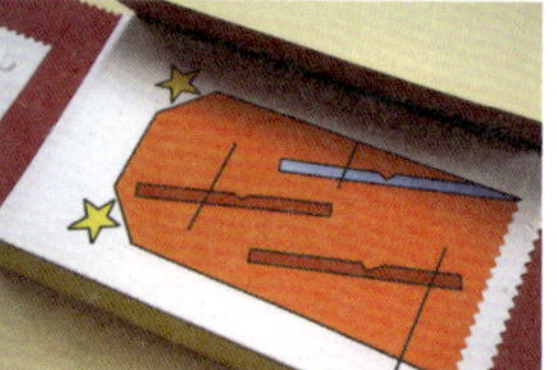

– Above, Beyond, Below, 1985, Fruitmarket Gallery Edinburgh, 32 pp., 17.8 x 14 cm. © ADAGP, Paris, 2024.
– Bookmark, Printed Matter Books by Artists. © ADAGP, Paris, 2024.
– EARTH TO EARTH ASHES TO ASHES DUST TO DUST, 1970, Panza's presentation of the work at Villa Menafoglio Litta Panza, Varese (photographed in 1977). Photo: Giorgio Colombo, Milan. © ADAGP, Paris, 2024.

Avec ce qui est sans doute sa première œuvre d'art dématérialisée, *UNE SÉRIE DE PIQUETS PLANTÉS DANS LE SOL À INTERVALLES RÉGULIERS POUR FORMER UN RECTANGLE — DE LA FICELLE TENDUE D'UN PIQUET À L'AUTRE POUR DÉLIMITER UN QUADRILLAGE — UN RECTANGLE SOUSTRAIT À CE RECTANGLE*, Weiner arrive à la conclusion que «LA PIÈCE NE DOIT PAS NÉCESSAIREMENT ÊTRE RÉALISÉE[18]» après l'utilisation, par un groupe d'étudiants, du pré où la pièce était installée pour une partie de football américain, ce qui a endommagé cette dernière :

> Lorsque je suis arrivé et que je l'ai examinée, il ne me semblait pas que les Philistins aient particulièrement endommagé la pièce. Et c'en était décidé. À partir de ce moment, la décision était basée sur l'émotion, alors qu'elle était auparavant intellectuelle. À ce moment précis, une transition vers le plan des émotions a eu lieu, lorsque j'ai réalisé que cela n'avait pas d'importance. Et cela n'était certainement pas une raison pour aller se battre avec quelqu'un.[19]

Weiner ne doit pas nécessairement réaliser la pièce si le rectangle qu'il soustrait est de la même taille que celui dont il a été retiré.

L'ŒUVRE D'ART DÉMATÉRIALISÉE

Entre 1973 et 1977, Giuseppe Panza di Biumo, collectionneur important et soutien de la première heure de Weiner, a installé l'œuvre *DE LA TERRE À LA TERRE, DE LA CENDRE À LA CENDRE, DE LA POUSSIÈRE À LA POUSSIÈRE* (1970) sur le palier d'une cage d'escalier de sa villa de Varèse, en Italie. Panza a fait transférer le texte en Letraset sur papier, puis l'a encadré dans un cadre baroque extravagant :

> Je l'ai finalement rencontré [Panza] après son acquisition de nombreuses pièces, et je lui ai posé la question évidente : comment les montrait-il à d'autres personnes ? Il a dit : «Eh bien, je voulais vous en parler, et j'ai essayé ceci et cela, j'ai essayé de les faire imprimer, etc.» Finalement, j'ai convenu avec lui, étant donné que nous avions de si bonnes conversations, qu'il pouvait présenter les pièces comme il le souhaitait. Il a trouvé un architecte qui l'a mise sur le mur. Je suis arrivé chez lui pour voir la collection, et il y avait une de mes pièces qui était peinte ou réalisée d'après transfert, je n'ai jamais pu le dire, sur le mur. Je pense que j'ai été un peu secoué, j'ai marché dans la ville de Milan pendant un moment, et j'ai réalisé que c'était aussi bien qu'autre chose. Ce n'était pas quelque chose que j'avais trouvé, c'était quelque chose qui avait été décidé par quelqu'un d'autre qui utilisait la pièce. Je pense que j'en avais aussi assez de transporter ces papiers froissés tapés à la machine.[20]

L'utilisation du langage et donc du graphisme pour présenter la pièce a plusieurs conséquences qui sont inhérentes au travail de Weiner et à son idéologie :

> Si vous réalisez un objet unique, l'acheteur, le nouveau propriétaire, peut le mettre à la cave et donc, en gros, l'acheter pour qu'il ne circule plus. Certaines œuvres d'art ont été rachetées de cette manière, car leur contenu idéologique était, que cela ait été justifié ou

18 — Troisième point de la *Déclaration d'intention*, 1969.
19 — Anne Rorimer, "Lawrence Weiner: Language as Object," in Lawrence Weiner et al., *LAWRENCE WEINER: WORKS FROM THE BEGINNING OF THE SIXTIES TOWARDS THE END OF THE EIGHTIES* (Amsterdam: Stedelijk Museum, 1988), p. 14.
20 — Gumpert, "Lawrence Weiner: Early Work," in *Having Been Said*, p. 123.
21 — Robert C. Morgan, "A Conversation with Lawrence Weiner," in *Having Been Said*, p. 102.

> it was something that just came about by someone who was using the work. I think I was also tired of carrying these wrinkled typewritten papers.[20]

The use of language—and therefore of graphic design—as a presentation of the artwork, has a few consequences that are inherent to Weiner's work and ideology:

> Now, if you make a unique object, the buyer, the new owner, can put it in the basement and so basically buy it out of circulation. There has been art bought off in this way because its ideological content was either paranoidly or legitimately contrary to some industrialist's beliefs.[21]

Or, as stated in an interview with Carles Guerra about the nature of Weiner's work in relation to poetry:

> I know why I use language. I use language because I find that I can then work with the general aspects of material. But if you look at the time, mid-sixties, all over the world artists were beginning to use language. I think it was just one of those realizations that suited the times. It meant that you could communicate your work to somebody in Paris when you didn't have the funds to go to Paris. Somebody in Rome could communicate to you. It became almost a material necessity, but for me it became a material choice...[22]

It is important to stress that Weiner's innovation is not so much that he started to work with language, but rather that he took advantage of the particular effects of graphic design and the typographic representation of language.

"ME, JOSÉ" AIN'T ENOUGH

Over the years, Weiner has received many questions about his work in relation to graffiti for obvious reasons, and he has in general been dismissive of them.

> I found myself in the *Barrio* in Los Angeles trying to give a seminar to kids who wanted to talk about art and language, just like people here, but they were talking about graffiti. Graffiti. OK, I make work, I put it outside, in language, I guess it is graffiti of a kind. They asked me, "How do you judge when a society will allow you to

20 — Gumpert, "Lawrence Weiner: Early Work," in *Having Been Said*, p. 122.
21 — Robert C. Morgan, "A Conversation with Lawrence Weiner," in *Having Been Said*, p. 102.
22 — Carles Guerra, "The Only Thing That Knows Its Own Essence Is the Thing Itself," in *Having Been Said*, p. 336.

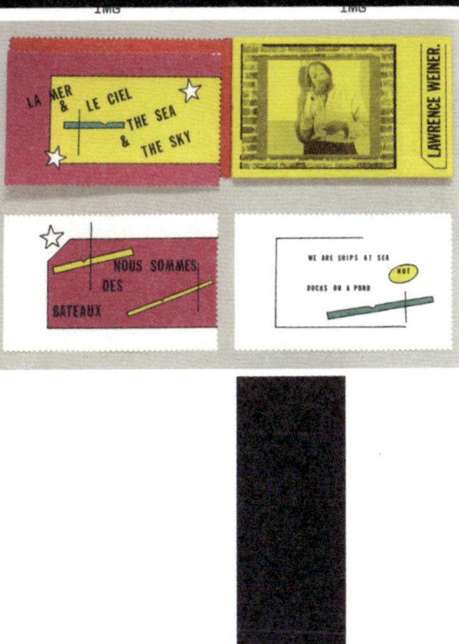

LA MER ET LE CIEL, 1985, portfolio comprising ten color screen prints on white calico, Eric Linard Publisher, Strasbourg, 15.5 x 25.5 x 7 cm. © ADAGP, Paris, 2024.

sur les côtés des bateaux, et ce sont aussi des signes qui sont utilisés pour indiquer le niveau de l'eau. Mais ils ne sont pas exactement utilisés de la même manière, ils sont utilisés d'une manière légèrement différente… [43]

Un peu plus loin dans l'entretien, Weiner introduit un autre concept :

LW … Et peut-être que mes dessins et mes petites poésies sonores, comme vous voudrez les appeler, sont…
DS Vos petites…?
LW Des poésies sonores. Ces petites choses en rapport avec ce que l'on apprend en faisant de l'art. Vous exprimez votre état existentiel. La poésie sonore, c'est ce que font les musiciens lorsqu'ils veulent utiliser la musique pour exprimer une émotion qui n'a rien à voir avec la musique. Mais appelez cela comme vous voulez. Ce ne sont que des dessins et ils utilisent le langage lui-même comme un dessin. [44]

Dans la conclusion d'un texte sur la pièce *5 ÉLÉMENTS 2 FOIS*, Martin Van der Koelen tente d'attribuer une signification à la présentation graphique particulière du travail de Weiner :

… ses textes sont souvent combinés avec des éléments graphiques formels. On peut y voir des parenthèses, les symboles « + », « & », « = », ainsi que des rectangles ou des ovales encadrants, des lignes de division qui rappellent souvent les traits de fraction mathématiques. Souvent, une partie de l'écriture est aussi cursive. Plus ces ajouts semblent forts, plus l'aspect visuel est souligné, plus ces textes se présentent de manière directe et évidente comme des œuvres d'art individuelles, indépendamment de toute référence à des objets (artistiques) extralinguistiques. On peut reconnaître le contexte suivant : moins on a l'impression d'avoir affaire à une description d'une œuvre d'art ou de sa production, c'est-à-dire à des concepts pour des objets non linguistiques, plus les textes concrets deviennent eux-mêmes des objets d'art…
Si l'on peut déduire des déclarations de Weiner que la présentation visuelle de ses œuvres est secondaire par rapport au texte lui-même, son effort et le soin qu'il exige pour la formation et la réalisation du texte est néanmoins remarquable. Ainsi, lorsqu'une œuvre est réalisée et rendue publique, la forme de la présentation en constitue bien une composante essentielle. [45]

Benjamin H. Buchloh développe ce point dans l'hommage posthume qu'il a rédigé pour Artforum :

Le fait que les phrases de Weiner déploient souvent tout le potentiel combinatoire des ordres syntaxique, lexical, grammatical et typographique du langage (par exemple, ses jeux avec des caractéristiques typographiques comme l'esperluette, les signes mathématiques, les parenthèses ou les crochets) n'a pas été reconnu comme une source de subversion supplémentaire. C'est précisément dans le glissement des significations apparemment établies qui en résulte, dans l'équivalence ou l'alternance rapide entre deux significations, ou dans l'indécision que ces constructions induisent chez le lecteur, que Weiner invite les spectateurs/lecteurs à faire leurs propres choix constitutifs, à agir en tant que sujets pleinement participants à la fois à l'intérieur et à l'extérieur des règles des structures linguistiques données (tout comme il est inévitable qu'ils opèrent simultanément à l'intérieur et à l'extérieur du régime du langage lui-même). [46]

43 — Schwarz, "Interview with Lawrence Weiner" in *Having Been Said*, p. 195.
44 — Schwarz, "Interview with Lawrence Weiner" in *Having Been Said*, p. 195.
45 — Gappmayer and van der Koelen, *LAWRENCE WEINER 5 Elements 2 Times*, p. 9.
46 — Buchloh, "LAWRENCE WEINER (1942–2021)," p. 134.

A little bit later in the interview, Weiner introduces another concept:

LW …And perhaps my drawings and my little tone poems, as you want to call them, are…
DS Your little…?
LW Tone poems. These little things to do with the things you learn from the making of art. You express your existential state. Tone poem—it's what musicians do when they want to use music to express an emotion that has nothing to do with music. But call it what you will. They are just drawings and using language itself as a drawing. [44]

In the conclusion of a text on the work *5 ELEMENTS 2 TIMES*, Martin van der Koelen tries to ascribe meaning to the particular graphic presentation of Weiner's work:

…his texts are often combined with graphic formal elements. One can see brackets, the symbols '+', '&', '=', as well as framing rectangles or ovals, dividing lines often reminding of mathematical fraction-strokes. Many times, part of the writing is cursive, too. The stronger such additions appear, the visual aspect is stressed, the more direct and self-evident these texts present themselves as individual works of art, independent from any reference to extra-linguistic (artistic) objects. One can recognize the following context: the weaker the impression is that we have to do with a description of a work of art or its production, that is with concepts for non-lingual objects, the more concrete texts themselves become objects of art…. If it can be derived from Weiner's statements that the visual presentation of his works is secondary to the text itself, yet then his effort and the care he demands for the formation and realization of the text is remarkable. So when a work is realized and made public, the form of the presentation then does constitute a rather essential component. [45]

Benjamin H. Buchloh expands on this in the obituary he wrote for *Artforum*:

The fact that Weiner's sentences often deploy the full combinatory potential of the syntactic, lexical, grammatical, and typographical orders of language (e.g. his games with typographic features such as ampersands, mathematical signs, parentheses, or brackets) has not been recognized as an additional source of subversive intent: It is precisely in the resulting slippage of seemingly prescribed meanings, in the equivalence or rapid alternation of two meanings, or in the indecisiveness that these constructions induce in the reader that Weiner invites spectators/readers to make their own constitutive choices, to perform as fully participatory subjects both inside and outside the rules of the given language structures (just as it is inevitable that they operate simultaneously inside and outside the regime of language itself). [46]

WE ARE SHIPS AT SEA,
NOT DUCKS ON A POND

LW I was very impressed by Pollock because they looked like star maps, and it turns out that they were; they were an attempt to find one's place in the world—Wow! As a kid, you got it right! I didn't know at the time. [47]

44 — Schwarz, "Interview with Lawrence Weiner" in *Having Been Said*, p. 195.
45 — Gappmayer and van der Koelen, *LAWRENCE WEINER 5 Elements 2 Times*, p. 9.
46 — Buchloh, "LAWRENCE WEINER (1942–2021)," p. 134.
47 — Emily McDermott, "Artists at Work: Lawrence Weiner," *Interview Magazine*, September 2015. Online at: https://www.interviewmagazine.com/art/artists-at-work-lawrence-weiner (retrieved 22/5/2024).

– MOI + TOI & NOUS, 1993, Le Nouveau Musée, Institut d'Art Contemporain, Villeurbainne, 30.5 x 25 cm, 24 pp. © ADAGP, Paris, 2024.
– Displacement, Catalogue and artist book from the exhibition Displacement at Dia, April 1991–February 1992. © ADAGP, Paris, 2024.
– MOI + TOI & NOUS, 2018. Poster, 60 x 40 cm. Reactivation of a work from the exhibition Specific and General Works, Nouveau Musée, 1993. © ADAGP, Paris, 2024.

MOI
+
TOI
&
NOUS

A+ ARCHITECTURE IN BELGIUM

A+ 311: Circular Plans introduces a refreshed graphic and editorial structure for the long-running architecture magazine. Designed to balance familiarity with quiet provocation, the issue splits the publication into a projects section and a thematic dossier. The design integrates seamlessly into architectural vernacular while asserting a clear, contemporary visual voice.

DESIGN	SIZE	PUBLISHER	FEATURES
Studio de Ronners & Anagramme	206mm x 280mm / 210mm x 300mm	CIAUD (Centre d'Information pour l'Architecture, l'Urbanisme et le Design)	Staple-bound sections held together by elastic band, offset insert

A+311
CIRCULA+R PLANS
Project
URA YVES MALYSSE KIKI VERBEECK
HOOFDKANTOOR PLEEGZORG, LEUVEN
Tekst: Emmanuel van der Beek
Foto's: Filip Dujardin
Pleegzorg Vlaams-Brabant en Brussel kreeg een nieuw onderkomen op een merkwaardige plek aan een steenweg. Het gebouw refereert aan de modernistische villa en diens spanning tussen stilstaan en bewegen, tussen thuiskomen en vertrekken.
Het is een merkwaardig stukje steenweg. De weg snijdt er door de heuvel, waarvan de twee helften worden gestut door betonnen keerwanden. Wie hier Leuven binnenrijdt, komt geheimzinnige wegen tegen: rechts naar het Lemmensinstituut, een kunstschool en naar Gasthuisberg, het grote ziekenhuis, links naar het postmoderne KBC-gebouw. Het is de rafelrand van Leuven, moeizaam op de bergen gebouwd.
Precies op die plek heeft Pleegzorg Vlaams-Brabant en Brussel een nieuw hoofdkwartier, in een ensemble dat een stuk kleiner is dan de complexen in de buurt. Vanaf de steenweg zie je een van de gebouwen liggen. Het is een witte doos op felblauwe kolommen. Het geheel staat op een betonnen sokkel, twee bouwlagen hoog, die in de heuvel geschoven lijkt. In de sokkel verdwijnt een weg.
Boven is het beeld anders. Daar krijgt de witte doos een benaderbare schaal. De sokkel is er aan het zicht onttrokken. Je ziet nu dat het niet één gebouw is, maar drie gebouwen zijn, die URA voor Pleegzorg Vlaams-Brabant en Brussel heeft ontworpen. Er is het grote paviljoen, dat onderdak geeft aan kantoren en dat je vanaf de steenweg kunt zien. Er is een kleiner paviljoen, vooral met gesprekslokalen. En er is het kleinste paviljoen, één bouwlaag hoog, voor het onderhoudspersoneel. De drie witte gebouwen maken van de ruimte ertussen een plein.
Het grootste paviljoen knipoogt zonder schroom naar Le Corbusiers Villa Savoye (1928): een witte balk op kolommen, een transparante begane grond met ramen in een halve cirkel. Het plan mag een stuk minder spannend zijn dan dat van zijn modernistische voorbeeld, de referentie werkt omdat ze de tweepool toevoegt waar het programma om vraagt: een open, logistieke onderwereld en een huiselijke, naar binnen gekeerde bovenwereld.
Het kleinere paviljoen valt op door zijn zwierige dak. Onder het dak zit een zaal waar ontmoetingen plaatsvinden met kinderen, ouders, pleegouders en verzorgers. Een groot gordijn – een kunstwerk van Valérie Mannaerts – kan de onderste ramen afsluiten zonder de ruimte te verduisteren. De naar binnen gekeerde volumes aan weerszijden van de zaal geven onderdak aan spreekruimtes en kantoren.
De drie paviljoenen delen een vormentaal die eigen is aan URA: robuust en eenvoudig, vanzelfsprekend bijna. Witte tegels en felblauwe accenten zoals trappen, deuren en borstweringen verwijzen naar de villa die ooit op deze plek heeft gestaan. Op elke schaal maakt het gebouw de tweestrijd zichtbaar die bij het programma hoort: een tweestrijd tussen stilstaan en bewegen, tussen thuiskomen – altijd tijdelijk – en vertrekken, in één zwierige beweging de steenweg op.
4
A+311
VOLUME 52 (2025) N 1 NL / FR € 25

A+311
CIRCULA+R PLANS
20
A+311
In 1971 ontwierp Simone Guillissen-Hoa het Maison de la Culture in Doornik, dat in 1980 werd voltooid in samenwerking met Winance, Ginion en Pirson. In 2024 renoveerde a practice het gebouw om het terug te brengen naar zijn oorspronkelijke staat.
A practice
Maison de la Culture, Doornik
21
VOLUME 52 (2025) N 1 NL / FR € 25

36

A+311 CIRCULA+R PLANS

EDITO

ESSAYS

INTERVIEW

OPINIE

ISSN 1375-5072 / VOLUME 52 (2025) N 1 NL / FR € 25

ARCHITECTURE IN BELGIUM

A+ ARCHITECTURE IN BELGIUM
Tweetalig tijdschrift (FR/NL)

SOCIOTYPE JOURNAL, ISSUE #2

Sociotype Journal, Issue #2 celebrates ad hoc creativity through eclectic cultural essays. Typeset using all 48 styles and four optical sizes of Sociotype's hybrid gothic typeface, Rework, it explores topics ranging from hobby tunnelling and gorpcore upcycling to amateur conservation, murderabilia and serial art vandalism.

DESIGN	SIZE	PUBLISHER	FEATURES
Nic Carter, Joe Leadbeater, Alicia Mundy, Indiya Tupe	210mm x 275mm x 18mm	Sociotype	Section-sewn binding, soft cover, four-colour litho printing with neon Pantones, foiled and embossed cover

Out

PHOTOGRAPHIC OBSERVATIONS FROM THE ALLEYWAYS OF HONG KONG
BY MICHAEL WOLF

the
back

common
ground

What do desire paths
tell us about our yearning
to walk on the 'wild side'?

Build it and they will come – that's how the old saying goes, though cows wouldn't agree. Design, of systems or buildings or garments or anything else that starts with an idea, has two fundamental points of origin. Start with the thing, or its intended user? Proponents of each revile the other, and it's a schism which runs deep as any ideological difference.

WORDS: EMILY WATKINS

Artist Nicky Hirst modestly refers to her practice as 'pointing at stuff and conflating things'. But surely the ability to see like an artist – that is, to perceive significance in things that most would overlook – must be equal parts superpower and curse? How exhausting to be subject to a perpetual Baader-Meinhof phenomenon, seeing meaning everywhere. These images, from four individuals and one duo, might record everyday trivialities, but they also resonate with beauty, humour, and a sense of slippery profundity.

ROAD (RE) WORKS

WORDS: NIC CARTER

Since 2016, NICKY HIRST has recorded 'beautifully misaligned' manhole covers for her image series *#youhadonejob63*. Each one offers evidence of a job done, if not properly, then properly enough (except, of course, when the errant cover happens to scramble the tactile paving that acts as a guide for the visually impaired). Whether down to carelessness or subversive intent, there's a certain delight to these small hiccups in the orderly fabric of our urban infrastructure. Each one is a quiet moment of visual poetry, full of disruptive ambiguity.

DANIEL EATOCK collects snapshots of vehicle repairs, in which a section of bodywork has been replaced by an identical part from another vehicle of the same model, but different colour. Some of the transplants are a hair's breadth away from invisibility, while others appear to gleefully revel in their patchwork aesthetic, sporting go-fast stripes or old commercial graphics. Eatock likens them to the Japanese art form of *kintsugi*, where pottery repairs are illuminated rather than disguised. Are these repaired vehicles in fact richer for their modifications and patina of experience?

Under the guise of *@wallswalls*, Moscow-based SVETLANA FEOKTISTOVA and NAZAR ISSUE record buffs – street graffiti, imprecisely overpainted by the authorities, leaving patches of colour adorning the streets like accidental Poundshop Rothkos. The buffs provide only the very skimpiest illusion of civic order. It's the swiftness of the authorities' retaliation that speaks loudest: the state must not be undermined. However their task appears to be of Sisyphean proportions, as the rapid layering of buff on buff on buff pays testament to the tenacity of both parties involved.

Among the street level curiosities recorded by STEPHEN BURKE, are the colourful hieroglyphics left by highway workers to denote the presence of underground cabling and pipes. These marks are symptomatic of the kind of parallel existences that often occur within cities. In this case, the highway worker and artist, their worlds overlapping but almost entirely separate. Where one reads utilitarian information, the see other pure abstraction, dancing across the tarmac.

Finally MATT CALDERWOOD's shuttered windows and doorways sealed with board, concrete, and brick. Blinded to the world outside, these sad, occluded apertures resemble burial vaults for the memories of their erstwhile inhabitants and past industries. And yet, in the half-hearted attempts to replicate brickwork patterns, or bricks turned 90° to fill awkward gaps, there's a sense of absurdity that undercuts the pathos. All the while, the incongruously crisp edges of fresh mortar offers a vivid reminder of the inevitable passage of time. ●

REWORK - VERSION 1.001
WEIGHTS & OPTICAL SIZES

Optical Sizes At Scale

The four optical sizes of Rework, shown at their appropriate scales of usage.

Rework's Design Space

Rework's full family of font styles, mapped to show their relative proximity in weight as well as their optical size

From Minuscule to Monumental

Subtle adjustments of proportion and scale are more pronounced with each ascending optical size: with letterforms becoming more condensed, spacing tightens, ascenders + descenders shorten, the contrast increases, and Rework's apertures begin to close up.

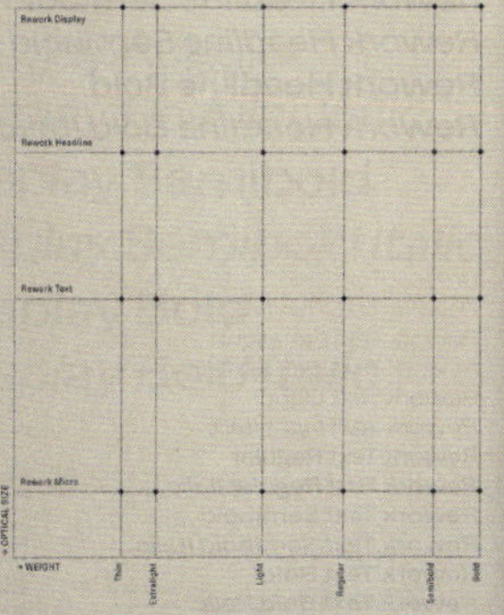

REWORK - VERSION 1.001
WEIGHTS & OPTICAL SIZES

TYPEONE MAGAZINE ISSUE 10

TYPEONE Magazine – Issue 10 marks five years in print with an expanded 182-page edition, examining not only what type looks like, but what it means within contemporary culture. Featuring interviews, essays and spotlights, each contribution is set in a typeface designed by its subject, creating visual diversity within a rigorously structured grid.

DESIGN	SIZE	PUBLISHER	FEATURES
Studio Ground Floor	223mm x 297mm x 10mm	TYPE01 Ltd	Perfect binding, various paper stocks

BEHIND THE ZINE

PRODUCTION & PROCESS

FEATURING

RISOTTO

For a growing number of creators and producers, printing is no longer the default choice for publishing and sharing work as it once was. This shift has sharpened the importance and relevance of production quality, as printed matter is now expected to earn its place in the world while competing for our dwindling attention spans. Decisions around paper, ink, format, and printing method are no longer neutral; in fact, they play a crucial role in shaping how a publication is read, valued, and remembered.

In zine culture in particular, production is often inseparable from content. As zines offer a tactile experience both visually and physically, the choices made in their production can reinforce urgency, intimacy, authenticity, or the power of a simple message. Although modern printing methods offer greater efficiency and accessibility, many zine makers continue to favour processes that foreground materiality and labour, prioritising intention and expression over speed or scale.

RISOTTO — CELEBRATING THE SLOW BEAUTY OF PERFECT IMPERFECTIONS

At a time when images circulate endlessly and cheaply, RISOTTO's philosophy is rooted in slowness, effort, and presence. Through attention to material, labour, and constraint, the studio's work champions production not merely as a means to an end, but part of the message itself: a way of signalling care for ideas, audiences, and the communities that form around shared artefacts. From its base in Glasgow, the team focuses on Risograph printing as both a production method and a way of thinking about publishing, collaboration, and accessibility — occupying the precious space between making and sharing.

For the uninitiated, Risograph printing relies on spot colours—applied one layer at a time—to produce outcomes that are often visibly imperfect. Slight misalignments, variations in ink density, and the interaction between translucent inks are inherent to the process. Rather than being errors, these characteristics are often welcomed as part of the final result.

"I first discovered Risograph printing at art school in New York, and fell in love with the texture and the limitations," founder Gabriella Marcella explains when asked about the studio's origins. "There was something honest about it. You could see how it was made."

When she returned to Scotland, access to Risograph printing was limited, as there were no public facilities or studios offering the process as part of their services. To explore the medium further, she found and installed a second-hand machine during her final year as a student at the Glasgow School of Art, where RISOTTO was born and initially functioned as a small print room. Besides using it to produce personal work, she also took on printing jobs — an approach that helped cover costs and keep the machine running.

From the outset, this dual role has shaped the studio's identity. Printing for other people was not seen as separate from experimentation, but as a way of sustaining the medium and techniques. As posters, zines, booklets, and flyers passed through the machine,

FOR THE PERSON
WHO HAS EVERYTHING
JAN

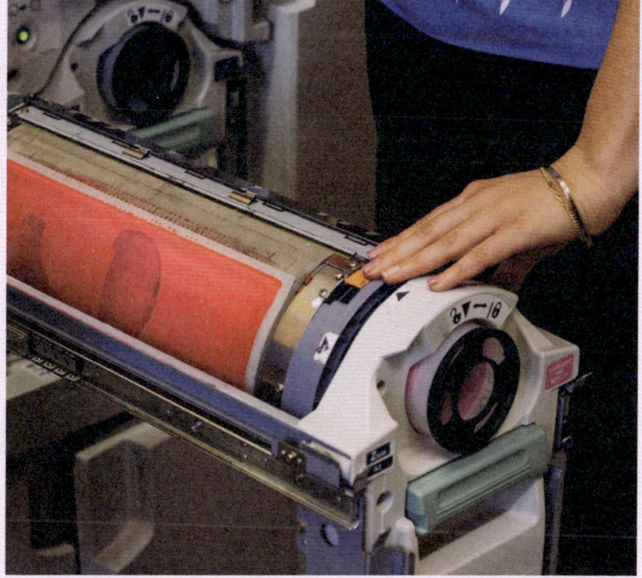

"KEEP PRINT ACCESSIBLE, KEEP IT PLAYFUL, AND USE THE MACHINES TO EXPERIMENT AND PRODUCE NEW WORK."

— GABRIELLA MARCELLA, RISOTTO

each project contributed to a growing understanding of what Risograph printing could do and how it could be used in different contexts. Over time, the small print room evolved into a more formal setup, then into a space that also accommodated a shop and workshops. Despite these changes—which were gradual, pragmatic, and shaped by circumstance rather than by a fixed plan—Gabriella's goals have remained consistent across the years.

"[My] motivation is the same as day one," she says. "Keep print accessible, keep it playful, and use the machines to experiment and produce new work."

This emphasis on accessibility is reflected in the studio's approach to zines and self-publishing. RISOTTO avoids rigid definitions — instead treating the zine as a flexible category that is shaped by intent. Rather than prioritise volume or commercial viability as others are wont to do, it sees zines as printed objects that enable their creators to communicate their messages authentically and directly without the mediation of large institutions or market-driven pressures.

While their earlier incarnations often featured photocopied pages and raw aesthetics, contemporary zines take many forms that include carefully produced, small-run publications that employ a variety of printing methods and materials. Instead of regarding this as a departure from the spirit of zine-making or zine culture in general, the studio acknowledges this evolution as an expansion of it.

"Over time, [the definition of zines] has stretched to include more considered objects," Gabriella notes. "The attitude is more important than the format. A zine can be quite polished now, but it should still feel like it came straight from an individual."

This focus on authorship and voice informs how RISOTTO approaches every project, whether self-initiated or commissioned. The studio is less concerned with producing a uniform aesthetic than with supporting a wide range of visual languages — acting as a conduit that brings ideas to life through the machines. This constant flow of work has made collaboration central to its practice. Artists, designers, musicians, charities, and community groups regularly use its facilities to meet different needs while sharing know-how and discussing ideas.

One of the most sustained expressions of this collaborative approach is RISO CLUB, a postcard subscription project initiated by the studio where four artists are invited to create new work each month. These works are then printed and sent out to subscribers. While the format is deliberately modest to ensure production is manageable and to allow for a wide range of contributors, the project has grown significantly, involving nearly 400 artists from different countries and backgrounds over the years.

"The club is run for love, not profit, which is important," Gabriella explains. "Keeping it affordable means the work can travel far and stay accessible; and it also keeps the focus on the relationships it has built, rather than on sales."

For RISOTTO, this non-profit approach to the club reflects a broader philosophy where independence is not defined by isolation from clients or institutions, but by the ability to make decisions based on curiosity and intuition. Just like the zines the studio produces, autonomy is actively protected and passion is central to its work.

"ONCE YOU UNDERSTAND HOW THE MACHINE AND COLOUR LAYERS WORK, YOU REALISE YOU DO NOT NEED BIG BUDGETS OR A REFINED IDEA TO EXPRESS YOUR IDEAS."

— GABRIELLA MARCELLA, RISOTTO

Although it now operates as a registered company, with the responsibilities that entails, many of its projects continue to originate from internal interests. The decision to remain relatively small has been a purposeful one, allowing the team to stay closely involved in production and avoid the administrative complexity that often accompanies growth.

"I've chosen to keep the studio small and focused, so we can all be involved in the making, and less about management," Gabriella shares. "Risograph is often associated with low cost, but the labour behind it is very real. The machine might be affordable compared to commercial presses, but the work is intensive."

This closeness to production is particularly important given the nature of Risograph printing. Besides taking into account the temperamental nature of the machines themselves, inks can behave differently depending on paper choice and unexpected issues are common. In addition to preparing each layer separately, colours must be tested and adjusted, and prints are often trimmed, collated, and bound by hand. The result is that value is carried less by how many are produced and more by attention.

For Gabriella, this labour is not something to minimise, but something that gives the work its weight — which is why RISOTTO makes the efforts involved visible rather than hiding it. Committed to openness and transparency, it sets realistic expectations and timelines with clients by first ensuring they understand the technical considerations in detail. Workshops also play a central role in education, through which the studio guides participants through the entire production process. Besides teaching skills, these sessions are designed to build confidence — encouraging participants to experiment, accept mistakes, and view outcomes as part of a learning process rather than as finished products. They are also able to exchange prints, talk about their practices, and make connections that extend beyond the session itself.

"I want people to leave with two things: a sense of empowerment and a sense of play," Gabriella says. "Once you understand how the machine and colour layers work, you realise you do not need big budgets or a refined idea to express your ideas."

Echoing their workshop approach, RISOTTO's relationship with Risograph printing is shaped by an acceptance of constraint. Rather than attempting to overcome the limits on colour use, format, and paper choice that the machines impose, the studio integrates the variability into the design process — driven by Gabriella's interest in systems and her belief that clear frameworks create space for experimentation.

To the team, budget, time, and distribution are the parameters that call for thoughtful navigation. If a project cannot accommodate an additional ink colour, visual depth could be achieved through overprinting or paper selection. If a publication needs to fit through a letterbox, the format is adjusted accordingly. These decisions often result in clearer, more focused outcomes.

This way of working also informs RISOTTO's ethos on sustainability. Rather than framing it as a separate initiative, the studio embeds it into everyday decisions — prioritising uncoated, recycled, or FSC-certified papers; minimising waste through efficient sheet usage; and reusing offcuts for secondary products such as notepads.

In a broader context, Gabriella observes that zines and small publications are increasingly expected to justify their existence. As audiences become more conscious of waste and storage, printed matter is no longer produced simply for novelty. While this shift has introduced new challenges within self-publishing, the studio views it as a positive development. By encouraging greater thoughtfulness around content, format, and circulation, it seeks to challenge the perception of zines as "disposable" items — foregrounding them instead as intentional, durable documents that can record events, archive ideas, and circulate knowledge.

"YOU FEEL THE PAPER, YOU SENSE THE LABOUR OF MAKING IT, AND YOU ARE MORE LIKELY TO KEEP IT. I LIKE USING DIGITAL AS THE INVITATION, AND PRINT AS LEGACY."

— GABRIELLA MARCELLA, RISOTTO

As such, the team does not shy away from digital platforms — instead using online tools as complementary parts of a wider ecosystem that support engagement, sharing, and international reach. Gabriella recognises that digital spaces have made it easier to find like-minded communities, while also noting that this ease often comes at the expense of slowness — a quality defined by the tactile presence of paper and ink, and by the awareness that the object has been physically made, encouraging readers to slow down and spend more time with it.

"A printed zine asks for a different kind of attention," she says. "You feel the paper, you sense the labour of making it, and you are more likely to keep it. I like using digital as the invitation, and print as legacy."

RISOTTO's own visual language — what Gabriella calls their "internal grammar" — has been shaped by years of working with Risograph printing. Because each colour is applied separately, designs are developed in layers, with careful consideration of how colours will interact. The translucency of Risograph inks encourages bold shapes and flat colour areas, while texture emerges through paper choice and ink density rather than through digital effects. Misregistration, often considered a flaw in other printing processes, is anticipated and incorporated — contributing to a sense of movement and individuality.

Due to its experience with these processes, the studio has a growing body of internal knowledge, including preferred ink combinations, halftone techniques, and methods for achieving gradients. Drawing from both commissioned work and educational activities, it has applied its approach across a wide range of projects, including collaborations with international brands such as Apple, Mini, Puma, and Swatch. Clients are often drawn to the team's use of colour, pattern, and process-driven aesthetics, and commissions are approached with an emphasis on aligning client objectives with RISOTTO's methods.

"I see Risograph as a bridge between DIY photocopy culture and bespoke screen-printing," Gabriella muses. "It allows small studios and individuals to produce work with a tactile, 'printed' quality, without needing to jump to huge print runs or larger budgets."

When asked about her favourite project to date, Gabriella recalls RISOTTO's workshops delivered in partnership with Pinterest in Cannes. For this project, the studio temporarily relocated to a beach setting, hosting up to 200 participants per day over four days. The challenge was to design an experience that remained personal and hands-on despite the scale of the location.

Achieving this required careful planning and system design. Workflows were structured to allow participants to create individual prints within limited time slots, and the movement of people through the space was choreographed as carefully as the printing process itself. The success of the project demonstrated that the team's approach could adapt to larger contexts without losing its emphasis on participation and making.

Looking ahead, RISOTTO is focused on consolidating its activities within a new studio space or HQ to create new possibilities that include more workshops, talks, and exhibitions. Another key upcoming milestone for the team is the 100th issue of RISO CLUB, with plans underway for an exhibition to collate the work of all 400 contributing artists to date, allowing audiences to experience the project as a physical archive rather than as individual mailings.

"What excites me is the idea of RISOTTO as both a production space and a place to host," Gabriella says. "It feels like the right moment to open the doors a bit wider and let more people into the process."

Part of risograph's continued relevance is a matter of timing. According to Gabriella, as creative work has become increasingly digital, there has been a growing appetite for things that feel physical, imperfect, and locally made — qualities that Risograph printing embodies. The process is also inherently social: a single machine can support an entire community of makers, encouraging studios to emerge not only as service providers, but also as shared spaces for experimentation. She sees the resulting global network of small studios expanding, forming an informal yet deeply connected ecosystem.

In parallel, RISOTTO will continue to operate as it always has — grounded in material practice, shaped by collaboration, and attentive to the communities that gather around it. When production is understood not as a closed system but as a shared rhythm of machines in motion, hands at work, and decisions made together, print is no longer merely the end-point. An active, unfolding process shaped by tools, constraints, and conversation, each project becomes an invitation to slow down, participate in the act of making, and find connection in the perfect imperfections left behind.

BEHIND THE ZINE

PUBLISHING & PLATFORM

FEATURING

NIEVES

HATO PRESS

Portrait of Benjamin Sommerhalder
by Stefan Marx

The act of printing may seem deceptively simple — where ink meets paper, pressure leaves a trace, and repetition slowly builds form; yet between these basic actions exists a wide range of possibilities. From the digital methods that prioritise speed and volume to Risograph printing, where colour layers through misalignment and chance, each technique carries its own rhythm, and none of these processes replace the others. Instead, they coexist, offering different ways of thinking and forming a shared language of print.

In that sense, what comes next for publishing is not a single direction, but many — and zines remain a space where these futures are tested first. As old machines find new uses, new technologies will borrow the logic of older ones and allow makers to move freely between control and accident, so that errors become features, limitations become style, and process stays visible. In a time when content can vanish with a simple scroll on a screen, zines will continue to insist on touch, time, and presence — showing that beyond polish or permanence, they will thrive in their ability to adapt, remain accessible, and stay firmly physical.

NIEVES — KEEPING THE COMMITMENT TO CONTINUITY ALIVE

When Benjamin Sommerhalder talks about publishing, he rarely describes it as a technical pursuit or an industry, returning to feelings like curiosity, excitement, and conviction instead. For him, it is less about prominence than about proximity — to the work, to the artist, and to the moment something comes into being. It is this sensibility that has shaped Nieves from its earliest days and continues to inform its place within contemporary zine and independent publishing culture.

Emerging from a desire to participate — that is, to make rather than observe — the publishing house did not begin as a fully formed idea. In the late 1990s, while studying graphic design in Switzerland, Benjamin started a magazine called Zoo. At the time, magazines were still the primary way cultural information was being circulated, and Zoo combined interviews, drawings, and short texts in an authentically fluid way that was closer to a zine than a lifestyle publication, borrowing as much from skate and music magazines as from art publishing.

Rather than treating it as a business or a stepping stone toward something larger, Benjamin simply wanted to publish what he wanted — and that meant taking responsibility for the entire process, from editing and design to printing and distribution. In 2001, a friend running a similar project suggested they combine distribution efforts, if only to make that part of the work more manageable. That practical decision became the seed of what would become Nieves.

"What motivated me wasn't a business plan or a clear long-term vision," he reflects. "It was really just a strong desire to publish and the idea of having my own publishing house. I'd already been doing zine projects with friends before that, and those experiences were important. Over time, the focus shifted — from magazines to zines, and later toward artists' books — but the project grew very organically. It was driven by curiosity, financial limitations, and the feeling that this was something I really wanted to keep doing."

Because resources were limited, titles were printed in short runs and timelines were always tight — but rather than boiling them down to obstacles or failures, these modest circumstances moulded the character of the publishing house, where continuity mattered more than growth. Publishing one book made it possible to publish the next, and if a project paid for itself, that was enough.

Zines naturally became central to this rhythm. As small, informal publications could be produced quickly and distributed directly, zines offered a way of working that felt immediate and unencumbered by expectation — requiring neither permission nor polish. Although Nieves later expanded its focus to include artists' books, these did not replace zines but rather extended the range of what was possible.

(i)

In the background, the wider context around zines was shifting, becoming increasingly visible and more broadly recognised. What once existed largely on the margins entered more stores, fairs, and collections. Today, the term "zine" applies to a wider and sometimes contradictory range of printed objects — from photocopied pamphlets to offset-printed catalogues and luxury editions. To Benjamin, however, the boundaries remain deliberate.

"For me, a zine is still a small edition produced using alternative or simple printing techniques: photocopy, Risograph, silkscreen," he explains. "It's important that it stays intimate, direct, and slightly rough around the edges. As soon as a publication becomes a larger edition and is offset printed, it loses the character of a zine for me. At that point, I call it a book, even if it's still staple-bound."

Even within the broader context, this distinction speaks to the importance of preserving the artist's relationship to process, scale, and time. In the simplest sense, a zine can be defined less by how it looks than by the conditions of its making. Zine-makers can respond to a moment by creating and sharing their work quickly — passing it directly from one set of hands to another with more flexibility.

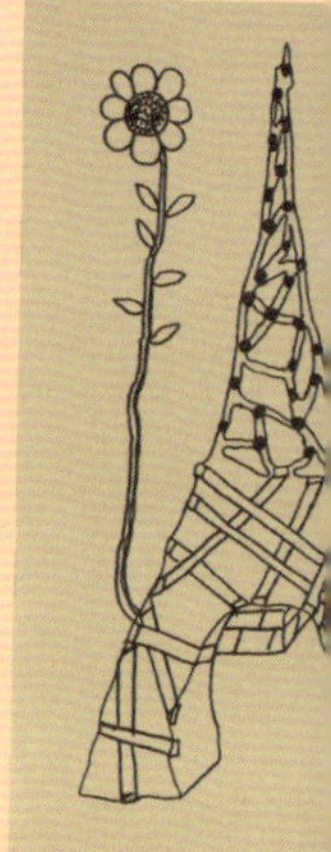
(iv)

This emphasis on process extends to how Benjamin works with artists. Rather than be driven by themes or curatorial agendas, projects at Nieves begin with a personal response. To that end, he is drawn to work that resonates intuitively — even if he cannot immediately articulate why.

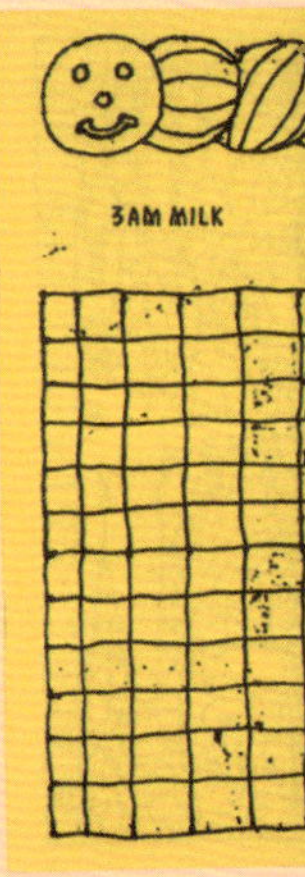

(vii)

Zines:
(i) 'Curves' by Mimi Laquidara
(ii) 'Himaa draws Stefan, Stefan draws Himaa' by Stefan Marx, Masanao Hirayama
(iii) 'Collectionneuse' by Annette Messager
(iv) 'Veistospuisto (Sculpture Garden)' by Jaakko Pallasvuo
(v) 'Martin Wong Was Here' by Martin Wong
(vi) 'Chronicle of a Tremor' by Andrea Heller
(vii) '3AM Milk' by Jim Stoten
(viii) 'Bookstore' by Kyle Field
(ix) 'IRIS' by Emi Ueoka

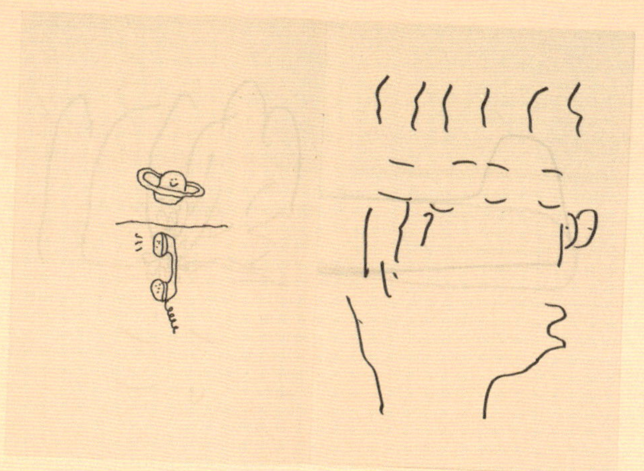

(ii)

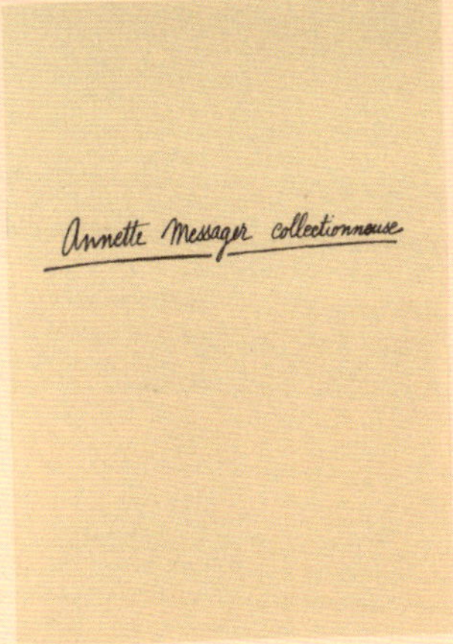

(iii)

(v)

(vi)

(viii)

(ix)

"IT'S IMPORTANT THAT IT STAYS INTIMATE, DIRECT, AND SLIGHTLY ROUGH AROUND THE EDGES."

— BENJAMIN SOMMERHALDER, NIEVES

"I'm drawn to work that touches me in some way, even if I can't always explain it," he says. "Originality, openness, and a strong sense of curiosity are important to me. I'm much less interested in whether someone is well known and much more interested in whether the work feels honest and convincing."

Often, Benjamin approaches an artist with a rough idea of how a piece of work might take shape – but that idea is never fixed, which means that the format evolves through exchange and trust. Rather than treat collaboration simply as a step in the process, he sees it as the process itself. Books like This Is Not My Cat by Takashi Homma or Going to Love You by Mark Gonzales are testaments to his outlook, as they were developed through extended back-and-forth, with sequencing, paper choice, and scale shifting until the publication felt inevitable rather than merely resolved.

"I don't really see myself as someone who produces content," Benjamin muses. "I work with artists whose work I admire and want to publish. Usually, I already have some idea in my head of how a book or zine could work, but that idea almost always changes through conversation. The publication really emerges through dialogue."

Over time, these collaborations have grown into a wide network of lasting relationships, with some artists returning to Nieves repeatedly to build on their last project. These sustained exchanges are key to how he understands publishing – not as a series of isolated releases, but as an ongoing practice. The cumulative effect of repeated collaborations often matters more than any single title.

One such collaboration is with artist Stefan Marx, whose work he cites as a recurring source of inspiration. Their shared history has produced numerous outcomes, ranging from quick, photocopied zines to more substantial artists' books. Stefan's direct language, graphic economy, and openness to imperfection align closely with Nieves' publishing ethos.

Ultimately, what Benjamin values most in these projects is their lack of overdetermination. The work does not try to explain itself or justify its existence; instead, it simply exists as a confident entity in its own terms. This philosophy extends to how the team navigates constraints more broadly.

"Constraints have always been part of Nieves," he reflects ."Limited budgets, small editions, simple printing methods – they can be restrictive, but they're also productive. I strive for perfection, but because the print runs are small and the printing methods relatively affordable, a lot of pressure is taken away. Within those limits, there's actually a lot of freedom."

Graphic design, in this context, is deliberately understated. Benjamin often describes his role as almost invisible. Rather than impose a visual identity, he sees his main goal as to create enough structure for the work to live and breathe comfortably, where typography is functional, layouts are clear, and sequencing follows the logic of the material rather than an external design system. The foundation to this approach and way of working lies in independence.

"INDEPENDENCE MEANS BEING ABLE TO WORK AT MY OWN PACE AND FOLLOW MY INSTINCTS."

— BENJAMIN SOMMERHALDER, NIEVES

"Independence means being able to work at my own pace and follow my instincts," he says. "It also means saying no many times, even to good projects, in order to stay focused. Of course, Nieves exists because of collaborations and networks, but the core decisions remain personal, and that's very important to me."

International relationships have also played a key role in shaping Nieves. From the beginning, Benjamin has been interested in finding compelling work wherever it exists. Travel and collaborations abroad—particularly in Japan—introduced him to different attitudes toward publishing and craftsmanship, where artists often emphasised paper quality, binding, and pacing. These experiences continue to reinforce his belief in small editions, careful production, and long-term thinking, while affirming that publishing does not need to follow a single dominant model.

More recently, he has become increasingly interested in working with artists from regions less immediately connected to Western publishing circuits, including South America, parts of Africa, the Middle East, and South Asia. Building these relationships takes time, but that slowness is part of their value. While publications from these collaborations often resist categorisation—combining photography, drawing, and text in ways that challenge standard formats—he believes they should be rooted in curiosity, respect, and listening to make them meaningful in today's digital-first era.

"A zine is physical, direct, and intimate. You don't need much money, infrastructure, or permission to make one, and that simplicity is very powerful," Benjamin explains. "In a world where so much is fleeting and screen-based, a zine offers something slow and tangible. It creates a moment of pause, a physical encounter that asks for time and attention."

Digital media, he also acknowledges, has transformed how work is shared and discovered - which is why Nieves has begun offering parts of its zine back-catalogue as downloads. Instead of viewing them as a replacement for print, the publishing house uses these platforms as a way of extending the life and accessibility of work originally produced in smaller numbers, so that the digital versions function more as archives than substitutes.

As zine culture continues to evolve, Benjamin remains optimistic but grounded. Looking ahead, he imagines a publishing landscape in which independent voices continue to matter, and in which print is valued not out of nostalgia, but through care and intention - allowing digital and physical formats to co-exist thoughtfully.

Photo: © Nicole Bachmann

Within this changing landscape and amid its uncertainties, Nieves will continue much as it always has: steady, intuitive, and committed to the act of publishing itself. Rather than growing bigger or moving faster, Benjamin returns to the spirit that formed the publishing house from the beginning, drawing on the same impulses that guided him years ago. This outlook is perhaps most clearly felt in a simple, recurring experience.

"There isn't one single moment," he shares, "but the feeling of opening a box from the printer captures a lot of what Nieves is about for me. That mix of excitement, fear, and hope hasn't changed since the beginning. And if a publication comes out exactly as it should, that moment makes all the uncertainty worthwhile."

五木田智央作品集
横尾忠則
OUR LIFE BOOK KENTARO OKAWARA
ISSUE 10 NEW TYPE DESIGN
Volume 2
A S Books
HATo Press

HATO PRESS — THE PRESS AS A LIVING LAB

In 2009, two graduates of Central Saint Martins—Jackson Lam and Ken Kirton—faced a question familiar to almost every young creative emerging into an uncertain world: how do you carve out space to experiment when the structures around you feel inaccessible, expensive, and indifferent? Their answer was characteristically direct: if the architecture didn't exist, they would build it themselves.

What they built was Hato Press – named for the Japanese word for pigeon. Inspired by the spirit of the bird that persists in any environment, their press was defined from the outset by modesty, community and accessibility. Rather than something that was done at the last step of a creative project, they set out to bring printing into the creative process – letting the printer become a living tool to shape the work while it was being made.

"We wanted to be as common and resilient as the city birds we saw every day," the founders explain. "Starting Hato was our way of supporting our own practice while simultaneously lifting others up. It wasn't just about the ink on the paper; it was about the empowerment that comes with having the tools to materialise a thought. We wanted to take the mystery out of the production process and replace it with a collaborative dialogue. If you had an idea, Hato was the place where that idea could become a physical reality, overnight if necessary."

At the heart of Hato Press is the Risograph and the question of why—in an age of near-infinite digital reproduction—a machine that prints in layers of deliberately imprecise ink has become culturally meaningful.

Risograph printing, like screen printing, translates image files into physical dots through a stencil-based process. Misregistration, smudging, and roller marks are not defects but the medium's signature. Each print is subtly unique and the spontaneity is not simulated; it cannot be, because it arises from physical reality rather than digital intent.

For Hato Press, this materiality is inseparable from the ethos of independent publishing. In a landscape saturated with frictionless digital content, the imperfect Riso-printed zine offers something genuinely scarce: tangibility. "It's difficult to replicate this spontaneity in pixels," the founders note, "because it needs to be added with intention, and it's that lack of intention that makes physical print so unique."

This tension between digital abundance and physical singularity sits at the heart of contemporary independent publishing. Hato Press has navigated it not by rejecting the digital, but by understanding what print can offer that pixels cannot.

"PLAY SITS AT THE HEART OF BOTH THE STUDIO AND THE PRESS. AT ITS SIMPLEST, PLAY IS ABOUT CURIOSITY AND A SENSE OF ENJOYMENT — APPROACHING IDEAS WITH OPENNESS RATHER THAN PRESSURE."

— HATO PRESS

Their output ranges from artist books and zines to food and film projects like the Studio Cookbook series that documents the go-to recipes of creatives while in the studio, as well as Cooking with Scorsese, a wry archival project documenting recipes in films where food plays a central role in the story — from the fried egg on bread in Hayao Miyazaki's Castle in the Sky, to the handmade dumplings in Ang Lee's Eat Drink Man Woman.

"Play sits at the heart of both the studio and the press," the founders explain. "At its simplest, play is about curiosity and a sense of enjoyment — approaching ideas with openness rather than pressure. We try to move through briefs without over-forcing outcomes, allowing space for unexpected connections and intuitive decisions to surface. That mindset keeps the work alive."

To that end, research at Hato Press is not primarily analytical; it is immersive. It happens in exhibitions, in libraries, through films and music. All these are forms of creative play, and often lead to new breakthroughs and discoveries compared to a typical research process.

This approach is visible in their ongoing zine series, which since 2020 has invited a different creative to work within the constraints of the medium each month. What the project revealed, they note, was the remarkable breadth of what a zine can be: a colouring book, a calendar, a poem, a lookbook, a manifesto. Ultimately, through play, they give themselves the permission to follow their instincts and stay experimental, collaborative, and responsive.

The question of what small presses offer that larger publishers cannot is, at this moment in publishing history, genuinely urgent. The consolidation of major publishing houses,

[P. 263] 'Bread As' by Lexie Smith

flour
5g SALT
10g carob
65-75g water (85)
oil
600g flour
water
oil

the dominance of algorithmic retail platforms, and the narrowing commercial logic of mainstream publishing have created conditions in which singular, experimental, or politically marginal voices find it increasingly difficult to exist without compromise.

Hato Press's perspective on this is nuanced like the issue itself: large publishers "inevitably operate within layers of structure — commercial expectations, market positioning, brand legacy." None of this is inherently negative, but it "can make it harder for singular or emerging voices to exist without compromise." What small presses offer in contrast is proximity, flexibility, and trust — the ability to shape projects around the work itself rather than around predetermined formats or sales projections.

Yet they are careful not to romanticise the margins. What feels missing in the current landscape, they argue, is not creativity but visibility. "Independent publishing still tends to be framed as operating on the margins, celebrated within certain circles but not always given equal weight by mainstream media, bookstores, or wider audiences." Greater recognition and infrastructure for small presses would not diminish their independence; it would amplify the artists they support. “With more space and attention, independent presses could have an even broader cultural impact while retaining the independence that makes them necessary,” the founders explain.

This is where independent bookstores, book fairs, and artist-led spaces become structurally important. For Hato Press, these are not simply distribution channels but cultural mediators – spaces that contextualise and champion independent publishing

[Left to Right] 'Breakfast Food for Dinner' by Haydée Touitou, 'Visible Vehicle Repairs' by Daniel Eatockdellatur

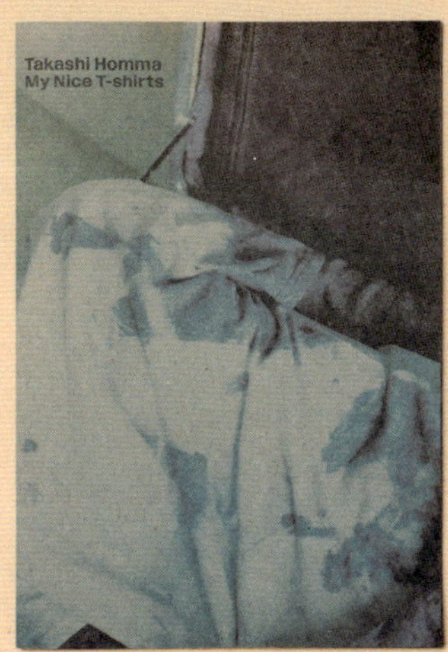

[Left to Right] 'Eyes Wide Open' by Emma Larsson, 'My Nice T-Shirts' by Takashi Homma

"WE DIDN'T JUST START A PRESS, WE STARTED A CON-VERSATION THAT WE'RE STILL HAVING FIFTEEN YEARS LATER."

— HATO PRESS

in ways that larger retail environments cannot. "They don't just distribute our books," they note. "They actively shape the ecology in which independent voices can be seen, discovered, and taken seriously."

Today, Hato Press operates differently from how it once ran. Working on a project-by-project basis, it now produces a small number of carefully considered collaborations alongside self-initiated books. The decision to step back from full commercial operations was, paradoxically, a return to origins: to the experimental, dialogue-driven spirit that motivated the founding.

Their studio and press continue to inform one another. Some artists who initially came to the former as clients—such as Pio Abad and Larry Achiampong—have since moved into publishing projects with the latter. This shift from commercial relationship to closer collaboration have been, as the founders describe it, "a huge compliment".

Looking ahead, Hato Press imagines their role expanding beyond the production of books into events, exhibitions, and digital sharing — acting as platforms and conveners for voices and forms that don't easily fit elsewhere. In a fast-moving creative ecosystem, they see this kind of independence and responsiveness as necessary.

"We didn't just start a press," they reflect. "We started a conversation that we're still having fifteen years later." In a publishing landscape that can feel increasingly driven by scale and algorithmic logic, that conversation—modest, persistent, and genuinely open—feels more valuable than ever.

BEHIND THE ZINE

EVENTS & EXPOSURE

FEATURING

TOKYO ART BOOK FAIR

PAGEMASTERS

MUSEUM OF
CONTEMPORARY
ART TOKYO
TABF
TOKYO ART
BOOK FAIR 2025
DEC 11—14, 19—21

In the age of influencers, the word "exposure" is everywhere, but meaningful visibility is harder to come by. Digital platforms promise reach while controlling who gets seen and for how long, feeding attention spans that are increasingly fragmented, short-lived, and shaped by algorithms that reward frequency, polish, and alignment to trends. For many creatives and independent publishers, this has made competing for audience share a constant, draining task — one that rarely leads to sustained engagement or genuine connection.

This is why visibility rooted in presence matters — and why zines continue to hold relevance. By taking a different approach, they offer a slower, more intentional form of exposure that values context over scale. Instead of fighting for attention, work is discovered through browsing, conversation, and chance at events and fairs where a reader picks something up because it resonates, not because it has been pushed into their feed. Ultimately, this means of exposure supports communities rather than metrics, so that encounters can become collaborations and knowledge is shared in a truly organic and authentic way.

TOKYO ART BOOK FAIR: WHERE BOOKS MEET PEOPLE

Every year, for a few days, the Museum of Contemporary Art in Tokyo's quiet Kiyosumi Shirakawa neighbourhood shifts its rhythm. The wide corridors fill with the sound of pages being turned, conversations unfolding across tables, and people pausing—sometimes for a long time—over books they have never seen before. Visitors travel from across Japan and from around the world, drawn by a shared curiosity and a quiet excitement for printed matter. During the Tokyo Art Book Fair, the museum feels less like a place to pass through and more like a gathering point, where the simple act of holding a book becomes a reason to stay, talk, and connect.

Tokyo Art Book Fair (TABF) grew out of a very specific moment. In 2008, Hiroshi Eguchi, then the owner of the Tokyo bookstore Utrecht, took part in the New York Art Book Fair as an exhibitor. Experiencing the energy of the fair from inside the booths left a strong impression on him — in particular, the direct, face-to-face exchanges where people were not just buying books, but talking, sharing ideas, and spending time together.

Back in Tokyo, that experience stayed with him. Together with organiser Naoko Higashi, Eguchi began imagining what a similar platform might look like in Japan. The aim was not to copy the New York fair, but to create something that made sense locally: something open, accessible, and rooted in Tokyo's existing art and publishing scenes. In 2009, the first edition took place under the name ZINE'S MATE: TOKYO ART BOOK FAIR 2009, held across two spaces in the city's trendy neighbourhood Omotesando—EYE OF GYRE and Vacant—and organised by a small group of volunteers.

From the beginning, TABF was conceived as a place to meet. What started modestly has grown steadily year by year, with the venue changing over time and the scale expanding naturally alongside its community. As its director since 2015, Yusuke Nakajima, explains:

"A book fair isn't only about selling books. It's about creating a space where people can encounter ideas, cultures, and each other." That idea continues to shape the fair today.

Since its launch, TABF has grown into one of the largest art book fairs in Asia. In its 15th edition in 2025, it was held over two separate weeks for the first time, with each week featuring a different lineup of exhibitors. Approximately 560 exhibitors participated, and the event attracted about 38,000 visitors in total. Tokyo plays an important role in how TABF functions. As a city, it is both densely local and internationally connected. Visitors can travel in from across Japan, while overseas exhibitors often see the fair as an entry point into the Japanese publishing world. TABF sits comfortably in this overlap.

"Tokyo is quite accessible," Nakajima says. "People from different regions and countries can gather here fairly easily." This physical accessibility allows TABF to become a meeting point between local makers and international publishers, without one dominating the other.

Rather than positioning exposure as scale or numbers, TABF focuses on presence. Exhibitors stand behind their tables, books in hand, ready to talk. Visitors are encouraged to slow down, flip through pages, ask questions. "When you meet the person who made the book, your relationship to it changes," Nakajima notes. "You don't just see the object; you understand the intention behind it." This kind of exposure is difficult to replicate online. TABF places value on the experience of encountering printed matter in person, where weight, texture, and sequencing matter just as much as content.

[PP. 268–271] Photos: © Hajime Kato. 2025

"A BOOK FAIR ISN'T ONLY ABOUT SELLING BOOKS, IT'S ABOUT CREATING A SPACE WHERE PEOPLE CAN ENCOUNTER IDEAS, CULTURES, AND EACH OTHER."

— YUSUKE NAKAJIMA, TOKYO ART BOOK FAIR

Photo: © Hajime Kato. 2025

"ZINES ARE DRIVEN BY THE DESIRE TO EXPRESS SOMETHING DIRECTLY, THAT HASN'T REALLY CHANGED OVER TIME."

— YUSUKE NAKAJIMA, TOKYO ART BOOK FAIR

Within the fair, this energy is especially visible in the ZINE'S MATE AREA — a section dedicated to emerging artists and independent creators. The area reflects TABF's long-standing connection to self-publishing cultures, from zines and mini-comics to more experimental printed matter.

Zines have always been part of TABF, but in recent years their presence has grown more visible. Nakajima sees this as a natural development. "Zines are often the first step for many young artists," he explains. "They're light, flexible, and easy to start with." Compared to art books, which often require longer production cycles and institutional support, zines allow for immediacy. They can be personal, experimental, or even unfinished. TABF treats these qualities as strengths rather than shortcomings. "Zines are driven by the desire to express something directly," Nakajima says. "That hasn't really changed over time." At the fair, zines sit alongside established publishers and internationally recognised imprints. This proximity gives emerging makers a sense of belonging within a larger publishing ecosystem. Exposure here does not mean hierarchy — it means being part of the same conversation.

While TABF welcomes large crowds, the organisers pay close attention to how people actually interact within the space. Over the years, they have introduced small gestures and programmes designed to encourage conversation rather than passive browsing.

"There are many moments that happen outside of the main event," Nakajima explains. Exhibitors-only gatherings held after public hours create quieter spaces for exchange. A simple card game, where participants earn a free drink by talking to others, lowers social barriers. "It sounds small," he says, "but these kinds of things make it easier for people to connect." The Talent Award, introduced more recently, shifts attention towards recognition rather than competition. Selected by invited judges across two weekends, the award highlights publishers whose work resonates with the fair's values. "It's a way to celebrate what people are doing," Nakajima notes, "not to rank them." Talks, workshops, and exhibitions also play an important role. They provide context that books alone sometimes cannot. "A book can communicate a lot," Nakajima says, "but hearing someone speak about their process or history adds another layer."

International exchange has become increasingly central to TABF. In recent years, nearly half of the exhibitors have come from overseas, reflecting the growing interest in Tokyo as a meeting point for art book cultures across Asia, Europe, and beyond.

TABF maintains close relationships with art book fairs around the world. These connections are informal but sustained, built through repeated encounters and shared values. "We often invite other fairs to introduce their local scenes in Tokyo," Nakajima explains, mentioning cities such as Bangkok, Singapore, and Seoul.

At the same time, TABF actively brings Japanese publishers overseas. This two-way movement is important. "Exposure shouldn't only go in one direction," Nakajima says. "It works best when it's reciprocal."

The Guest Country programme reflects this approach. Rather than following trends, selections are shaped by long-term perspectives and ongoing conversations. "We think about what kind of publishing culture we want to introduce at that moment," Nakajima explains. The goal is not to present a fixed image of a country, but to show publishing as a living practice.

Held at the Museum of Contemporary Art Tokyo (MOT), TABF exists within a public, civic setting. For Nakajima, this is significant. "Being in a museum changes how people see books," he says. Art books and zines are encountered not as niche products, but as cultural works with their own histories and contexts. Exhibitions staged alongside the fair extend this idea. Projects such as Yes Yes Yes: Revolutionary Press in Italy 1966–1978 placed historical zines next to later developments, tracing decades of publishing practice. "We wanted to show that zines have always been connected to social movements and ideas," Nakajima explains. By situating these exhibitions within the fair, TABF encourages visitors to think about continuity rather than novelty. Exposure becomes something that unfolds over time, linking past and present.

As TABF has grown, questions around scale and independence have become more pressing. For Nakajima, independence is closely tied to balance. "We try not to rely too heavily on any single company or institution," he says. Maintaining equal relationships allows the fair to stay flexible and open. Needless to say, with growth comes responsibility too. Diversity of publishers and perspectives is welcomed, but the organisers also work to maintain a clear sense of direction. "Honesty and sincerity are important," Nakajima notes. "If people trust the fair, they're more willing to take part."

TABF also exists within a broader ecosystem of bookstores and publishing spaces across Tokyo — from large-scale bookshops to specialist photography and zine stores, as well as neighbourhood independents shaped by the tastes of their owners. For many international visitors, the fair becomes a starting point for exploring the city through its book culture, moving beyond familiar areas and into everyday local landscapes.

Today, TABF's identity is widely recognised, and interest in expanding the format continues to grow. While the organisers do not feel the need to replicate the fair elsewhere under the same name, they are open to the idea of more opportunities for people to encounter art books and zines.

"At the end of the day," Nakajima reflects, "we hope that people who come to the fair leave with a deeper interest in books." Whether as readers, makers, or organisers, exposure at TABF often becomes the starting point for longer journeys.

By focusing on encounters rather than spectacle, Tokyo Art Book Fair continues to show how events can shape the way zines are seen, shared, and carried forward.

[P.275] Photos: © Hajime Kato. 2025

GUEST
COUNTRY
ITALY

PageMasters ZineFair
2025
6th - 7th September // Saturday 12-8 PM // Sunday 11-6 PM
FREE ENTRY
(and always will be!)
x160
independent
Titles
x44
Publishers
Tables
Music from
East Anglia
Records &
Anu
Performances
&
Talks
Workshops
from:
Anu Ambasna
Tommy Brentnall
Mandy Merzaban
ArtHub Studios, New Cross, Stanley Street, London, SE8 4BL

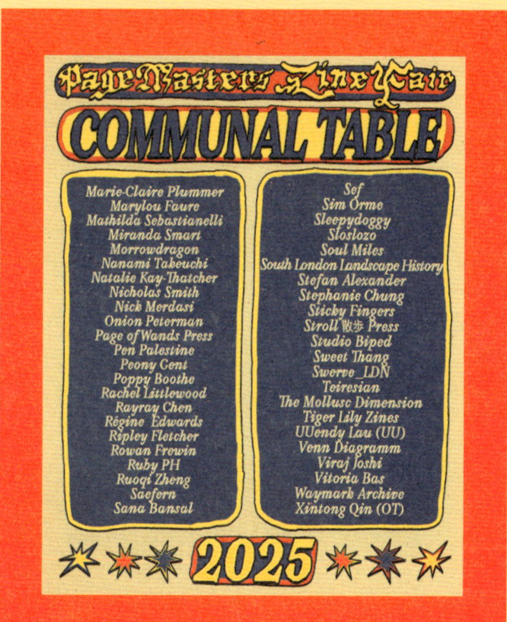

PAGEMASTERS — THE DEFIANT COUNTERCULTURE OF CLOSENESS IN A DIGITAL WORLD

In a time when culture is largely consumed through platforms and systematically assessed by brands and corporations, the continued relevance of the zine feels quietly radical. Inconvenient by design, zines demand physical presence, intention, and time — both to make and to engage with. They carry voices that are often sidelined elsewhere, conveying ideas that are too specific or too personal to survive algorithmic filtering.

Historically, this is precisely what gave zines their power. They have long belonged to countercultures and anti-populist, anti-capitalist movements, created with the intention of reaching and resonating with people who were marginalised or silenced. When mainstream channels were hostile, inaccessible, or exclusionary, zines offered an alternative by being cheap to produce, difficult to control, and quick to circulate. While the digital age has made it easier than ever to publish one's innermost thoughts with a click, zines continue to grow as a parallel route to exposure as we know it — one rooted in proximity rather than views, and resistant to the pressures of constant optimisation.

Within this route, PageMasters has carved out its own place. Based in Lewisham, the Risograph studio has become a key node in London's DIY publishing ecosystem. Rather than chasing visibility through likes or trending posts, it focuses on building infrastructure around print — not only to produce objects with material presence, but to support the conditions that allow independent publishing to thrive. That means providing access

"ANYTHING CAN BE A ZINE, BUT MOSTLY IT'S PRINTED EPHEMERA WITHOUT A 'PROPER' SPINE, DISTRIBUTED CHEAPLY, USUALLY CONTAINING VALUABLE OR SUBVERSIVE INFORMATION."

— PAGEMASTERS

to tools, shared knowledge, and spaces where people can engage without the pressure to "perform" for commercial results.

However, rather than an attempt to disrupt an industry, the studio was born as a response to hitting a wall. Both its founders, Jordan Taylor and Justin Bailey, were working at another print company when it became clear that the space for experimentation had closed — and the exciting possibilities that came with building something they could truly call their own became impossible to ignore.

That decision to walk away rather than be confined to someone else's limits continues to define PageMasters, where independence is central to its ethos. The freedom to choose projects, set terms, and prioritise long-term relationships over short-term gains while accepting precarity as part of the deal—as they often did in the early years—is an approach that closely mirrors how Jordan defines the zine itself: "Anything can be a zine, but mostly it's printed ephemera without a 'proper' spine, distributed cheaply, usually containing valuable or subversive information."

This absence of a spine is symbolic, as zines are not meant to sit neatly on shelves and be revered; they are meant to move and change hands unencumbered, slipping freely between people and places with the same ease as the ideas and content they carry. This mobility still underpins the studio's role today as a space for unfiltered expression.

As digital culture has intensified, this physical circulation has become more meaningful. In the online realm, exposure is abstract — where it is possible to reach thousands of people and still feel unseen. Zine culture, however, offers a different economy of attention: when someone picks up your work at a fair, the interaction is direct, the feedback is immediate, and the exchange is human.

[Right] Photos: © Holly Revell

Arts Club

Photo: © Holly Revell

This is where PageMasters' role becomes crucial. Independent publishing rarely survives on individual effort alone; it depends on relationships, shared resources, and trust built over time. Through its studio, workshops, and events, it has gradually helped shape a network that extends far beyond its physical space — made up of repeat collaborators, returning artists, former students, and grassroots projects: people who rely on one another not just for production, but for advice, access, and mutual support. In a sector defined by uneven funding, this kind of infrastructure becomes essential, allowing work to circulate even when institutional backing is absent.

"A good thing about collaboration is that it helps you understand who you shouldn't work with, and more importantly, who you absolutely should," Jordan explains. "Over the past eight years, we have built a wide network of collaborators, long-term clients, students who have gone on to set up their own businesses, and community projects we have supported across the UK. When people receive funding, they come to us for support, and when they don't, we still help where we can. Over time, this has grown into a solid community locally, nationally, and internationally, which is worth more than gold."

For Jordan, collaboration quickly moves beyond shared creative intent into questions of labour, resources, and responsibility. Working together means being clear about what a project demands, not just aesthetically but materially. Without that clarity, even the most aligned partnerships can become strained.

"IF YOU STICK WITH SOMETHING LONG ENOUGH, IT STARTS TO WORK EVENTUALLY."

— PAGEMASTERS

In print, those realities are immediate. Every decision carries costs in time, money, and production, and those pressures shape what collective effort looks like in practice. Rather than fight against reality, the studio views it as a structuring force — one that determines scale, pace, and how work ultimately circulates.

Much of this labour happens away from personal projects. Long periods are spent supporting other creators, maintaining infrastructure, and keeping the studio viable. Creative autonomy is less a constant state than something returned to intermittently, informed by the practical experience the team has accumulated along the way.

"I always recommend checking artist union rates of pay and bringing them into the conversation early," Jordan shares. "It grounds discussions in something concrete and fair. It's also worth remembering that many people working in the arts likely already come from wealth, and that's simply a reality you have to acclimatise to without letting it make you bitter. If you stick with something long enough, it starts to work eventually. There are long stretches where we're not focused on our own work at all, but when we do return to personal projects, we have a wealth of approaches to draw from, shaped by the many different ways we engage with print through the commercial side of the business."

The duo's perspective also shapes how the team thinks about success. Rather than being a statement or ideal, it functions as a practical way of working that allows them to adjust and respond to changing pressures without having to answer to anyone else. After years of colouring within the lines, this has become less about avoiding responsibility and more about being able to make decisions and change direction when needed.

This adaptability shines through in PageMasters' events, particularly the PageMasters Zine Fair. Thriving as a fully self-funded DIY endeavour since September 2025, it counts the South London Gallery as a recurring venue partner — a testament to the studio's dedication to putting in the work.

The structure of the fair also challenges common ideas of exposure, reframing it as something shared rather than competed over. Instead of relying only on individual tables—which can be expensive, intimidating, or hard to access—a communal table offers another way for people to participate. The studio also buys stock upfront, removing the risks of sale-or-return arrangements and slow wholesale systems. For many makers, it is the first time their efforts are supported without being expected to sell everything themselves — a key part of the magic Jordan finds in these fairs.

When asked about print versus digital, Jordan sidesteps the debate: "At this moment in time, who cares? The world is on fire. I am less concerned about print versus digital and more interested in people sharing information through new, alternative or old-school methods. That said, I will always choose physical over digital because that's what interests me. I believe people want something offline, not delivered through oligarchic platforms."

Workshops have become a central part of PageMasters' offerings, serving as an important way the studio connects with wider audiences. Sitting alongside its fairs as a practical entry point, they are often the first time someone encounters Risograph printing as something they can actively use, rather than simply admire from a distance. Instead of asking people to arrive with finished work, the team invites participants into the process itself. Students, self-publishers, and commercial clients occupy the same space, helping to level the field and widen who feels able to create and distribute.

"Education demystifies the process," Jordan says. "Editing, preparing files, and sending work to print all become much clearer the more you practice. You don't need to be an expert to make a good zine."

This hands-on practice often leads directly to visibility. Participants leave workshops with something tangible to share—zines, posters, or small editions that circulate through fairs, studios, and personal networks—alongside the skills and confidence to keep making more. At a deeper level, they also tap into a wider cultural mood: many participants arrive frustrated by polished systems that feel distant or inaccessible, and leave with a renewed sense that publishing can be immediate, imperfect, and personal.

Jordan sees this shift reflected in the work that passes through PageMasters: "I genuinely believe we are moving towards a world where copyright, at least as we know it, will not exist. Memes are a perfect example. Trends come and go, so it's best to just focus on what excites you — what you have the will to work on."

When thinking about the future, they describe their ambitions as "delusional." The long-term dream is to build a school that could rival traditional art education: practical, collaborative, and rooted in making rather than prestige. For now, that vision exists in fragments—co-ops, fairs, workshops—but the direction is clear. Holding space at this scale comes with emotional demands and managing burnout remains a work in progress, but they approach it pragmatically.

"I do what I can," Jordan muses. "If I can be of help to a community or an individual, fabulous. If not, no hard feelings. I always go the extra mile so I know I did what I could. Sometimes projects collapse in on themselves, and sometimes they grow their own legs and run off — which is beautiful. Both are totally normal."

From this beauty emerges a simple truth: zines have grown not in spite of the modern media landscape, but because of it. As culture becomes louder, faster, and more exploitative, the pull of small, self-directed work becomes stronger. Beyond exposure, it offers a more meaningful sense of connection — and in a world that is seemingly growing more divided, that closeness is powerfully countercultural.

BEHIND THE ZINE

CULTURE & COMMUNITY

FEATURING

RAUM FÜR ILLUSTRATION

ZINE COOP

Anytime

In recent years, zines have re-entered cultural conversations not as a revival, but as a persistence. Existing somewhere between art object, publication, and social gesture, they operate outside the conventions of institutional publishing while remaining deeply engaged with contemporary culture. Rooted in DIY traditions, subcultures, and political self-expression, zines continue to evolve – absorbing new visual languages and concerns about the world around us without surrendering their independence.

What defines zine culture, however, is less the format itself than the way it circulates and the relationships it produces. Zines move through hands rather than platforms: exchanged at fairs, mailed between cities, donated to libraries, or left to be found. Their distribution relies on trust, proximity, and shared interest rather than algorithms. Within this slow circulation, community is not declared but formed through shared labour, informal networks, and a willingness to operate at the margins of sustainability. The spaces that support zines are often fragile by design – held together by friendship, commitment, and the belief that cultural value does not require commercial viability in order to endure.

RAUM FÜR ILLUSTRATION — MAKING ROOM FOR PEOPLE THROUGH A LIVING PRACTICE

Raum Für Illustration did not start out with the grand ambitions of building a community cornerstone or a cultural infrastructure. More simply, the idea of its inception blossomed from the layouts, deadlines, and disciplined routines of editorial life in the German magazine world, where print design not only sits alongside content as decorative flourishes, but also serves as an important means of organising thought for easier consumption.

While the emphasis on structure, clarity, and responsibility has long shaped Germany's publishing landscape, it exists in sharp contrast to the country's indie arts and culture scene, which foregrounds experimentation. Although these two sides of the coin are what make the cultural sector itself exciting, independent initiatives still operate largely outside the security of institutional support, relying on short-term funding, voluntary labour, and spatial arrangements that are often temporary. It is within this tension—between stability and vulnerability—that the studio would eventually find its place.

For almost a decade, Raum Für Illustration founder Philipp Schultz worked at ZEIT Verlag, one of Germany's most respected publishing houses. As a well-established institution that places great trust in its readers, ZEIT had long been defending printed matter as something worth time, money, and attention, even as the industry around it began to shrink due to the proliferation of screens. By the time he became art director of ZEIT Leo, the publisher's children's magazine, Philipp was already deeply entrenched in German print culture.

ZEIT Leo occupied a special place within the ecosystem. As a magazine for children, it allowed for the kind of visual freedom that was rare elsewhere. Instead of treating illustration as a mere accessory, the magazine utilised it as a central narrative tool not only to attract young readers, but also to provoke curiosity, explain ideas, and carry meaning independently of the copy.

"I was given a lot of freedom to relaunch ZEIT Leo and focused strongly on using illustrations," Philipp recalls. "As a result, a large part of my work involved reviewing illustration portfolios – and I was completely hooked on the many possibilities that illustration offers."

Over time, this immersion reshaped how he thought about images. As hundreds of portfolios passed through his hands, he was exposed to a field far broader than the narrow glimpse typically visible in mainstream magazines – where political illustration sat alongside poetic abstraction, and quiet observational drawings appeared next to bold graphic gestures. As a loose, expansive language of its own, illustration opened up a new universe that exceeded the editorial frameworks meant to contain it.

Meanwhile, German publishing was also shifting as a whole, with smaller print runs, tighter budgets, and related jobs becoming more precarious. In response, large media groups began consolidating their power, while independent publishers struggled for survival. The concentration of ownership among prominent groups such as Axel Springer further narrowed the space for dissenting voices, alternative aesthetics, and novel formats – shifting attention away from innovation toward the question of how long stability could be maintained.

In parallel, the indie arts and culture scene was quietly under pressure. Artist-run initiatives found homes in old factories and temporary spaces, often rooted in strong relationships with local communities – but as rents rose and cities changed, they were gradually pushed aside. Long-standing cultural venues vanished and once-vibrant cultural environments were replaced by commercial developments, making non-institutional efforts harder and far more expensive to sustain.

Against this backdrop, illustration continued to circulate online, appear in advertising, and emerge in self-published projects. This growing gap between how much illustration existed and how little physical space there was to encounter it played no small part in pushing Philipp to leave ZEIT Leo and start something of his own. Although moving on from a stable position was not an easy decision, staying on felt like standing still.

"After three years as art director, I wanted to explore new spaces for and with illustration – to break out of the constraints of my magazine; so I took the plunge into self-employment," he says.

Initially, Raum Für Illustration was meant to function as a design studio focused on client work and illustrative solutions. The public dimension arrived later—almost by accident—via a sticker show Philipp organised to help get the studio noticed. Stickers were chosen for practical reasons: they were affordable to produce, easy to display, and accessible across ages. But they also carried strong cultural meaning, especially in the music, skateboarding, and activist communities.

Ultimately, the exhibition proved effective – and people came, stayed, and returned. The atmosphere felt different from the transactional rhythm of client briefs, and when the

[PP. 284–285] 2023 Zine Salon (Library Auswahl)
[P. 287] Kogan Kult Cult City Exhibition

"AFTER THREE YEARS AS ART DIRECTOR, I WANTED TO EXPLORE NEW SPACES FOR AND WITH ILLUSTRATION – TO BREAK OUT OF THE CONSTRAINTS OF MY MAGAZINE."

— PHILIPP SCHULTZ, RAUM FÜR ILLUSTRATION

Zine Library 2019 Photos: © Michael Kohls

show ended, the question was no longer how it might be repeated, but whether stopping made sense at all. The subsequent move to a space with a larger storefront propelled the situation further. Raum Für Illustration was no longer hidden behind a doorbell or an appointment; passersby could look in, replacing intention with curiosity. To maximise use of the window, Philipp then added a modest shop and began a publishing arm to sustain it. Zines followed naturally, and with them came a small but steady group of visitors who began to recognise one another, linger, and treat the space less as a destination and more as somewhere to come back to.

This development echoed a broader shift within German print and pop culture. Since the early 2000s, zines had slowly found their way into the public eye after years confined to punk scenes, political collectives, and underground cultures. Cities such as Berlin, Hamburg, Leipzig, Cologne, and Düsseldorf saw the growing emergence of small fairs,

independent bookshops, and self-organised festivals. Events like Miss Read in Berlin or the Hamburg Comicfestival became meeting points for artists, designers, illustrators, and writers dissatisfied with both mainstream publishing and purely digital formats.

For Raum Für Illustration, the definition of a zine was never rigid, with photocopied booklets sitting beside books printed with attention to detail. Independently published works across illustration, comics, design, photography, and fine art formed the heart of its collection, offering something other publications increasingly could not: autonomy. They enabled people to create without permission, pitch decks, or market forecasts, where the content could be personal, unique, and even unfinished. In a cultural economy driven by visibility and metrics, zines continue to create a safe space for feminist, queer, and other underrepresented voices to thrive.

According to Philipp, the shop's zine library began with an exhibition featuring zines from around the world in 2019, after which they remained stored in boxes until 2024, when they were brought out as part of another four-part exhibition series. It was through this series that they finally found their permanent place in the shop, and the library's index on the website was created.

"I wasn't expecting much," he admits. "We had only been around for a few months and were completely unknown. [In the end,] we received more than 600 zines from 25 countries. I was overwhelmed and incredibly happy about the love from the community. That was the moment I knew I was on the right track."

Today, the library holds over 2,100 publications from more than 45 countries, with most of them being donations. Instead of adhering to an acquisition budget, curatorial hierarchy, or thematic strategy, the collection reflects the richness of relationships. Political zines coexist with diary-like ones while conceptual projects sit alongside playful visual experiments, forming a diverse archive of contemporary independent publishing.

[Top to Bottom] Zine Library 2025

"I WAS OVERWHELMED AND INCREDIBLY HAPPY ABOUT THE LOVE FROM THE COMMUNITY. THAT WAS THE MOMENT I KNEW I WAS ON THE RIGHT TRACK."

— PHILIPP SCHULTZ, RAUM FÜR ILLUSTRATION

While community is often invoked as a buzzword, it has manifested in practical ways at Raum Für Illustration – where volunteers eventually became regulars, regulars became collaborators, and people showed up not because they were paid, but because the space mattered to them. Philipp credits two collaborators in particular—Alica Naimark and Erik Müller—for shaping it profoundly.

"Without them, Raum Für Illustration would be a completely different place," he says. "Out of love for the space and the projects, they both started as volunteers. I later hired them because they were so involved and ran the shop so efficiently."

Over the years, interns from South Korea, Italy, France, England, Spain, and Hungary have passed through, each leaving behind traces of their own references and working ethos. Without branding or formal declarations, these influences accumulated quietly and were absorbed organically, mirroring how culture circulates today: through friendships, recommendations, and shared enthusiasm rather than official channels.

This mode of operation also reflects broader realities within Germany's indie arts and culture sector. Much of what sustains it is informal: unpaid labour, emotional investment, and networks that grew over time. While independence allows for artistic freedom and experimentation, it also exposes projects to constant uncertainty, where funding often fluctuates, planning security is minimal, and access to affordable space is increasingly rare – vulnerabilities that Philipp understands.

"People are more willing to spend €30 on a print than €18 on a zine," he notes. "I find that really unfortunate, but that's how it is. A zine disappears on a shelf; a print hangs on the wall like a trophy."

Since 2024, the team has rarely held exhibitions, due to a growing focus on print work and a lack of time and space. While Philipp describes this as a sad turn of events, it has also made room for new possibilities. In an increasingly digital world, Raum Für

[Top] Kogan Kult Cult City Exhibition

Illustration continues to insist on physical presence. Zines are objects with weight, texture, and smell, and browsing them together produces conversations that rarely happen online. Social media remains necessary for visibility, but Philipp approaches it with scepticism – viewing it both as a blessing for its ability to connect people worldwide and a curse because of "the d*mned algorithm". To him, digital platforms function as invitations and print remains the destination where things settle.

"I'm totally old school about that," he says. "For me, a zine is something tangible. An object. E-zines don't interest me at all – they're something completely different."

At the end of the day, Raum Für Illustration does not position itself as a benchmark, nor does it profess to hold a blueprint for community-building. It is the outcome of specific conditions, relationships, and decisions – a testament to how publishing can exist outside institutions, how autonomous practice survives amid structural instability, and how a room—through care, trust, and shared effort—can become a place where people stay, not because they have to, but because they want to.

"I think it's always important to stay curious and keep your heart and eyes open," Philipp concludes. "And for me, friendship is key. You can't do it alone."

ZINE COOP — CULTURE, COMMUNITY, AND COLLECTIVE CARE IN HONG KONG'S ZINE SCENE

In a city where value is often measured in speed, scale, and financial return, zines move differently. They are slow, small, and resolutely personal. In Hong Kong, few have done more to protect and nurture this way of working than ZINE COOP, an indie publishing collective that has quietly become one of the city's most important cultural platforms for zine-making. Since its founding in 2017, ZINE COOP has operated not simply as a distributor or organiser, but as a form of community infrastructure; creating spaces where people can gather, share, and speak in their own voices.

Founded by Beatrix Pang and Forrest Lau, later joined by Jason Li, ZINE COOP emerged at a time when zines were still largely invisible within Hong Kong's mainstream creative landscape. While there were small, underground pockets of comic-makers and self-publishers, there was little sense of a connected scene. For the founders, the solution was not to immediately build a brand or platform, but to build relationships first. As Beatrix reflects, "At the beginning, there weren't many people making zines in Hong Kong. We felt that if we wanted anything to grow, we had to build a community first, because only when people gather together can things really move forward."

Before ZINE COOP officially existed, its members had already been travelling to art book fairs around the world, observing how zine cultures in places like Japan had developed strong, self-sustaining ecosystems. Around the same time, alternative printing methods such as Risography and letterpress were beginning to take root in Hong Kong, thanks to studios like Ink'chacha and Odd One Out. These technologies lowered the barrier to entry, making small-run, experimental publishing more accessible. ZINE COOP formed within this moment — less as a reaction to a trend, and more as a response to a shared need for connection.

The founders' own paths into zines were shaped by different creative backgrounds, but shared a similar impulse: making something despite limitations. Beatrix, who comes from photography and poetry, encountered zines through working with limited resources. "I didn't even really know what a zine was at first," they admit. "I think a lot of creatives don't. For me, it came from having limited resources and still wanting to make something — that's when zines started to make sense." During a short residency in the United States, they produced a foldable zine from a single sheet of paper, collecting poems written during that period as a way to record fleeting moments.

editions produced in collaboration with Ink'chacha. Jason, meanwhile, came to zines through comics and online exchanges. "I didn't think of my comics as zines at first," he recalls. "It was only after talking to Forrest that I realised — oh, this actually counts. That realisation was really empowering."

Together, these varied entry points shaped a shared understanding of zines as a medium without rules, and one that prioritises expression over polish and intention over scale. Rather than positioning zines as a niche product, ZINE COOP treats them as an open-ended practice: flexible, personal, and shaped by whoever chooses to participate.

The community that gathers around ZINE COOP reflects this openness. It includes designers, illustrators, photographers, and comic artists, many of whom are introverted and deeply committed to their practice. Within this community, zines become a way to speak without having to be loud.

Beyond creative disciplines, ZINE COOP actively works to uplift voices that are often marginalised within Hong Kong's cultural landscape. Ethnic minority communities, migrant workers, LGBTQ+ groups, and second-generation immigrants all form part of the collective's extended network. Beatrix points out that while Hong Kong is often described as a melting pot, visibility remains uneven. "There are so many people coexisting in the city—ethnic minorities, migrant workers, immigrants—who don't really have channels suited to their languages and experiences," they say. "For instance, mainstream publishing favours Cantonese and English, leaving few outlets for South and Southeast Asian voices."

Inclusivity, for ZINE COOP, is not an abstract principle but a practical one. "Inclusivity doesn't just happen automatically," Beatrix explains. "We have to constantly think about who might be left out, and how we can invite them in." This thinking shapes everything from open application processes to the provision of on-site translation between English and Chinese, ensuring that events do not default to a single language or audience.

DIVE INTO ZINE YO! installation, ZINE COOP © 2026.

"WE FELT THAT IF WE WANTED ANYTHING TO GROW, WE HAD TO BUILD A COMMUNITY FIRST, BECAUSE ONLY WHEN PEOPLE GATHER TOGETHER CAN THINGS REALLY MOVE FORWARD."

— BEATRIX PANG, ZINE COOP

ZINE COOP measures success not through metrics, but through presence. At their most recent Zine Fest in 2025, every applicant is accepted, even when this means extra labour for the organisers. Events are built through layered programming, including workshops, talks, and informal exchanges stacked together to encourage organic interaction. The work is demanding, but it remains sustainable because it is grounded in enjoyment. As Jason puts it, "There are only three of us, so manpower is always a challenge. But we've always said we'll only keep doing this if it's still fun — and so far, it is."

In a city defined by speed and constant redevelopment, zines have taken on an additional role: that of informal archives. Members of the ZINE COOP community use photography, mapping, illustration, typography, and writing to document places and practices that may soon disappear. Jason notes that zines are uniquely suited to this task. "Zines are great

[PP. 296–297] ZINE YO! FEST installation, ZINE COOP © 2026. Photo: soft ground production

"WITH ZINES, YOU CAN DOCUMENT THINGS THAT MIGHT DISAPPEAR JUST BY PAYING ATTENTION."

— FORREST LAU, ZINE COOP

for preservation because you don't need permission," he says. "You can make something small and personal, just for yourself, without going through an official publishing process."

Forrest's Typography Walk in Causeway Bay, a hand-crafted zine mapping 72 typographic landmarks across the neighbourhood, embodies this archival impulse. "I see myself as an archiver in an ever-changing city," he explains. "With zines, you can document things that might disappear just by paying attention." For him, zines also function as a quiet form of resistance. In a city that emphasises so much on financial gain, zines are a way to go against that and to preserve some sense of humanity, sincerity, and care.

Some of ZINE COOP's most meaningful work has taken place in workshops. Forrest recalls sessions with elderly women in community centres and students with special learning needs, where creativity emerged in unexpected forms. "Zines are a very democratic medium," he reflects. Beatrix speaks of collaborations with Narrative by Us and a workshop held in London with Filipino domestic workers. In that session,

Zine Exhibition + Programs
小誌展 + 各式節目
9.20–10.12
Zine Market 小誌市集
9.20–21，10.11–12
DESIGNTRUST
信言設計大使
ZINE COOP
ZINE YO FEST 節
尖沙咀重慶大廈地庫慶方
Garage, B/F, Heath, Chung King Mansion, TST

[P. 298] ZINE YO! FEST poster, ZINE COOP © 2026. Design: Forrest Lau

[P.299] Zine collection, ZINE COOP © 2026.

participants explored the theme "Why We Are All Here," producing zines that reflected shared experiences of migration, labour, and displacement. "That's when I realised how systemic these stories are — and how much zines can hold," Beatrix says.

Looking ahead, ZINE COOP remains cautious but hopeful. Future ideas include shared authorship on social media, clearer resources for first-time zine-makers, and continued experimentation with decentralised formats such as virtual zine festivals. Larger dreams — residencies, study trips, longer-term engagements — are balanced against the realities of space, funding, and energy in Hong Kong. "Zine-making isn't a lucrative business," Beatrix acknowledges, "but capital isn't the only way to bring people together."

What ultimately sustains ZINE COOP is trust. The founders describe one another as both collaborators and sources of support, and this ethos extends outward into the wider community. In choosing care over growth, ZINE COOP offers a model of cultural practice rooted not in productivity or visibility, but in people.

In a city that moves relentlessly forward, their work reminds us that culture can also be held; gently, collectively, and with intention.

BIOGRAPHY & CREDITS

ADD TO CART

Add to Cart is a collaborative project by 0.1 and The Object that examines the ideas of object, tradition, and collection through books produced in a range of formats, using publishing as a medium to explore how everyday items are preserved, interpreted, and recontextualised.

PP. 042–045, 128–133

ALFIE WHEATLEY

Alfie Wheatley is a graphic designer and art director whose practice spans commercial and self-initiated work. Alongside projects for global brands, his personal work explores DIY culture through zines and publications, drawing on football, music, and rave subcultures, with a strong focus on print-led experimentation informed by his experience in advertising and brand campaigns.

PP. 084–087

BIANCA FORISCHI

Bianca Forischi is a Brazilian graphic designer and illustrator whose work combines digital and analogue techniques. Guided by intuition, her practice embraces imperfection, expressive brushwork, and vibrant colour. Influenced by Latin American vernacular design, she draws on its humour, ornamentation, and maximalism to capture the energy and freedom of everyday visual culture.

PP. 073–075

BROOS STOFFELS

Broos Stoffels is an independent graphic designer and art director based in Brussels. Working across analogue and digital media, his practice focuses on their intersection through the creation of visual systems for identities, publications, campaigns, and websites. He also co-runs Aubergine Press, an independent publishing house producing illustration-led publications featuring his own work and that of other artists.

PP. 088–091
Riso Printing: Harry Studio

PP. 092–095
Illustration: Lukas Verstraete

CAN CAN PRESS

Can Can Press is a creative studio and publishing label based in Mexico City, specialising in visual identity and editorial design. Their practice centres on collaboration and multidisciplinary experimentation, shaping art and design projects through a thoughtful, process-driven approach that values exchange, dialogue, and collective creativity.

PP. 114–121

CAN YANG

Can Yang is a London-based designer and academic who approaches publishing as a critical, experimental medium. Her research explores knowledge production through image–text juxtaposition, examining how meaning is shaped and reshaped across languages and cultures. Drawing on image theory and visual epistemology, she foregrounds underrepresented knowledge systems. She studied at the Rhode Island School of Design and the Royal College of Art, and teaches in London.

PP. 062–063, 137–139

CHEN LUO

Chen Luo is a graphic designer and educator based in Maryland. She is a thesis adviser in the MFA Graphic Design programme at MICA and co-founder of Body&Forma, a collective practice that bridges language barriers through publishing and performative workshops. Her work reconfigures reading and writing into bodily acts, transforming static materials into participatory and communal forms of publishing

PP. 146–149

CHENGJIE LI (NLIEECHI)

Born in Sichuan and based in Kyoto, Chengjie Li (Nlieechi) is a graphic designer and zine artist who creates personal works such as art books and zines. His practice combines graphic design and photography, with a strong interest in silkscreen and Risograph printing. He was a nominee for the TOKYO TDC Prize and recognised in Award360's Best 100 in 2024.

PP. 014–019, 026–029, 048–051
Special Credit: Akinobu Oda (Hand Saw Press Kyoto)

PP. 150–153
Special Credit: SD Print

DTAN STUDIO

DTAN Studio works where precision meets spontaneity, exploring the space between digital clarity and analogue warmth. Embracing misalignment, hand-cut textures, and film grain, the studio treats imperfection as a visual language; celebrating human touch, curiosity, and the depth of crafted presence.

PP. 178–181
Creative Direction: John Caponi
Photography: Francis Broek

ÉLISE RIGOLLET OFFICES

Élise Rigollet Offices is a creative practice and design studio founded by Élise Rigollet in 2018. The studio develops cohesive visual and conceptual narratives across brand identity, art direction, and both print and digital design.

PP. 038–041

EMPIRE BOOKS

Empire Books is a publishing imprint founded in 2015 by Sacha Léopold and François Havegeer of Syndicat. Their cross-disciplinary practice explores originality, reproduction, and print processes through books, visual identities, and exhibitions, drawing on extensive expertise in printing and manufacturing while collaborating closely with contemporary artists and art institutions.

PP. 226–229

EXTENSIVE PUBLISHING—COPYRIGHT/RESERVED

Extensive Publishing is the independent publishing arm of experimental studio COPYRIGHT/RESERVED, founded in 2023. It explores books and objects as interdisciplinary spaces for experimentation, operating as both publisher and Risograph print studio. Alongside its own titles, it supports peers by producing and distributing books, posters, and zines on demand.

PP. 024–025

FOR&ST

for&st is an award-winning design studio founded on the principle of "design for story", viewing design as a tool for shaping experience beyond aesthetics. Its work has received international recognition from organisations including D&AD, Tokyo TDC, and iF Design, and is held in the permanent collection of Columbia University.

PP. 222–225

GRAFIS NUSANTARA

Grafis Nusantara is a platform dedicated to archiving vintage Indonesian labels and stickers, highlighting the archipelago's rich visual culture as a source of knowledge and reference. Through digital archives and social curation, it creates greater access and appreciation for Indonesian graphic artefacts.

PP. 182–195

HATO PRESS

Hato Press is a London-based independent publisher, Risograph printing studio, and design agency founded in 2009 by Ken Kirton and Jackson Lam. Originally established to make printing more accessible, it fosters creative community through collaborations, workshops, and publishing artist zines, children's books, and curated work.

PP. 260–266

HOLYCRAP

Holycrap is a family art collective founded in 2011, using printed publications as a form of personal expression. Through their long-running Rubbish Famzine, they share collective voices and perspectives, earning international recognition including D&AD and Cannes Lions, and receiving Singapore's President's Design Award for Design of the Year in 2015.

PP. 196–199
Printing: Allegro Print
Editor: Claire Lim
Junior Creatives & Illustrators: Renn and Aira Lim

PP. 200–209
Printing: Dominie Press
Paper: RJ Paper
Editor: Claire Lim
Junior Creatives & Illustrators: Renn and Aira Lim

HOUTH

HOUTH, founded in Taipei in 2014, is a creative studio specialising in brand strategy and design. A member of AGI (Alliance Graphique Internationale), its work has been recognised by Tokyo TDC and featured in TOP in Asia. Known for bold colour, experimental graphics and inventive typography, HOUTH pursues solutions that blur the boundary between art and commerce.

PP. 122–125, 140–143

HOWFUL

HOWFUL is a designer with nearly a decade of experience, running a studio while developing independent brands. Trained in Industrial Design, his practice explores the intersection of graphic, visual and product design within branding. He focuses on systems of expression rather than fixed outcomes, and runs Risograph workshops that treat printing as an experimental, process-driven practice.

PP. 052–053, 104–105

HSIAN-JUNG CHEN

Hsian-Jung Chen is a Taipei-based ceramic artist whose work draws inspiration from everyday life. Through processes of amplification and reduction, he transforms familiar subjects into geometric forms and vivid colours. By blurring the boundary between art and function, his practice encourages viewers to reconsider their relationship with everyday objects.

PP. 020–023

JONATHAN MAK

Jonathan Mak is a Hong Kong–based graphic designer working across interaction design, branding, and multimedia art. His practice includes collaborations with global brands and cultural institutions, alongside personal projects such as zines and music translations, with his work recognised by awards including D&AD, Cannes Lions, and the Type Directors Club.

PP. 058–061
Drawings & Words: Jonathan Mak's Parents
Printing: flip & roll

KOSEKO DESIGN & PRESS

KOSEKO DESIGN & PRESS is an experimental graphic design studio based in Kyoto, founded by Tomoyuki and Yafa Koseko. Working in visual communication, the studio draws on psychology, philosophy, and semiotics, presenting research-led outcomes through publications and exhibitions, with work shown at international art book fairs across Asia.

PP. 154–157
Residency Support: Hyperwave

LONELY KIDNEY

Lonely Kidney is a visual artist working across graphic design and illustration. Her practice explores surreal imaginings shaped by her personal experiences and observations. Challenging conventional ideas of beauty, she combines discordant and imperfect elements into a considered chaos. A subtle sense of humour runs throughout, reflecting the playful spirit underpinning her work.

PP. 126–127

LUANA LLOYD

Luana Lloyd is an art director and illustrator whose practice focuses on making digital experiences more tangible through print. In her personal work, she experiments with unconventional typography and disrupted reading rhythms, using writing itself as a visual and conceptual tool.

PP. 070–072
Special Credit: Pedro Moreira

MEANTIME

Meantime is an independent magazine from Singapore that documents stories lost to time. Published biennially, each issue centres on a distinct theme, with topics ranging from love and ghost stories to humorous, bad, and breakup narratives.

PP. 210–217
Printing: Allegro Print
Paper: RJ Paper

MEW IMASHUKU

Born in 2000, Mew Imashuku works across poetry, performance and media art. Through tactile interventions such as pressure, heat and vibration, she explores bodily fragmentation in homogenised urban spaces. By involving others, her devices destabilise bodily boundaries, creating new relational possibilities while confronting the ethical tensions inherent in shared sensation.

PP. 158–163
Printing: Inuuniq Print Co., Ltd.
Binding: Hakushodo
Special Credit: Kumonodaira Sanso LLC

NIEVES

Nieves is an independent publishing house based in Zurich. Founded in 2001 by Benjamin Sommerhalder. it focuses on publishing artist books and zines.

PP. 252–259

NOPATTERN STUDIO

NoPattern Studio is the practice of Chicago-based artist and designer Chuck Anderson. Founded in 2004 when he was 18 and self-taught, his work is recognised for vibrant colour and hybrid digital-physical processes. Anderson has collaborated with major brands like Apple, Vans, and Microsoft, and is currently Creative Director at Ernie Ball, while continuing his independent art and zine practice.

PP. 106–109

NÚRIA BALINHA

Núria Balinha graduated with a degree in Fine Arts (Multimedia) from the University of Porto in 2023. In 2022, she undertook an Erasmus semester at the Eugeniusz Geppert Academy of Fine Arts in Wrocław. She is currently completing a Master's in Editorial Design at Elisava, Barcelona. Her work is driven by a fascination with colour, its energy and unpredictability.

PP. 064–065, 076–077, 082–083

PAGEMASTERS

PageMasters is a queer-owned South London Risograph printing studio and publishing house offering affordable printing services alongside art book publishing, weekly workshops, and a community zine fair.

PP. 276–282

PAY2PLAY

PAY2PLAY is a small graphic design studio based in Beijing, founded in 2019 by Sun Xiaoxi and Wang Lang. Working across editorial design, exhibition identities, packaging, and branding, the studio is driven by experimentation, with a particular interest in exploring new forms, materials, and the boundaries of graphic design.

PP. 174–177

PETR PERSIK

Petr Persik is an independent designer focused on self-initiated printed matter. His practice centres on zines as a space for experimentation and direct expression, where content, material, and format evolve together. Working intuitively, he treats design as part of the message, producing fast, honest projects rooted in personal observations and everyday life.

PP. 078–081

RACHEL SENDER

Rachel Sender is an editorial illustrator based in Rotterdam. Her work draws on close observation of human behaviour, using warmth and humour to engage audiences. After training in Barcelona, she established her practice in the Netherlands, combining client work with teaching at the Willem de Kooning Academy and community building for local illustrators.

PP. 100–103
Riso Printing: Teuntje Fleur
Screen Printing: Michael van Kekem

RAUM FUER ILLUSTRATION

RAUM FÜR ILLUSTRATION (Space for Illustration) is a gallery, shop, zine library, Risograph printing and design studio in Hamburg, St. Pauli, founded by Philipp Schultz.

PP. 284–293

RISOTTO

Founded in 2012 by Gabriella Marcella, Glasgow-based RISOTTO is a design and print studio specialising in vibrant and sustainable Risograph stationery, posters, and custom prints with a bold, fluorescent aesthetic.

PP. 242–250

RIVERSBED

Yang Qiao Ran is a graphic designer and visual artist who founded the design studio Riversbed in 2018. Her work explores shape and colour through abstract compositions, with particular attention to spatial proportion and boundaries. Through this process, she reflects on the delicate balance between the self and the external world.

PP. 134–136
Typeface: ABC Diatype
Monoprinting: KAWA SUMI
Print Photography: Sydney Sie

SITING YAO

Siting Yao is a graphic designer and independent publisher based in London. A Central Saint Martins graduate, her practice centres on Risograph printing and independent publishing. Through research-led projects, she explores queer culture and works to amplify the voices and experiences of Chinese queer communities through print.

PP. 054–057

SOCIOTYPE

Sociotype is a design-led type foundry founded in 2021 by London studio SOCIO, producing versatile type families. Its annual Sociotype Journal functions as a readable type specimen, with each issue themed around the typeface used. Recent issues explore makeshift creativity and ideas of home, set in the foundry's Rework and Onsite font families.

PP. 234–237

SOMETHINGMOON DESIGN

SomethingMoon Design is a graphic design studio based in Macau, founded by Chiwai Cheang. Alongside the studio's practice, Cheang is active in publishing, writing, event planning, music production, and running a bookstore, situating design within a broader cultural and creative context.

PP. 164–173

STUDIO DE RONNERS

Studio de Ronners is a graphic and digital design agency with an international team. The studio develops visual identities, campaigns, websites, motion, and editorial design for cultural institutions, public bodies, and commercial clients, combining strategic insight with artistic sensibility to create clear, meaningful, and distinctive communication.

PP. 230–233
Artistic Director of A+: Amaryllis Jacobs
Editor-in-Chief of A+: Eline Dehullu
Cover Photography: Stijn Bollaert
Printing: die Keure

STUDIO ELANA SCHLENKER

Studio Elana Schlenker is a medium-agnostic design practice founded by Elana Schlenker in 2011, working across disciplines to develop concept-led projects that adapt fluidly to different formats and contexts.

PP. 218–221
Illustration: Katharina Kulenkampff

TESS SMITH-ROBERTS

Tess Smith-Roberts is an illustrator whose work is defined by humour, bold shapes and playful colour. Drawing inspiration from still life painting, awkward dates and food, her illustrations span editorial, advertising and product design, with clients including The New Yorker, It's Nice That, Sydney Opera House and Innisfree.

PP. 096–099
Special Credit: Risa Nakazawa (The Bee's Knees)

TOKYO ART BOOK FAIR

TOKYO ART BOOK FAIR launched in 2009 as Japan's first book fair specialising in art publications. As the biggest event of its kind in Asia, it aims to champion and lead art publishing culture across the region.

PP. 268–275

TYPE01

TYPE01 is a magazine offering a contemporary perspective on graphic design and typography. Founded in 2020, it uses type as a conceptual starting point to explore culture, business, technology, and design, combining editorial depth with experimental layouts to document typographic history while advancing contemporary practice.

PP. 238–240

TYRONE WILLIAMS

Tyrone Williams is a photographer from Northampton whose work transforms everyday urban scenes into abstract, graphic images. Blending photography with digital experimentation, he explores colour, form, and texture through both traditional and manipulated processes. His practice includes numerous self-published zines and books, and he is a joint winner of BBC Four's Great British Photography Challenge.

PP. 110–113
Designer: Sam Hutchinson

PP. 144–145
Designer: Wataru Otaki

VICTORIA ROSSELLI

Victoria Rosselli is a multidisciplinary designer and art director based in Brooklyn, New York. With eight years of experience, she works across print and digital for agencies, brands, and publications. As Deputy Art Director at The Wall Street Journal Magazine, she oversees print, digital stories, and illustration, alongside a personal practice centred on Risograph-printed matter.

PP. 066–069
Printing: SVA Riso Lab

WAN CHAOFAN

Wan Chaofan is a photographer born in Hebei in 1991 and a Doctor of Arts graduate of Tokyo University of the Arts. His practice explores relationships between people, landscape, and spirit. He has published the "Yes, the River Knows" photobook series, received multiple photography awards, and his work is held in the Kiyosato Museum of Photographic Arts.

PP. 046–047
Designer: Tang Yayi

WUTHIPOL UJATHAMMARAT

Wuthipol Ujathammarat is a Bangkok-based self-publishing artist, graphic designer, and curator. Working through initiatives including Aperture Brought Me Here and Wuthipol Designs, his practice explores photographic narrative and conceptual documentary, using publication design to examine how images alone can construct stories beyond traditional photographic forms.

PP. 010–013
Printing: Cyberprint Group

PP. 030–033
Production: Studio2B

PP. 034–035
Production: Haptic Edition

ZINE COOP

Founded in 2017 by Beatrix Pang and Forrest Lau, ZINE COOP is the first collective and platform in Hong Kong dedicated to promoting zine culture through grassroots publishing and DIY creativity.

PP. 294–299

ACKNOWLEDGEMENTS

WE WOULD LIKE TO THANK ALL THE DESIGNERS AND COMPANIES WHO WERE INVOLVED IN THE PRODUCTION OF THIS BOOK. THIS PROJECT WOULD NOT HAVE BEEN ACCOMPLISHED WITHOUT THEIR SIGNIFICANT CONTRIBUTION TO ITS COMPILATION. WE WOULD ALSO LIKE TO EXPRESS OUR GRATITUDE TO ALL THE PRODUCERS FOR THEIR INVALUABLE OPINIONS AND ASSISTANCE THROUGHOUT THIS ENTIRE PROJECT. ITS SUCCESSFUL COMPLETION ALSO OWES A GREAT DEAL TO MANY PROFESSIONALS IN THE CREATIVE INDUSTRY WHO HAVE GIVEN US PRECIOUS INSIGHTS AND COMMENTS. AND TO THE MANY OTHERS WHOSE NAMES ARE NOT CREDITED BUT HAVE MADE SPECIFIC INPUT IN THIS BOOK, WE THANK YOU FOR YOUR CONTINUOUS SUPPORT THE WHOLE TIME.

FUTURE EDITIONS

IF YOU WISH TO PARTICIPATE IN VICTION:ARY'S FUTURE PROJECTS AND PUBLICATIONS, PLEASE SEND YOUR WEBSITE OR PORTFOLIO TO WE@VICTIONARY.COM.